ESSENTIALS OF COMPARATIVE POLITICS

ESSENTIALS OF COMPARATIVE POLITICS

PATRICK O'NEIL

University of Puget Sound

W. W. NORTON & COMPANY

NEW YORK • LONDON

W. W. Norton & Company has been independent since its founding in 1923, when William Warder Norton and Mary D. Herter Norton first published lectures delivered at the People's Institute, the adult education division of New York City's Cooper Union. The Nortons soon expanded their program beyond the Institute, publishing books by celebrated academics from America and abroad. By mid-century, the two major pillars of Norton's publishing program—trade books and college texts—were firmly established. In the 1950s, the Norton family transferred control of the company to its employees, and today—with a staff of four hundred and a comparable number of trade, college, and professional titles published each year—W. W. Norton & Company stands as the largest and oldest publishing house owned wholly by its employees.

Manufacturing by Courier Companies
Book design by Martin Lubin
Production manager: Diane O'Connor

Library of Congress Cataloging-in-Publication Data

O'Neil, Patrick H., 1966–
    Essentials of comparative politics / Patrick O'Neil
      p. cm.
    Includes bibliographical references and index.

ISBN 0-393-97654-8 (pbk.)

  1. Comparative government. 2. State, The. 3. Capitalism. 4. Democracy.
    5. Post-communism. I. Title.

JF51.O54 2003
  320.3—dc21
                                                    2003042148

W. W. Norton & Company, Inc., 500 Fifth Avenue, New York, N.Y. 10110
www.wwnorton.com

W. W. Norton & Company Ltd., Castle House, 75/76 Wells Street, London W1T 3QT

2 3 4 5 6 7 8 9 0

CONTENTS

5 Authoritarianism 119

6 Democracy 147

7 Advanced Democracies   176

10 Globalization

LIST OF MAPS

PREFACE

The past fifteen years have seen a dramatic transformation of comparative politics: the end of the Cold War and the collapse of the Soviet Union, the spread of democracy around the world, the rise of new economic powers in Asia, and the deepening of globalization. For a time, many considered these changes to be unmitigated progress that would bring about a decline in global conflict and produce widespread prosperity. For Americans in particular, however, September 11, 2001, cast doubt on this belief, as the uncertainties of the future seem to portend more risk than reward. It is increasingly difficult to sustain the notion that, as the last superpower, the United States or any country can function without a good understanding of the billions of people who live outside its borders. We ignore the world at our peril.

This textbook is meant to contribute to our understanding of comparative politics—the study of domestic politics around the world—by investigating the most central ideas and questions that make up this field. It begins with the most basic struggle in politics—the battle between freedom and equality. How can these two ideals be reconciled or balanced? How this struggle has unfolded across place and time represents the core of comparative politics, and this book will consider this struggle throughout its chapters. In addition to this guiding theme, this textbook emphasizes the importance of institutions. Human action is guided fundamentally by the institutions that people construct, such as culture, constitutions, and property rights. Once established, these institutions are influential and persistent—not easily overcome, changed, or removed. How these institutions emerge and how they affect politics are central to this work.

With these ideas in place, this book tackles the basic institutions of power: states, markets, societies, democracy, and authoritarianism. What are states, how do they emerge, and how can we measure their capacity, autonomy, and efficacy? How do markets function, and what kinds of relationships exist between states and markets? How do societal components such as nationalism, ethnicity, and ideology shape political values? What are the main differences between democracy and authoritarianism, and what explains why one or the other predominates in various parts of the world? These are a few of the questions this book will attempt to answer.

Once these concepts and questions have been explored, subsequent chapters will apply them directly to various political systems: the advanced democracies, communist and postcommunist countries, and newly industrializing and less-developed countries. In each of these the basic institutions of the state, markets, society, and democracy or authoritarianism shape the relationship between freedom and equality. What basic characteristics lead us to group these countries together? How do they compare with one another, and what are their prospects for economic, social, and democratic development? Finally, the discussion of globalization in the final chapter asks students to consider how the institutions of politics and the battle over freedom and equality may be transformed by a globalized world.

The format of this text is different from those of most textbooks in this field. Traditionally, comparative politics textbooks have been built around a set of country studies, with introductory chapters for the advanced, postcommunist, and less-developed worlds. Although such textbooks can provide a great deal of information about a wide range of cases, the trade-off is often a less thorough consideration of the basic grammar of comparative politics. We might know who the prime minister of Japan is but have less of an understanding of, say, political culture, mercantilism, or state autonomy—all ideas that can help us make sense of politics across time and place. This text strives to fill this gap; it is designed to be alongside traditional case studies to help draw out broader questions and issues. By grasping these concepts, arguments, and questions, students will better understand the political dynamics of the wider world.

This thematic approach to the essential tools and ideas of comparative politics is supported by a strong pedagogy that clarifies and reinforces the most important concepts. Building on the central theme of the struggle between freedom and equality, a "Matrix of Freedom and Equality" diagram in each chapter plots the institutions and political systems discussed in relation to these two values. "Global Comparisons" illustrate key points with real-world data from several countries; "Comparing Concepts" contrasts related terms and concepts; timelines and thematic maps show important political developments over time and around the globe; and "In Focus" boxes summarize a range of ideas that students will want to review.

Many people have contributed to this work. The text itself is inspired by Karen Mingst's *Essentials of International Relations*. When W. W. Norton first published this work in 1999, I was struck by its concision and came to the conclusion that comparative politics would benefit from a similar kind of text. At Norton, Peter Lesser first encouraged me to submit a proposal for this textbook, and Roby Harrington asked me to develop the initial chapters, championed its publication, and provided important feedback at many stages. Robert Whiteside provided early editorial support, with Ann Marcy taking over that task as the work drew closer to completion. Ann, Rob, and Roby all held me to a high standard of writing and argumentation, which was at times frustrating and demanding—precisely what I needed. My great thanks to them. My thanks, too, to Carey Schwaber for helping to develop the artwork and to Traci Nagle for her meticulous copy-editing.

In addition to the people at Norton, many fellow academics have helped improve this work. Most important have been my own colleagues at the University of Puget Sound, in particular Don Share and Karl Fields. Over the past few years Don, Karl, and I have team taught introductory comparative politics, and working with these two outstanding teachers and scholars helped generate many of the ideas contained in this book. Don and Karl were also kind enough to use draft chapters of this text in their courses and provided a great deal of feedback and numerous suggestions. I am fortunate to have such valuable colleagues. Additional important input has come from Karen Mingst, whose own work gave her a valuable perspective and helped focus this text. I have also benefited from the input of Douglas Durasoff (Seattle Pacific University), Cynthia Enloe (Clark University), Damian J. Fernandez (Florida International University), Michael Fleet (Marquette University), David Leheny (University of Wisconsin), Andrew Milton (University of Puget Sound), Vincent Wei-Cheng Wang (University of Richmond), and Bruce Wilson (University of Central Florida). I thank them for their words of encouragement as well as their sharp critiques.

Finally, I would like to thank the students of the University of Puget Sound for their questions and insights; the administration of the university for their support of this project; and my wife, Jayne, for her patience with me during this long task.

PATRICK O'NEIL
Tacoma, Washington
July 2002

AFRICA, 2003

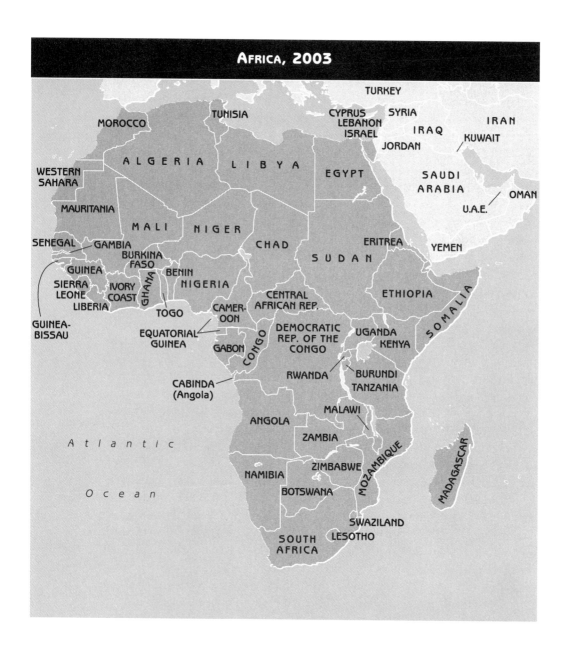

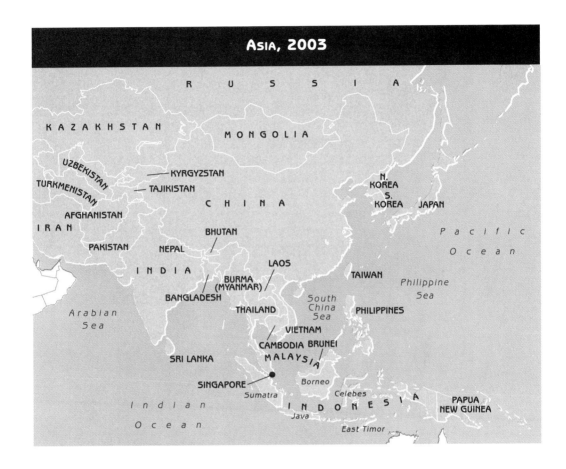

ASIA, 2003

RUSSIA

KAZAKHSTAN

MONGOLIA

UZBEKISTAN

KYRGYZSTAN

TURKMENISTAN

TAJIKISTAN

CHINA

N.
KOREA
S.
KOREA   JAPAN

AFGHANISTAN

IRAN

Pacific

Ocean

PAKISTAN   NEPAL

BHUTAN

INDIA

LAOS

BURMA
(MYANMAR)

TAIWAN   *Philippine
Sea*

BANGLADESH

*Arabian
Sea*

THAILAND   *South
China
Sea*

PHILIPPINES

VIETNAM

CAMBODIA BRUNEI

SRI LANKA

MALAYSIA

SINGAPORE

Borneo

Sumatra   *Celebes*

PAPUA
NEW GUINEA

Indian

INDONESIA

Ocean

Java

East Timor

EUROPE, 2003

LATIN AMERICA, 2003

Atlantic Ocean

MEXICO

Gulf of Mexico

BAHAMAS

PUERTO RICO (U.S.)

VIRGIN IS. (U.K./U.S.)

CUBA

DOM. REP.

BARBUDA

GUADELOUPE (FR.)

JAMAICA

DOMINICA

BELIZE

HAITI

ST. LUCIA

MARTINIQUE (FR.)

GUATEMALA   HONDURAS

NETHERLANDS ANTILLES (NETH.)

ST. VINCENT AND THE GRENADINES

EL SALVADOR   NICARAGUA

GRENADA

COSTA RICA   PANAMA

TRINIDAD AND TOBAGO

VENEZUELA

SURINAME

GUYANA

FRENCH GUIANA

COLOMBIA

ECUADOR

PERU

B R A Z I L

BOLIVIA

Pacific Ocean

PARAGUAY

CHILE

URUGUAY

ARGENTINA

Atlantic Ocean

Falkland Islands (U.K.)

xix

ESSENTIALS OF COMPARATIVE POLITICS

INTRODUCTION 1

During the past two decades the world has seen an astonishing number of changes: the rise of new economic powers in Asia; the collapse of communist systems in Eastern Europe and the Soviet Union; the spread of democracy to new parts of the globe; the creation of new technologies such as the Internet and the World Wide Web; the deepening of international connections, commonly referred to as "globalization"; and the emergence of a new global terrorist threat. As a result of these profound changes, many of the traditional assumptions and concepts used to understand politics have been challenged. New economic forces are shifting wealth around the world, enriching some countries or regions while bypassing others. Technology is rapidly transforming societies everywhere, a change that is attractive to some but threatening to others. People appear to be interconnected as never before, although it is unclear whether this connection brings with it greater understanding and community, or inequality and conflict. The terrorist attacks of September 11, 2001, made us all too aware that the very innovations that make our modern world— skyscrapers and airplanes, e-mail and satellite television—can be turned against us. Politics seems torn by the acceleration of social and economic developments, calling into question the very notion of **sovereignty**—the ability of states to carry out actions or policies within a territory independently from external actors or internal rivals.

These changes are simultaneously fascinating, hopeful, confusing, and terrifying. For some, they represent the onset of a dramatic change in domestic and international politics that will bring an end to nationalism and narrow, parochial identities. These observers point to such developments as the European Union, a political and economic integration of fifteen countries that had waged two horrific wars against one another within the past century, killing tens of millions. Yet these countries are now so highly integrated that the majority of them have relinquished their own national currencies, replacing them with a single currency, the euro. The idea that European countries would ever again go to war against each other seems hard to accept.

Others are less enthusiastic about such developments. They see these changes as leading not to harmonization, but to increasing discord. As the speed of change increases and governments' ability to control them declines, these observers predict, a backlash will take form against the "homogenization" of the world. Conflict will re-emerge, not decline, as people seek to assert what is unique about themselves and to combat ideas they do not accept but cannot avoid. This conflict may take the form of ethnic conflict, as it has already in Yugoslavia or Indonesia; of domestic and international terrorism, as it has with Al Qaeda; or of public protests against globalization, such as the demonstrations in the United States and Europe against the World Trade Organization or the European Union.

Conflict because people don't want views forced on them

Although it is unclear in which direction politics is heading—greater cooperation or greater conflict, or even both at the same time—in order to make sense of these contradictory forces, we have to master the basic language of politics. Once we have achieved that we can draw our own conclusions about these momentous changes and their implications for politics in our own country and around the world.

IN FOCUS

FUNDAMENTAL QUESTIONS IN COMPARATIVE POLITICS

- How can political systems be compared?
- What are the limitations of the comparative method?
- How do institutions shape politics in various countries?
- How do different countries reconcile freedom with equality?
- Can a political system achieve high levels of both freedom and equality?

This chapter will lay out some of the most basic vocabulary of comparative politics. We will begin with the most basic questions: What is politics? How does one compare different political systems around the world? We will spend some time considering the methods of comparative politics and how scholars have approached the study of politics over time. As we shall see, over the past half-century political scientists have struggled not just with the challenges of analyzing politics, but also with whether this study can actually be a science. Exploring these issues will give us a better sense of the limitations, and possibilities, in the study of comparative politics. From here we will consider comparative politics through the study of institutions. **Institutions**—that is, organizations or activities that are self-perpetuating and valued for their own sake—play an important role in defining and shaping what is possible and probable in political life. In addition to looking at institutions, we will take up the theme of freedom and equality. If institutions shape how the game of politics is played, then the objective of the game itself is the optimal mix of freedom and equality. Must one come at the expense of the other? If so, which is more important? Can both full freedom and full equality be achieved? Or is neither desirable? With the knowledge gained by exploring these questions, we will be ready to take on the complexity of politics across the planet.

WHAT IS COMPARATIVE POLITICS?

Before we go any further we must identify what exactly comparative politics is. **Politics** is commonly defined as the struggle in any group for power that will give a person or people the ability to make decisions for the larger group. This group may range from a small organization up to an entire country or even the entire global population. Although politics can be found everywhere (we may speak of "office politics," for example, when we are talking about relations within a business), political scientists concentrate on the struggle for leadership and power for the community. Politics is essentially the struggle for the authority to make decisions that will affect the public as a whole.

Within political science, **comparative politics** is a subfield that compares this struggle across countries. By studying a wide variety of countries, comparativists hope to shed light on the countries under study as well as on our own political system. For example, one important question we will return to frequently is why some countries are democratic while others are not. Why have politics in some countries resulted in power being more dispersed among the people, while in other societies power has been concentrated in the hands of a few? Are these results a function of cultural values or economic development? Is one system superior to the other? These are not simply academic questions: democratic countries actively support the spread of like-minded regimes around the world, but if it is unclear how or why democracy comes about, it becomes difficult to promote. The comparative study of politics in a number of different circumstances can help us draw conclusions that no single case alone would provide. Moreover, the study of politics beyond our own borders helps place our own system in perspective, by highlighting alternatives to our own political order and, as a result, challenging our assumption that there is one right way to organize political life.

The Comparative Method

It is not enough, however, to simply broaden our horizons by studying politics around the world. *How* one makes comparisons between cases is equally important. If there is no criterion or guide by which we gather information or draw conclusions, then our studies become little more than a collection of random details. Comparativists must therefore rely on a **comparative method**—a means of making comparisons across cases. By comparing two or more countries, we seek to draw some generalizations about politics that could be valid in other cases.

This can be illustrated by returning to the example used above. If we are interested in why democracy has failed to develop in some countries, we can compare a number of nondemocratic countries and look for patterns or similarities among them, such as a low level of economic development or similar cultural values. By carrying out such studies, we may find a *correlation,* or apparent association, between certain factors or *variables*. Suppose that, upon investigation, we find that countries with a high rate of poverty are less likely to be democracies than countries where poverty is low. Egypt might be one example that would support this hypothesis; nearly a quarter of Egypt's population lives below the national poverty line, and political freedoms in Egypt are highly restricted. If we look at only this one case, then, poverty and authoritarianism appear to be *correlated*. But that correlation is not proof of anything. Correlation is not the same thing as *causality,* in which a change in one variable causes change in another. We do not know, in our simple case study of Egypt, whether poverty has led to authoritarianism, or whether authoritarianism has led to poverty. Is it the prevalence of poverty that has allowed authoritarian leaders to maintain control, or is the long tenure of authoritarian leaders the source of the country's poverty? Or might there be a third factor, such as certain cultural values or historical legacies, that causes both authoritarianism and poverty?

Finding the cause is rarely easy, for several reasons. First, political scientists are unable to control the variables in the cases they study. In our search for cause and effect relationships, in other words, we are unable to make true comparisons, since each of our cases is quite different. By way of comparison, imagine that a researcher wants to determine if increased exercise by college students leads to higher grades. In studying the

Correlation, Causation, and Germs: Dr. Ignac Semmelweis

In the 1840s, the Hungarian physician Ignac Semmelweis confronted a puzzle: in his Vienna hospital a high number of women died from infection after giving birth. Yet this was not true for women who were attended at the hospital by midwives; they had much lower rates of infection than those who were attended by student doctors. After controlling for all other variables, Semmelweis concluded that the only difference was that the student doctors worked on cadavers before seeing their patients. The doctor ordered students to wash their hands after working on cadavers, and the rate of infection plunged. Semmelweis's research was thus able to generate a clear cause-and-effect relationship, even though in the 1840s there was as yet no understanding that diseases were transmitted by germs. As you might imagine, similar discoveries are much more difficult in political science and comparative politics.

students who are her subjects, the researcher can control for a number of variables that might also affect grades, such as the students' diets, the amount of sleep they get, or any other factor other than exercise that might influence the results. By controlling for these differences, by making certain that all these variables are the same across the subjects with the exception of exercise, the researcher can carry out her study with greater confidence regarding causation.

But political science offers very few opportunities to control variables, since they are a function of real-world politics. Countries are amazingly diverse in terms of such things as economics, culture, geography, resources, and political structures, and it is difficult to control for these differences. At best, we might seek to categorize countries on the basis of specific factors, controlling as much as possible for variables that might otherwise distort our conclusions. If, for example, we want to understand why gun-possession laws are so much less restrictive in the United States than in most other industrialized countries, we would be well served to compare U.S. laws to laws in other countries that have similar historical, economic, political, and social experiences, such as Canada and Australia.

This observation leads us to a second problem, however: political scientists are often hampered by a limited number of cases. In the natural sciences, research is often conducted with a huge number of cases—

studies of hundreds of stars, or thousands of individuals. This breadth allows researchers to select their cases in such a way as to control their variables, and the large number of cases also prevents any single unusual case from distorting the findings. But in comparative politics in particular we are limited by the number of countries in the world—fewer than 200 at present. If we attempt to control for differences by trying to find a number of cases that are similar (for example, industrialized democracies), our total body of cases may fall to thirty or fewer. Cases are also limited by time. For example, one current debate in international relations focuses on whether democratic countries tend not to go to war against other democracies, but because the history of modern democracy is so short (most democracies have developed only in the past fifty years), critics contend that we simply do not have enough data (or a long enough time frame) to draw such a conclusion.

A third problem in studying comparative politics concerns how we access the cases that we do have. Even with the limited number of countries available to study, research is further hindered by the barriers that make countries unique. The information that political scientists seek is often not easy to acquire, necessitating work "in the field," conducting interviews or studying government archives in other countries. International travel requires time and money, and researchers may spend months or even years in the field. Information may be hard to acquire. Interviewees may be unwilling to speak on sensitive issues or may distort information to serve their own interests. Libraries and archives may be incomplete, or access to them may be restricted. As you might imagine, doing such research in more than one country is extremely challenging. A researcher may be able to read Russian and travel to Russia frequently, but if she wants to compare communism between the Soviet Union and China, she would also need to be able to read Chinese and conduct research in China as well. Few comparativists have the language skills, time, or resources to conduct field research in a number of countries. As a result, they often instead master knowledge of a single country, which limits the kinds of comparisons they can make.

Quantitative versus Qualitative Research

In part because of these limitations, some scholars have attempted to use a **quantitative method** in comparative politics—one that relies on statistical data (such as taxation rates or voter turnout rates) from a range of countries to construct hypotheses about politics. Since in the quantitative method variables that are under investigation are expressed in the form of numbers, mastery of a language or years of field research are much less necessary; data are generated by almost every country around the world, often using similar standards to determine things like inflation, population growth, or electoral outcomes. As opposed to those who study only one or two countries, quantitative researchers are able to draw from a large number of cases and control their variables more easily. However, such researchers are limited by those variables that can be expressed in quantitative terms and exist across a number of cases. Those who use the quantitative approach argue that their work adheres most closely to a true comparative method, unlike those who may study only one or a few countries. Many quantitative researchers believe that their approach represents the future of the field, where questions about politics will be answered and puzzles solved.

quantitative method

argument for quant. methods

Other comparativists reject such approaches, embracing instead a **qualitative method**, which stresses that one cannot truly understand a country or region unless one is steeped in its history and culture. Limiting one's research to numerical variables raises the problem that such data may itself be skewed or incomparable: just because something is expressed in numbers does not mean that it is objective or accurate. Furthermore, the quantitative approach restricts the kinds of questions that can be asked, thereby precluding the more complex but important aspects of politics. As the political scientist Philip Converse put it, "what is important to study cannot be measured and what can be measured is not important to study."[1] The qualitative approach tends to focus much more on the unique aspects of countries, and its adherents are generally more skeptical that a comparative method like that seen in the natural sciences can be achieved.

COMPARING CONCEPTS
QUANTITATIVE METHOD VS. QUALITATIVE METHOD

Quantitative method	Gathering of statistical data across a large number of countries in order to look for correlations and test hypotheses about cause and effect. Emphasis on breadth over depth.
Qualitative method	Mastery of a limited number of cases through the detailed study of their history, language, and culture. Emphasis on depth over breadth.

In short, political scientists are limited as to the comparisons they can make and the conclusions they can draw. They struggle with both explanation and prediction. They wish to determine *why* events happen in comparative politics—Why are there revolutions? Why does democracy emerge?—but knowing *why* does not necessarily mean we know *when* events will come about. In seeking to understand, few comparativists would claim that they can predict an event except in the most general terms. This difficulty is not all that unusual: just because I understand how the stock market works does not mean I know when it will go up or down.

Given all these disagreements and limitations, is it worth our time to study comparative politics at all? Yes, absolutely. Qualitative methods create an in-depth knowledge of a country or countries, and quantitative methods can provide a broader analysis across regions and time. Both are valuable for at least two reasons. First, we ignore the outside world at our peril. One could argue that Americans failed to fully understand the threat of terrorism because they failed to understand the internal political dynamics of the Middle East, which played a major role in motivating the attacks of September 11. By mastering the internal complexities of other countries and investigating patterns of politics around the world, we can better ascertain those countries' internal dynamics and how they may affect us. Second, by understanding politics in a comparative setting, we arm ourselves with the knowledge necessary to make informed political choices about our own lives. How is our political system similar or dissimilar to others? What are the advantages or disadvantages of various systems? Which do we prefer and why? Political choices are based not on abstract ideas, but on very real examples and alternatives. Thus comparative politics has very practical and important applications.

DEBATES IN COMPARATIVE POLITICS

Debates within any field over how best to approach the subject are a normal part of intellectual progress; in Western political science, intellectual debates can be traced back at least 2,000 years to ancient Greece—in particular, Athens. Then as now, political thought revolved around notions of the public interest, of how to construct rules and goals to serve society's broader needs and desires. Most relevant for comparativists is the work of the philosopher Aristotle (384–322 B.C.E.). Aristotle departed from his political-philosopher predecessors, such as Plato (428–348 B.C.E.), who concentrated on abstract questions such as what would constitute the ideal political system. Instead, Aristotle conducted comparative research on existing political systems, eventually gathering and analyzing the constitutions of 158 Greek city-states. Aristotle's objective was less to determine the ideal political system than to understand different forms of politics that actually existed and their relative strengths and weaknesses. With this approach Aristotle conceived of an *empirical* (that is, observable and verifiable) science of politics with a practical purpose: statecraft, or how to govern. Aristotle was the first to separate the study of politics from that of philosophy.[2]

However, Aristotle's early approach did not immediately lead to any real science of politics. For the next 1,800 years discussions of politics remained embedded in the realm of philosophy, with the emphasis placed on how politics should be rather than on how politics was actually conducted. Ideals, rather than conclusions drawn from evidence, were the norm. Only with the works of the Italian Niccolò Machiavelli (1469–1527) did a comparative approach to politics truly emerge. Like Aristotle, he sought to analyze different political systems—those that existed around him as well as those that had preceded him in history, such as the Roman Empire—and even tried to predict their relative success and failure as a result. These findings, he believed, could then be applied by statesmen to avoid their predecessors' mistakes. Machiavelli's work reflects this pragmatism, dealing with the mechanics of government, diplomacy, military strategy, and above all, power.[3] Most notable is Machiavelli's conclusion that ideals have no place in politics, since the quest for power will inevitably conflict with moral values. It is this emphasis that leads us to use the contemporary (if misleading) term "Machiavellian" to refer to someone cunning and devious, operating without normal moral standards.

Because of his emphasis on statecraft and empirical knowledge, Machiavelli is often cited as the first modern political scientist, paving the way for other scholars. In the late sixteenth and early seventeenth centuries, authors such as Thomas Hobbes and John Locke followed in Machiavelli's footsteps, advocating particular political systems on the basis of empirical observation and analysis. They were followed in the eighteenth century by such scholars as Jean-Jacques Rousseau and Baron de Montesquieu, whose studies of the separation of power and civil liberties would directly influence the writing of the American Constitution and others to follow. The work of Karl Marx and Max Weber in the nineteenth and early twentieth centuries would further add to political science with analyses of the nature of political and economic organization and power. All these developments reflected widespread changes in scholarly inquiry. Machiavelli's writings came at a time when the medieval order was giving way to the

Renaissance, with its emphasis on science, secularism, and real-world knowledge over abstract ideals. The resulting work over the next four centuries, such as Isaac Newton's study of physics in the seventeenth and eighteenth centuries and Charles Darwin's work on evolution in the nineteenth reinforced the idea that politics, like any other area of knowledge, could be developed as a logical, rigorous, and predictable science. During those centuries, a number of major thinkers took up the comparative approach to the study of politics, which increasingly retreated from moral or religious foundations.

By the early twentieth century, the study of politics had changed dramatically into a discipline not unlike that which we know today. However, in spite of great strides, the field remained limited. In comparative politics, scholars and students focused their attention on a few modern political structures, primarily those in Europe. Moreover, comparativists tended to concentrate on static description over explanation or prediction, on *how* politics worked in these countries rather than *why*. But this approach to comparative politics was eventually shaken by international events: the rise of fascism and communism, World War II, and the Cold War. Each of these events raised important questions that political scientists could not easily answer: Why had Germany fallen prey to fascism, and Russia to communism? Could democracy be installed in countries like Germany and Japan? How could Soviet power be kept in check?

Consequently, after World War II comparative politics was embraced by a new generation of scholars who believed that the field must become a true science. Their conviction was in part shaped by a new wave of technological change and enthusiasm about progress. Nuclear power, space travel, computers, and television generated a common view that economics, society, and politics were being transformed dramatically—and for the better—through scientific advancement. Science would lead politics, and not vice versa. In addition, comparative politics was influenced by international relations. With the emergence of the United States and the Soviet Union as superpowers after World War II, the onset of the Cold War, and decolonization in the developing world, many political scientists in the West (especially in the United States) saw their role in part as helping to strengthen the position of the capitalist democracies. By making sense of political development around the world, they believed, such knowledge could guide foreign policy in ways that would foster the development of economic and political systems similar to those in the West.

Comparative politics was thus not simply a quest for knowledge, but part of the battle between the new superpowers. In this sense, then, com-

Major Thinkers in Comparative Politics

Aristotle (384–322 B.C.E.)	First separated the study of politics from that of philosophy; used comparative method to study Greek city-states; in *The Politics*, conceived of an empirical study of politics with a practical purpose.
Niccolò Machiavelli (1469–1527)	Often cited as first modern political scientist because of his emphasis on statecraft and empirical knowledge; analyzed different political systems, believing the findings could be applied by statesmen; discussed his theories in *The Prince*.
Thomas Hobbes (1588–1679)	Developed the notion of a "social contract," whereby people surrender certain liberties in favor of order; advocated a powerful state in *Leviathan*.
John Locke (1632–1704)	Argued that private property is essential to individual freedom and prosperity; advocated a weak state in his *Two Treatises of Government*.
Charles Louis de Secondat, Baron de Montesquieu (1689–1755)	Studies of government systems led to his advocating the separation of powers within government in *The Spirit of Laws*.
Jean-Jacques Rousseau (1712–78)	Argued that citizens' rights are inalienable and cannot be taken away by the state; influenced the development of civil rights; discussed these ideas in *The Social Contract*.
Karl Marx (1818–83)	Elaborated a theory of economic development and inequality in his book *Das Kapital*; predicted the eventual collapse of capitalism and democracy.
Max Weber (1864–1920)	Wrote widely on such topics as bureaucracy, forms of authority, and the impact of culture on economic and political development; developed many of these themes in *Economy and Society*.

Comparative scholars liked western ideals

parative politics was a largely *conservative* discipline, taking capitalism and democracy as the ideal. This view represented not simply an abstract hope, but a core belief of comparativists known as **modernization theory**, which held that as societies developed, they would become capitalist democracies, converging around a shared set of values and characteristics. The

Societies would all evolve into capitalist democracies → modernization theory

United States and other Western countries were furthest ahead on this path, the theory assumed that all countries would eventually catch up—unless "diverted" by alternative systems such as communism.

During the 1950s and 1960s, comparativists expanded their research to include a wider number of cases, particularly in the developing world. Field research, supported by government and private grants, became the normal means by which political scientists gathered data. New computer technologies combined with statistical methods were also applied to this expanding wealth of data. Finally, the subject of investigation shifted away from political institutions (such as legislatures and constitutions) and toward individual political behavior. This trend came to be known as the behavioral revolution. **Behavioralism** hoped to generate theories and generalizations that could help explain and even predict political activity. Ideally, this work would eventually lead to a "grand theory" of political behavior that would be valid across countries.

By the late 1960s, however, the great hopes of comparative politics began to fade. New theories and sophisticated methods of analysis increased scholars' knowledge about politics around the world, but this knowledge in itself did not lead to the expected new breakthroughs. Those theories that had been developed, such as modernization theory, increasingly failed to match politics on the ground; rather than becoming more capitalist and more democratic, many democracies collapsed in the face of violent con-

COMPARING CONCEPTS
TRENDS IN COMPARATIVE POLITICS

Traditional approach	Emphasis on describing political systems and their various institutions.
Behavioral revolution	The shift from a descriptive study of politics to one that emphasizes causality, explanation, and prediction; places greater emphasis on the political behavior of individuals as opposed to larger political structures, and on quantitative over qualitative methodology; modernization theory predominant.
Post-behavioralism	Rejection of a grand theory of politics; criticism of modernization theory as biased and inaccurate; diversity of methods and political approaches, emphasizing such things as gender, culture, environment, and globalization.

behavioral bad things

flict, to be replaced by nondemocratic systems that in no way reflected Western expectations or ideals. What had gone wrong?

Some critics charged that the behavioral revolution's obsession with appearing scientific had led the discipline astray by emphasizing methodology over knowledge and technical jargon over clarity. Others criticized the field for its ideological bias, arguing that comparativists were interested not in understanding the world but in prescribing the Western model of modernization. At worst, their work could be viewed as simply serving the foreign policy of the developed world.

In the 1970s and 1980s, comparative politics became defined largely by ideological and methodological debates. Left and right accused each other of bias and distortion, while advocates of quantitative and qualitative methods argued over how to structure and use research. Yet even as these debates raged among scholars, new global developments were taking shape that would shake the foundations of comparative politics once again.

The first major development was rapid industrialization in Asia. During the mid-1980s the region attracted attention as countries such as Taiwan, South Korea, Singapore, and China produced increasingly sophisticated products for export, generating tremendous economic growth in the process. While Latin American, African, and even European and North American economies stagnated or declined, some Asian countries more than tripled the standards of living for millions of people within just a few decades. What explained this sudden growth? Was it due to particularly "Asian" cultural values, specific trade strategies, or perhaps the presence of nondemocratic governments that could withstand the harsh sacrifices necessary for development?[4]

A second major event was the collapse of communism in the Soviet Union and Eastern Europe. In the 1980s the new leader of the Soviet Union, Mikhail Gorbachev, embarked on a series of dramatic reforms intended to revitalize and liberalize communism. These changes also raised the possibility that, with more democratic practices in the Soviet Union, the Cold War might finally come to an end, although many feared that a revamped form of communism would in fact be more dangerous than before. In the end, the Cold War did draw to a close, but not in the manner expected. In 1989 the Soviet-controlled countries of Eastern Europe threw off communist rule, and by 1991 Gorbachev's reforms, rather than revitalizing the Soviet Union, led to the country's breakup. Soviet communism had been unable to reform itself, and with its demise, observers now wondered if capitalism and democracy would take root in these post-communist countries.[5]

A third and related development was what has come to be known as the "third wave" of democracy.[6] During the 1970s and 1980s, a large number of countries around the world, particularly in Asia, Latin America, and Europe, shook off authoritarian rule. What was the source of this relatively rapid and unexpected democratization? And would these fragile democracies survive, or again succumb to nondemocratic rule?

All three of these events challenged scholars of comparative politics, regardless of their methodological or ideological preferences. The collapse of communism pointed out the limitations of both the qualitative and the quantitative approach, since neither had foreseen the impact of reforms in the region, even when they were under way. Similarly, the rise of new economic powers in Asia challenged many radical views that had long argued that poorer countries could not progress because of their domination by advanced economic powers such as the United States and Europe. Finally, the dramatic spread of democracy forced all comparativists to rethink the very future of politics and the role of their field.

This is where we find comparative politics now. In light of the dramatic political changes of the past several decades, scholars such as Francis Fukuyama have gone so far as to say that we are now at the "end of history," meaning that the dramatic struggles between right and left,

The Collapse of Communism and Comparative Politics: Crisis and Critique

In the late 1980s and early 1990s, comparativists were stunned by the sudden and unanticipated collapse of communism in Eastern Europe and the Soviet Union. Why had scholars who had studied the region for decades not anticipated its collapse? One criticism was that as a result of the behavioral revolution, political scientists had misunderstood communist systems in their effort to draw comparisons across different cases. Based on their own understanding of capitalist democracies such as the United States, Western scholars viewed communist countries as flexible and dynamic systems much like their own, which was hardly the case. A second criticism accused many political scientists of presenting a distorted view of the Soviet Union as a result of their own sympathies with left-wing views. In either case, critics charged the discipline with having misled itself through both method and ideology. Whether or not such criticisms are accurate, as a result of the collapse of communism, comparativists who studied the region found themselves having to rethink their approach.

capitalism and communism, and authoritarianism and democracy are now at an end.[7] All countries, these scholars argued, will sooner or later become capitalist democracies, and the old ideological divides that separate domestic and international politics are drawing to an end. In other words, the modernization theory was right after all, if somewhat premature. But critics such as political scientist Samuel Huntington counter that the triumph of capitalism and democracy is far from certain. These systems are the product of the unique historical experiences of the West and will not easily transfer around the world, Huntington says. Indeed, in the absence of major ideological distinctions between countries, he believes political divisions will fall primarily along cultural, ethnic, and religious lines.[8] Still other critics, such as political theorist Benjamin Barber, question whether the triumph of capitalist democracy as practiced in the West is even desirable, pointing to its inequalities, the destruction of local cultures, and a growing backlash against globalization.[9] These debates have only intensified since the September 11 attacks. Some see in the terrorist attacks and the U.S. response a cultural conflict; others see an inevitable result of globalization; still others identify a last gasp against capitalism and democracy. Each explanation asks us to see the world in a different way and draws different conclusions about the nature of political conflict.

A GUIDING APPROACH: POLITICAL INSTITUTIONS

A goal of this textbook is to provide a way to compare and analyze politics around the world in the aftermath of these tremendous changes. How can we organize our ideas and information? One way is through a guiding approach, a way of looking at the world that highlights some important features while de-emphasizing others. The guiding approach of this textbook is based on *institutions*, which were defined at the beginning of this chapter as organizations or patterns of activity that are self-perpetuating and valued for their own sake. In other words, an institution is something so embedded in people's lives as a norm or value that it is not easily dislodged or changed. People see an institution as central to their lives, and as a result the institution commands a great deal of legitimacy. Institutions serve as the rules, norms, and values that give meaning to human activity.

Consider an example from outside of politics. We often hear in the United States that baseball is an American institution. What exactly does this mean? In short, baseball is viewed by Americans not simply as a game, but as something valued for its own sake, a game that helps define American society.

Yet at the same time no American would say that soccer is a national institution. The reason is probably clear: soccer, unlike baseball, lacks the kind of public perception of its indispensability that baseball has. Whereas soccer is simply a game, baseball is part of what defines America and Americans. Even Americans who don't like baseball would probably say that America wouldn't be the same without it. Of course, just the opposite is true in Europe and much of Latin America, where soccer reigns as a premier social institution. As a result of this legitimacy and seeming indispensability, institutions command authority and can influence human behavior; we accept and conform to institutions and tend not to challenge them.

Another second example is more directly connected to politics. In many countries, democracy is an institution: it is not merely a means to compete over political power but a vital element in people's lives, bound up in the very way in which they define themselves. Democracy is part and parcel of collective identity, and some democratic countries and their people would not be the same place without it. If under threat, they would defend and might even die for it. In many other countries this is not the case: democracy is absent and unknown, or weakly institutionalized and unstable.

People in such countries do not define themselves by democracy's presence or absence, and as a result democracy's future there is insecure. This example indicates that there is no uniformity of institutions from country to country, and understanding this difference is central to the study of comparative politics.

What about a physical object or place? Can that, too, be an institution? Many would argue that the World Trade Center towers were an American institution—not just a set of office buildings, but structures representing American values. The same thing can be said about the Pentagon. When terrorists attacked these buildings on September 11, 2001, they did so not simply to cause a great loss of life, but also to clearly indicate that their hostility was directed against America itself—its institutions as they shape and represent the American way of life and the U.S. relationship to the outside world.

IN FOCUS

INSTITUTIONS . . .

- Are any organization or pattern of activity that is self-perpetuating and valued for its own sake.

- Embody norms or values considered central to people's lives, and thus are not easily dislodged or changed.

- Set the stage for political behavior by influencing how politics is conducted.

- Vary from country to country.

- *Examples:* baseball (in the United States), marriage, the World Trade Center towers

- *Common political institutions:* army, taxation, elections, the legislature

In general, however, institutions are not physical structures and are not so easily destroyed. Since they are embedded in each of us, in how we see the world and what we think is valuable and important, it is difficult to change or eliminate institutions. When institutions are threatened, people will rush to their defense. Although this bond helps create stability in society, one danger institutions pose is that people may come to resist even necessary change because they are stuck in "tried and true" ways that may no longer work.

Politics is full of institutions. The basic political structures of any country are composed of institutions: the army, the police, the legislature, or the courts, to name a few. We obey them not only because we think it is in our self-interest to do so, but because we see them as legitimate ways to conduct politics. Taxation is a good example. In many Western democracies, income taxes are an institution—we may not like them, but we pay them nonetheless. Is this because we are afraid of going to jail if we fail to do so? Perhaps. But research indicates that a major source of tax compliance is people's belief that taxation is a legitimate way to fund the programs that society needs. We pay, in other words, when we believe that it is the right thing to do, a norm. In contrast, in societies where taxes are not institutionalized, tax evasion tends to be rampant; people view taxes as illegitimate, and those who pay as suckers.

Institutions are a useful way to approach the study of politics because they set the stage for political behavior. Because institutions generate norms and values, they favor and allow certain kinds of political activity and not others. As a result, political institutions are critical because they influence politics, and how political institutions are constructed will have a profound effect on how politics is conducted.

In many ways our institutional approach takes us back to the study of comparative politics as it existed before the 1950s. Prior to the behavioral revolution, political scientists spent much of their time documenting the institutions of politics, often without asking how those institutions actually shaped politics. The behavioral revolution that followed emphasized cause and effect but turned its attention toward political actors and their calculations, resources, or strategies. The actual institutions were seen as largely unimportant. The recent return to the study of institutions in many ways combines these two traditions. From behavioralism, institutional approaches take their emphasis on cause-and-effect relationships, something that will be prevalent throughout this book. However, institutions are not simply the product of political behavior; they can and do have a powerful effect on how politics functions. In other words, institutions are not merely the *result* of politics, they can also be an important *cause*.

Recent events around the world may have led to a greater convergence of political and economic systems, but there is still a tremendous amount of variation that needs to be recognized and understood. This textbook will map some of the basic institutional differences between countries, acknowledging their diversity while pointing to some basic features that allow us to compare and evaluate them. By studying political institutions, we can hope to gain a better sense of the political landscape across the globe.

A GUIDING IDEA: RECONCILING FREEDOM AND EQUALITY

At the start of this chapter politics was defined as the struggle for power in order to make decisions for society. The institutional approach provides us with a way to organize our study by investigating the different ways in which that struggle can be shaped. Yet this begs an important question: People may struggle for political power, but what are they fighting for? What is it they seek to achieve once they have gained power?

At its core, the substance of politics is bound up in the struggle between individual freedom and collective equality. These are terms that mean very different things to different people, and so it is important to define each of them. *Freedom* is the ability of an individual to act independently, without fear of restriction or punishment by the state or other actors. It encompasses such concepts as free speech, free assembly, freedom of religion, and other civil liberties. *Equality* refers to a shared economic standard of individuals within a community, society, or country. In the figure on the following page, freedom and equality are laid out on two axes, showing their hypothetical relationship. One might imagine a situation in which both freedom and equality are high, as in the upper-left-hand corner; where freedom is high but equality low, as in the upper-right-hand corner; where equality is high and freedom is low, as in the bottom-left-hand corner; and where both equality and freedom are limited, as in the bottom right. Freedom and equality also affect political power. A greater emphasis on individual freedom is associated with a greater decentralization of political power, whereas a greater focus on collective equality is associated with a greater centralization of power.

Freedom and equality are thus interconnected, and the relationship between the two shapes political power. What is unclear, however, is

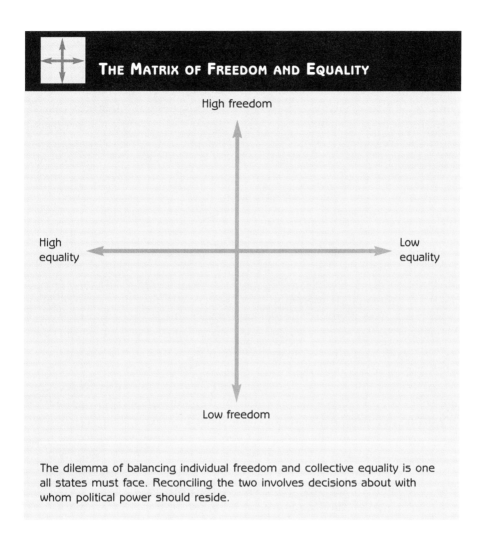

THE MATRIX OF FREEDOM AND EQUALITY

High freedom

High equality

Low equality

Low freedom

The dilemma of balancing individual freedom and collective equality is one all states must face. Reconciling the two involves decisions about with whom political power should reside.

whether one must come at the expense of the other. Greater personal freedom, for example, typically implies a smaller role for the state and limits on its powers to do such things as redistribute income through welfare and taxes. As a result, inequality may increase as individual freedom trumps the desire for greater collective equality. This growing inequality could in turn undermine democracy, if too many people feel as though the political system no longer cares about their needs. Even if this discontent is not a danger, there remains the question of whether society as a whole has an obligation to help the poor. The United States, as we shall see, has one of the highest degrees of both personal freedom and economic inequality in the world. Should this be a cause of concern?

On the other end, a primary focus on economic equality may erode personal freedom. Demands for greater economic equality may lead a government to take greater control of private property and personal wealth, all in the name of redistribution for the "greater good." Yet when economic and political powers are concentrated in one place, individual freedom may be threatened, since people control fewer private resources of their own. In the Soviet Union under communism, for example, all economic power was held by the state, giving it the ability to control people's lives—where they lived, the education they received, the jobs they held, the money they earned.

Are there other alternatives? Some argue that individual freedom and collective equality can in fact support one another, that by dramatically changing all political institutions and completely decentralizing power, people can have both freedom and equality. Still others reject both values, favoring the centralization of power in order to eliminate both individual freedom and collective equality. The logic of each of these arguments and their practical application will be considered over the subsequent chapters of this book.

In short, politics must constantly seek to balance individual freedom and collective equality. This inevitably leads to questions of power and the role of the people in political life. Who should be empowered to make decisions about freedom and equality? Should power be centralized in order to serve the community, or decentralized to serve the individual? Should power be fundamentally public or private? When does power become a danger to others, and how does one prevent this? Each political system must reconcile freedom and equality and, in so doing, determine where political power shall reside. And each political system creates a unique set of institutions to structure political power and shape the role that the people play in political affairs.

IN SUM: LOOKING AHEAD

Politics is the struggle for power in any organization, and comparative politics is the study of this struggle around the world. Over the past centuries the study of politics has evolved from philosophy to a field that emphasizes empirical research and the quest to explain and even predict politics. This approach has limitations: in spite of the earlier desire to emulate the natural sciences, comparative politics, like political sciences as a whole, has not been able to generate any "grand theory" of political behavior. Yet the need to study politics remains as important as ever; dramatic changes over the past twenty years have called on comparativists to provide insight on these developments.

Political institutions can help us organize this task. Institutions generate norms and values, and different configurations of institutions lead to different forms of political activity. Institutions can help us map the landscape of politics. If institutions serve as a map to political activity, then the goal of that activity is to reconcile the competing values of individual freedom and collective equality. All countries must strike a balance between these two forces, determining where power should reside and in whose hands. In the chapters to come, we will return to this question of freedom and equality, and to the way in which these values influence, and are influenced by, institutions. Armed with this knowledge, by the end of this course you will be able to draw your own conclusions about what combination of these values can or should be sought in order to construct a better political order.

NOTES

1 Philip E. Converse, "The Nature of Belief Systems in Mass Publics," in David E. Apter, ed., *Ideology and Discontent* (New York: Free Press, 1964), 206.

2 Aristotle, *The Politics,* trans. T. A. Sinclair (New York: Viking, 1992).

3 Niccolò Machiavelli, *The Prince,* trans. W. K. Marriott (New York: Knopf, 1992).

4 For an analysis of Asian development see Stephan Haggard, *Pathways from the Periphery: The Politics of Growth in the Newly Industrializing Countries* (Ithaca: Cornell University Press, 1990).

5 A good overview of the collapse of communism in the Soviet Union can be found in David Remnick, *Lenin's Tomb: The Last Days of the Soviet Empire* (New York: Random House, 1993).

6 Samuel P. Huntington, *The Third Wave: Democratization in the Late Twentieth Century* (Norman: University of Oklahoma Press, 1993).

7 Francis Fukuyama, *The End of History and The Last Man* (New York: Free Press, 1992).

8 Samuel P. Huntington, *The Clash of Civilization and the Remaking of World Order* (New York: Simon and Schuster, 1996).

9 Benjamin Barber, *Jihad versus McWorld: How Globalism and Tribalism Are Reshaping the World* (New York: Random House: 1995).

2 STATES

We begin our study of the basic institutions of politics by turning our attention to the state. This discussion is often difficult for Americans, who are not used to thinking about politics in terms of centralized political power. Indeed, when Americans think of the word "state," they typically conjure up the idea of local, not centralized, politics.[1] But for most people around the world "the state" refers to centralized authority, the locus of power. In this chapter we will break down the basic components of states and discuss how states help reconcile freedom and equality and distribute power toward that end. The chapter will define what states are and what they comprise, distinguishing a "state" from a "government" and a "regime." We will also consider the origins of states themselves. For most of human history, politics was built on organizations other than states, and myriad forms of authority existed around the world. Yet now only states remain. Why?

Once we have discussed the nature and origins of the state, we will look at some different ways in which states can be compared. This discussion will include an analysis of different forms of legitimacy, which gives a state power, and the actual levels of power itself. Can states be weak or strong? And if so, how would we measure their strength? To answer this question, we will make a distinction between *state capacity* and *state autonomy* and look at different cases in which the combination of the two differs. With these ideas more clearly in hand, we will return to our theme of individual freedom and collective equality, and the future of the state itself.

Defining the State

What exactly do we mean by the term "state"? Political scientists, drawing on the work of the German scholar Max Weber, typically define **state** in its most basic terms as the organization that maintains a monopoly of violence over a territory. At first glance, this may seem to be a rather severe definition of what a state is or does, but a bit of explanation should help flesh out this concept. One of the most important elements of a state is what we call **sovereignty**, or the ability to carry out actions or policies within a territory independently from external actors or internal rivals. In other words, a state needs to be able to act as the sole authority over its territory and the people who live there, setting forth laws, resolving disputes between people, and generating security.

In order to achieve this, states need power, typically (but not only) physical power. If a state cannot defend its territory from outside actors such as other states, then it runs the risk that other states will interfere, even to the point of taking its territory or destroying it outright. Similarly, if the state faces armed actors within its own territory, such as organized crime or rebel movements, it runs the risk that its rules and policies will be undermined. Thus, in order to secure control, a state must be armed. To protect against international rivals, states need armies. And in response to domestic rivals, states need a police force. In fact, the very word "police" comes from the old French word meaning "to govern."

IN FOCUS

The State Is . . .

- The monopoly of force over a given territory.
- A set of political institutions to generate and carry out policy.
- Typically highly institutionalized.
- Sovereign.
- Characterized by such institutions as an army, police, taxation, a judiciary, and a social-welfare system.

A state is thus an institution that seeks to wield the majority of force within a territory, establishing order and deterring challengers from inside and out. In so doing, it provides security for its subjects by limiting the danger of external attack and internal crime and disorder—both of which are seen as threats to the state and its citizens. In some ways, a state (especially a nondemocratic one) is a kind of protection racket—demanding money in return for security and order, staking out turf, defending its clients from rivals, settling internal disputes, and punishing those who do not pay.

But the state is not simply an armed body. Unlike criminal rackets, the state is made up of a large number of institutions that are engaged in the process of turning political ideas into policy. Laws and regulations, health care, unemployment insurance, environmental protection, transportation infrastructure, and public parks are but a few things that typically fall under the responsibility of the state. Moreover, the state is a set of institutions (ministries, departments, offices, army, police) that society deems necessary in order to achieve basic goals regarding freedom and equality. When there is a lack of agreement on these goals, the state must attempt to reconcile different views and seek consensus. And unlike a criminal racket, which people obey out of fear or pure self-interest, the state is valued for its own sake. The public views the state as legitimate, vital, and appropriate—who can imagine politics without it? States are thus strongly institutionalized and not easily changed. Leaders may come and go, but the state remains, even in the face of crisis, turmoil, or revolution. Although destruction through war can eliminate states altogether, even this outcome is unusual. Thus the state is defined as a monopoly of force over a given territory, but it is also the set of political institutions that transform ideas regarding freedom and equality into concrete action. It is, if you will, the machinery of politics, establishing order *and* turning politics into policy.

A few other terms that are often used with regard to political organization need to be defined here. Although often used interchangeably with the concept of the state, they are in fact separate institutions that help define and direct the state. First, we should make a distinction between the state and the idea of a **regime, which is defined** as the fundamental rules and norms of politics. More specifically, a regime embodies long-term goals regarding individual freedom and collective equality, and regarding where power should reside and how it should be used. At the most basic level, we can speak of a democratic regime or an authoritarian one. In a *democratic regime,* the rules and norms of politics emphasize a large role for the public in governance, as well as certain individual rights or liberties. Power in such regimes tends to be decentralized, and long-term goals tend to center around either balancing individual freedom and collective equality, or emphasizing freedom over equality. An *authoritarian regime,* in contrast,

IN FOCUS

A REGIME IS . . .

- Norms and rules regarding individual freedom and collective equality, the locus of power, and the use of that power.

- Institutionalized, but can be changed by dramatic social events such as a revolution.

- Categorized at the most basic level as either democratic or authoritarian.

- Often embodied in a constitution.

emphasizes a limited role for the public in politics. Power is centralized in the hands of the state, and long-term goals may vary. Individual freedom may be restricted in favor of greater collective equality, or both freedom and equality may be limited. Power may even be centralized merely for its own sake.

Even within democratic or authoritarian regimes, the basic rules and norms of politics may differ. The democratic regime of the United States is not the same as that of Canada; the authoritarian regime of China is not the same as that of Cuba. Some of these differences can be found in basic documents such as constitutions, but often the rules and norms that distinguish one regime from another are unwritten and implicit, requiring careful study.

Like the state, regimes are often institutions. Regimes do not easily or quickly change, although they can be transformed or altered, usually by dramatic social events such as a revolution or a national crisis. Most revolutions, in fact, can be seen as revolts not against the state, but against the current regime—to overthrow the old rules and norms and replace them with new ones. For example, France refers to its current regime as the "Fifth Republic." Since the French Revolution overthrew the monarchy in 1789, each French republic has been characterized by a separate regime, embodied in the constitution and the broader political rules that shape politics. In another example, South Africa's transition to democracy in the 1990s involved a change of regime, as the white-dominated system of apartheid has given way to one that provides democratic rights to all South Africans.

In some authoritarian countries where politics is dominated by a single individual, observers may use the term "regime" to refer to that leader, emphasizing the view that all decisions flow from that one person. Or as King Louis XIV of France famously put it, "*L'Etat, c'est moi*" (I am the state).

To recap, if the state is a monopoly of force and a set of political institutions to generate policy, then the regime is defined as the norms and rules regarding the proper balance of freedom and equality and the use of power. To use an analogy, if the state is the machinery of politics, like a personal computer, then one can think of a regime as its software, the programming that defines its capabilities. Each computer runs differently, depending on the software installed.

This brings us to a third term to add to our understanding of state and regime: government. **Government** can be defined as the leadership or elite in charge of running

IN FOCUS

GOVERNMENT IS . . .

- The leadership or elite in charge of running the state.
- Weakly institutionalized.
- Often characterized by elected officials such as a president or prime minister, or unelected officials such as a dictator.
- Limited by the existing regime.

the state. If the state is the machinery of politics, and the regime its pro-gramming, then the government acts as its operator. The government may consist of democratically elected legislators, presidents, and prime minis-ters, or it may be made up of dictators who gained offices through force or other nondemocratic means. Whatever their path to power, governments all hold particular ideas regarding freedom and equality and attempt to use the state to realize those ideas. But few governments are able to act with complete freedom in this regard. Democratic and even authoritarian governments must confront the existing regime, the norms and values of politics that have built up over time. Push too hard against an existing regime, and resistance or even outright rebellion may occur. For example, Mikhail Gorbachev's attempt to fundamentally transform the regime of the Soviet Union in the 1980s led to that country's breakup.

In part because of the power of regimes, governments tend to be weakly institutionalized—that is to say, those in power are not viewed by the pub-lic as irreplaceable, such that the country would collapse without them. In democratic regimes governments are replaced fairly frequently, and even

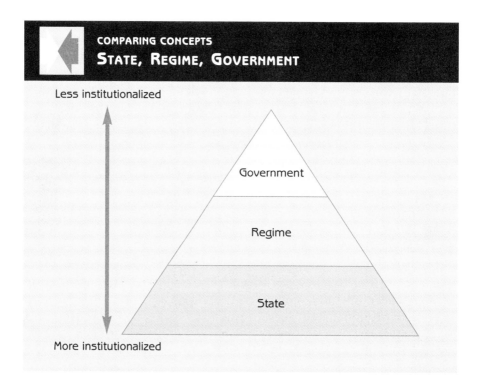

COMPARING CONCEPTS

STATE, REGIME, GOVERNMENT

Less institutionalized

Government

Regime

State

More institutionalized

in authoritarian settings those who rule are continuously threatened by rivals and their own mortality. Governments come and go, whereas regimes and states may live on for decades or even centuries.

Finally, we have the term **country**, which can be seen as shorthand for all the concepts so far discussed—state, government, regime—as well as the people who live within that political system. We will commonly speak about various countries in this textbook, and when we do, we are referring to the entire political entity and its citizens.

THE ORIGINS OF POLITICAL ORGANIZATION

So far we have noted that modern politics is defined by states, which monopolize force and execute policies. This political machinery is given direction by a particular regime, and by the government in power. Governments provide short-term goals regarding freedom and equality, and regimes provide a more institutionalized set of norms and values about politics. This combination of institutions is relatively new. For tens of thousands of years human beings have formed collective groups, ranging from relatively simple and fluid gatherings to highly complex systems that incorporate hundreds of thousands or millions of individuals and last for centuries. Tribes, bands, cities, empires took root anywhere that people settled, serving as fundamental forms of human organization. But as we look over the face of the earth in this new millennium we see that these various forms of political organization have for the most part disappeared. The globe is now clearly demarcated by only one type of political organization—the state—that over the past few hundred years has displaced virtually all other political structures. Almost no inhabitable territory or people on the face of the earth is not claimed by some state.

But where did states come from, and why have they displaced all other forms of political organization? Why are there no longer parts of the world controlled by city-states, tribes, or empires? In order to answer these questions we first need to go back into human history and discuss the origins of political organization. How human beings have come together and how they have organized their lives will also be a central issue later on as we look at the role of democracy and authoritarianism in the modern world. It would appear that states have been able to dispatch all other forms of political organization, in spite of the long history of these other forms. By understanding the origins and power of states, we can better grasp their functions in the modern world and understand that, just as human beings once existed without states, states might themselves be replaced in the future by some other form of political organization.

Archeology and history tell us that throughout history human beings have organized into political units, although their findings do not explain why human beings organized in the first place. For political scientists interested in current affairs, this original motivation may be of little concern, but for anthropologists and others focused on human history and social evolution, the question is important. There are a number of different and competing explanations as to why human beings organize. One important factor is probably environment and agriculture. Where people were able to domesticate plants and animals (a much more difficult process than one might imagine), they moved from a nomadic hunter-gatherer existence to one of sedentary living. Concepts that would have previously been meaningless, such as territory, crops, and homes, suddenly became life-or-death issues.

In addition, the rise of agriculture allowed for the creation of food surpluses, again a great change from the hunter-gatherer days. Food surpluses allowed for greater human specialization: some people could forgo farming and pursue other activities, such as making useful goods that could be exchanged for food and other items. But while agriculture and a sedentary existence created property and specialization, it also created, or at least increased, human inequality. In a system of greater specialization that relies on a wide array of talents, some will clearly benefit more than others; wealth and power inevitably become unequally distributed.

This time period is when political organization most likely had its beginning. Whereas in small bands or larger tribes there tends to be relative equality and communal decision-making, as societies grow larger, more specialized, and more unequal, they require new mechanisms to handle disputes. Those with economic surpluses seek to protect their riches from theft. Those without surpluses seek a greater share of the group's resources. And both fear attack by outside groups that might covet their lands, crops, and homes. Because of such human innovations as agriculture, the very concepts of individualism versus the collective, of freedom versus equality, first arose. Who gets what? Who has the right to do what? And how should these decisions be made and enforced? Reconciling freedom and equality in turn raised questions regarding the locus and use of power, and thus created politics.

Because of these changes political organizations formed in order to reconcile freedom and equality. These organizations could settle or prevent disputes between individuals, thus generating early notions of law and justice. Political organizations could also punish those found guilty of breaking rules and raise a military force capable of resisting invaders. These roles of punishing and defending paved the way for a monopoly of force. In order to carry out these activities, though, political organizations required revenue, creating the need for taxation. Clearly, then, many of the elements of modern politics emerged in the distant past.

One thing that remains unclear, however, is whether these political organizations emerged through consensus or through force. In other words, did political systems develop because some people managed to impose their will on others, installing themselves as chiefs or kings and using violence to impose their will? Or did people willingly form political systems as a way to overcome the anarchy that would otherwise result in a world that lacked central authority? In the absence of evidence, philosophers have long debated this issue. The philosopher Thomas Hobbes believed that human beings voluntarily enter into a "social contract" or agreement among themselves to create a single political authority to overcome anarchy. In return for giving up many of their rights, people were ensured security and a foundation on which to build a civilization. Jean-Jacques Rousseau, while also accepting the idea of the social contract, emphasized that this contract exists not between people but between ruler and ruled. Those in power are charged with providing security and liberty, and if they fail to do so, the people have the right to dissolve the social contract. Rousseau argued that political systems do not live up to their intention to serve society as a whole, since once established they inevitably generate inequality between the ruling elite and the masses. Karl Marx went even further, rejecting the very notion of a social contract. Instead, he viewed political organization solely as a tool of exploitation, a system by which those who gain economic power can maintain their spoils by oppressing those they have taken it from. In his view, if human beings were allowed to create a truly equal society, there would be no need for political organization or even politics.

As we shall see in later chapters, those who believe in the institutions of modern democracy reflect the view of politics as a consensus, with people willingly surrendering some of their power, in order to gain greater security and prosperity. However, they also assert that politics must serve the wishes of the public; when it does not, the public has the right to replace those in power. In contrast, those skeptical of modern democracy emphasize the coercive nature of politics; they doubt that the domineering state and the unequal relations it creates can be at all democratic. All politics reflects this tension between coercion and consensus. Each state balances the two differently, reflecting the tension between freedom and equality.

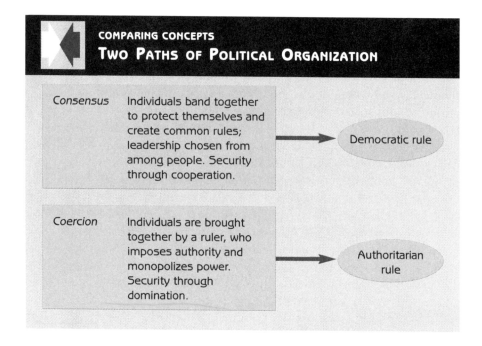

COMPARING CONCEPTS
TWO PATHS OF POLITICAL ORGANIZATION

Consensus   Individuals band together to protect themselves and create common rules; leadership chosen from among people. Security through cooperation.   →   Democratic rule

Coercion   Individuals are brought together by a ruler, who imposes authority and monopolizes power. Security through domination.   →   Authoritarian rule

Through a mixture of coercion and consensus, complex organizations began to emerge around 7,500 years ago, bearing the political hallmarks of politics that exist to this day, such as taxation, bureaucracy, laws, military force, and leadership. Some of these political units were relatively small, such as the city-states that emerged in ancient Greece some 2,700 years ago. In other cases large empires emerged, as in China, South America, the Middle East, and Africa. Across these political systems economic relations were based on agricultural production, with more specialized goods and trade as secondary activities. And unlike in modern countries, the borders of these early political systems were often undefined or unclear. Beyond their authority, large portions of the inhabited world possessed no form of complex political organization.

THE RISE OF THE MODERN STATE

This patchwork of differing political systems would eventually give way to the modern state, which would first arrive in Europe. Why the state first developed, emerged in Europe, and came to dominate the world is uncertain, but it may in part be due to historical chance and the curious advantage of backwardness. Two thousand years ago, Europe, like other parts of the world, was dominated by a single large empire—in this case, the Roman Empire. Spanning thousands of miles across western Europe to North Africa and Egypt, the Roman Empire developed a highly complex political system that tied together millions of people and generated an advanced infrastructure of cities, laws, trade, knowledge, and roads. After a thousand years, however, the Roman Empire eventually declined, succumbing to the pressures of overexpansion and increased attacks by rival forces. By the fifth century C.E., Rome itself was sacked by invaders.

As the Roman Empire collapsed, the complex political institutions and the other benefits that had extended across its territory largely disappeared, particularly in western Europe. The security generated by imperial control evaporated, replaced by roving bands of marauders. Roads and other basic forms of infrastructure people depended on eroded. Rules and regulations fragmented and lost their power. The knowledge and technology accumulated under the empire was lost or forgotten, and the advanced system

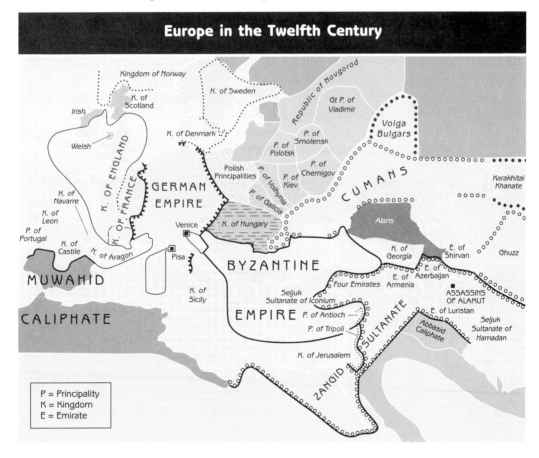

Europe in the Twelfth Century

P = Principality
K = Kingdom
E = Emirate

of trade and travel between communities came to an end. Much of western Europe reverted to anarchy, entering the period commonly known as the Dark Ages, from about 500 C.E. to about 1000 C.E.

Yet paradoxically, this period of dramatic decline and anarchy appears to have set the stage for the creation of the modern state. As the sociologist Charles Tilly has noted, in this highly fragmented, unstable, and violent environment, new political organizations began to develop, in constant competition with their rivals.[2] In some cases, these were simply thugs who realized they could earn a better living by controlling and taxing one group of people rather than by constantly pillaging from place to place. Warlords staked out relatively small areas of land that they could easily defend and consolidated control over these regions, fighting off rival groups. In other cases, the people appear to have banded together themselves to fight off bandit groups. As Tilly and others have concluded, the modern state emerged from or in reaction to what was essentially organized crime, with armed groups staking out turf, offering protection, and demanding payment in return.

The constant warfare among these numerous rivals seems to have generated a kind of rapid organizational evolution. Those groups that could quickly adapt survived, while less successful groups were conquered and disappeared. Rapid development was thus encouraged by a highly competitive and fluid environment.

Not only history, but also geography appears to have played a role in the rise of the modern state. The physiologist Jared Diamond has argued that Europe's close proximity to Asia and the Middle East provided benefits in the form of new plants, animals, and technical innovations that were otherwise unavailable to peoples in the Americas or Africa. At the same time, Europe's diverse geography hindered political centralization under a single language or culture.[3] Even at the height of the Roman Empire, much of central, northern, and eastern Europe had lain beyond the Romans' reach. Contrast this with China, where political power was centralized and institutionalized already by the third century C.E. Because China was more politically stable and lacked the kind of competitive environment seen in Europe, over time its institutions grew ossified, inflexible, and resistant to political, economic, or technological change.

Out of the constant warfare of the Dark Ages emerged a new form of political organization—the state—that possessed three important advantages over alternate forms. First, states encouraged economic development. Before and during the Dark Ages, most Europeans lived under an economic system based on subsistence agriculture. Property such as land tended to be monopolized by those in power rather than by those who worked it. Warlords could tie the people to the land (serfdom) and extract their labor and levy heavy taxes on those who produced nonagricultural goods. However, such economic conditions were counterproductive for society as a whole: individuals had little incentive to produce if the fruits of their labor were simply taken by others. Those rulers who created laws, regulations, and infrastructure that permitted and respected private property and individual profit, however, found that production grew, giving the ruler more resources to tax or borrow (and with which to make war).

Second, some rulers similarly encouraged technological innovation as a means of increasing their own economic and military power. As with private commerce and trade, rulers realized that new technologies would also stimulate economic development by providing new goods and services. When technological innovation was harnessed to commerce, economic development expanded dramatically. Technological change was thus viewed by some rulers not as a threat to their power but as a means to expand it. Many of the advantages that made Europe powerful as it set off to conquer the world—gunpowder, advanced mathematics, modern cartography, paper, astronomy—had actually originated in Asia and the Middle East. But the Europeans absorbed these innovations and put them to new uses. What mattered most was not *who* had discovered these things, but rather *how* these discoveries were encouraged or used by the state and society. Eventually, this access to technological innovation, combined with states willing to tolerate or encourage private enterprise, would set the stage for modern capitalism—a system of private property, free markets, and investment in the pursuit of wealth.

Third, through the creation of domestic stability, increased trade and commerce, and the development of infrastructure, states assisted in the homogenization of peoples living in their territories. The fact that people could travel more freely within the territory of their state encouraged interaction and the development of a shared culture. The state, through printed documents, education, and legal codes, also contributed to the standardization of language. People in Europe began to see themselves as belonging to a common ethnic identity that comprised shared cultural values. Instead of identifying with their trade, clan, religion, or town, people began to see themselves as English or French or German. Ethnicity would prove to be a powerful asset to the state, for it in turn fostered nationalism—a shared political identity. (We will discuss these concepts in detail in Chapter 3.)

Around 1500 C.E., states covered only 20 percent of the globe. But this was soon to change. Well organized and armed with technological advances, national identity, and economic resources, the states of Europe began to

TIMELINE: POLITICAL ORGANIZATION IN EUROPE

10th–9th centuries B.C.E.	Greek dark ages
8th–7th centuries B.C.E.	Beginning of Greek city-states, centralization of political power in Europe
6th–5th centuries B.C.E.	Establishment of Roman republic, first development of democracy in Athens
2nd–1st centuries B.C.E.	Roman conquest of Greece
1st–2nd centuries C.E.	Roman Empire expands across Europe and into the Middle East, zenith of centralized imperial power in Europe
3rd–4th centuries C.E.	Internal decline of Roman Empire, beginning of European dark ages, development stagnates
5th–6th centuries C.E.	Rome sacked by the Visigoths, widespread strife among competing European warlords
7th–8th centuries C.E.	Muslim armies enter Spain; Islamic world grows in power during a period of innovation and expansion
9th–10th centuries C.E.	Viking raids across Europe
11th–12th centuries C.E.	European crusades into Middle East, warfare begins to consolidate Europe into distinct political units
12th–13th centuries C.E.	Period of rapid innovation and development: mechanical clock invented; paper, compass adopted from Asia and the Middle East
14th–15th centuries C.E.	Voyages of exploration and early imperialism, early European states centralize, Islamic world stagnates
16th–17th centuries C.E.	Scientific revolution, modern states develop, modern identities of nationalism and patriotism develop

rapidly accrue power. As economic power grew, so did the ability of the state to manage ever greater numbers of people and ever more territory. Increased finances and state organization also allowed for the development of large, professional armies. Possessing the ability to conquer and control larger pieces of land, states began to defeat and absorb their rivals. Another major rival to state power, the Roman Catholic Church, was also defeated during this time. The Thirty Years' War (1618–48), in part a struggle between Roman Catholicism and Protestantism, culminated in the Treaty of Westphalia in 1648. Under this treaty, the authority of the pope over Europe's people and leadership was radically curtailed. Without this rival spiritual authority, states were free to direct religion within their own territory, subordinating the spiritual to the political. State sovereignty as we understand it today effectively dates from the Treaty of Westphalia.

At this same time, European states began to expand their economic, technical, and military powers beyond their own shores. During the seventeenth and eighteenth centuries Spain and Portugal took control of South America, while the Dutch, the French, and the British expanded state power into Asia. By the nineteenth century, nearly all of Africa had similarly been divided up among European states and incorporated into their far-flung empires.

The organizational structure of the state was thus imposed around the world by force. Yet as European control receded in the twentieth century, the structure of the state remained—indeed, states even grew in number. Although peoples all around the world resisted and eventually threw off European domination, they viewed the state as a superior—or at least inevitable—form of political evolution, and they adopted it for their own purposes. The world thus became a world of states: states set forth international boundaries and established international rules, and they became the primary actors in domestic and international politics around the world.

The rapid spread of states has not been without its drawbacks, however. Whereas Europe took several hundred years to create the modern state, much of the world has been forced to take up this form of organization more quickly, adopting it out of necessity. Yet the historical conditions of Africa or South America were radically different from those of Europe. Thus many new states lack the resources and organization that much older states have developed over centuries, and new states are often confronted with the challenge of controlling a territory where a multitude of peoples, languages, religions, and culture may coexist—problems that most European states solved only over the course of hundreds of years and at the cost of countless lives lost in battle. For better or worse, although Europe no longer directly rules over much of the earth, it has left us with the legacy of the state itself.

COMPARING STATE POWER

The discussion above showed that political evolution has been a lengthy and somewhat arbitrary process. Where conditions allowed for human beings to settle permanently, complex forms of political organization quickly formed, with features that reflect basic aspects of modern politics: freedom, equality, and the allocation of power. But only over the past few centuries has the state taken shape, forging new political, economic, and social institutions that have made it extremely powerful. States quickly eradicated all other forms of political organization and laid claim to all corners of the earth.

But in spite of this uniformity, not all states are the same. Some are powerful, effective, and stable; others appear weak, disorganized, and incapable of action. Moreover, a single state can have a commanding presence in one area but appear ineffectual in another. What explains this range of state authority and power? In order to answer this question and make effective comparisons, we need some more conceptual tools with which to work.

Legitimacy — *states, leaders need to be recognized*

The first concept to address is that of **legitimacy**, which can be defined as a value whereby something or someone is recognized and accepted as right and proper. In other words, a legitimate institution or person is widely accepted and recognized by the public. Legitimacy confers authority and power. In the case of states, we know they wield a great deal of coercive force. But is that the only reason that people recognize their authority? In fact, many people obey the law even when the threat of punishment is slight. Why? They view such behavior as "the right thing" to do. We pay our taxes, we do not litter, and we serve in the military not simply because of fear of punishment, but because we assume that the state has the authority to ask these things of us. Legitimacy thus creates power that relies not on coercion, but on consent. Without legitimacy, a state would have to use the continuous threat of force to maintain order—a difficult task.

How does a state become legitimate? Let us turn again to Max Weber, who argued that political legitimacy comes in three basic forms: traditional, charismatic, and rational-legal.[4] **Traditional legitimacy** rests on the idea that someone or something is valid because "it has always been that way." In other words, this legitimacy is built on the idea that certain aspects of politics are to be accepted because they have been accepted over a long period of time. In some way, they are seen as inseparable from the identity of the people themselves. Traditional legitimacy often embodies historical myths and legends, as well as the continuity between past and present. Rituals and ceremonies all help to reinforce traditional legitimacy, by providing actions and symbols that are ancient, unique, and dramatic. One good example is the legitimacy accorded to a monarchy. What makes a monarch a monarch? Typically a king or queen is not voted into office, but instead is a member of the monarchy by virtue of his or her birth. The kings of both Jordan and Morocco are considered to be direct descendants of the Prophet Muhammed, who established the Islamic faith in the seventh century C.E. They therefore enjoy a legitimacy that stems not just from political continuity, but from religion as well.

In short, traditional legitimacy is a system built on history and continuity. The longer a traditional political system has been in place, the more institutionalized it becomes, as it has the weight of history on its side. Change becomes difficult to imagine if an institution has existed "since time immemorial."

Charismatic legitimacy is in many ways the very opposite of traditional legitimacy. When we use "charisma" in everyday conversation, we usually are describing someone who is good-looking or perhaps a witty conversationalist. But in politics charisma means much more. Rather than relying on the weight of history and the continuity of certain roles or values, charismatic legitimacy is based on the power of ideas. These are typically embodied by one individual, who can move the public through these ideas and the manner in which she or he presents them. Some individuals possess a certain magnetism that surrounds both who they are and what they say. Jesus and Mohammed are perfect examples of charismatic figures who could gather huge followings through the power of their ideas. In a more modern and more sinister example, Adolf Hitler can also be viewed as a charismatic figure. If we look at pictures of Hitler today, we might think it strange that this unattractive man could so dominate a country and plunge Europe into genocide and war. Yet it is not physical appearance, but rather the force of ideas, that makes charisma possible.

As you can imagine, charismatic legitimacy is not institutionalized and thus is fairly tenuous, since it commonly dies with the individual who possesses it. But charismatic legitimacy often gets transformed into traditional legitimacy with the creation of rituals and values that are meant to capture the spirit and intent of the charismatic leader's power. This process may or may not directly involve the charismatic leader's descendants. Weber called this kind of institutionalization "the routinization of charisma."

In contrast to the first two forms of legitimacy, **rational-legal legitimacy** is based not on history or rituals (as in the case of traditional legitimacy), or on the force of ideas (as in charismatic legitimacy), but rather on a system of laws and procedures that are highly institutionalized. A leader or political official can be legitimate by virtue of the clear rules by which he or she came to office. Moreover, people obey the decisions of these actors because they believe that the rules the leaders enforce serve the public's interest. In this case, it is not the person who is important, or even that individual's particular values or ideas, but the title and office that he or she holds. The office is legitimate, rather than the person in it. Once that person leaves office, he or she loses authority.

As you have probably already guessed, the world of modern states is built on a rational-legal foundation. States rely on bureaucracies, paperwork, and thousands of individuals to make daily decisions on a wide range of issues. Ideally, the public accepts these decisions as the proper way to get things done, and they presume that these decisions are reasonably fair and predictable. For example, if there are elections, they accept the outcome even if their preferred candidate loses, and they obey the instructions of those who won. The 2000 presidential election in the United States is a perfect example of rational-legal legitimacy. After weeks of bitter disputes over who had actually won the election, the Supreme Court's intervention effectively ended the battle, and the Democratic candidate, Al Gore, agreed to abide by the outcome. In spite of denunciations by some that the election was illegitimate, the vast majority of Americans accepted George W. Bush as their president, even if they had not voted for him

COMPARING CONCEPTS
THREE TYPES OF LEGITIMACY

Type	Characteristics	Example
Traditional legitimacy	Built by habit and custom over time, stressing history; strongly institutionalized	Monarch (Queen Elizabeth)
Charismatic legitimacy	Built on the force of ideas and the presence of the leader; weakly institutionalized	Revolutionary hero (Vladimir Lenin)
Rational-legal legitimacy	Built on rules and procedures and the offices that create and enforce those rules; strongly institutionalized	Elected executive (George Bush)

(and the majority of voters had not). Legitimacy is not confined only to political actors within the state; our own individual legitimacy comes from a rational-legal foundation: our driver's license, identification numbers, passports, or voter registration cards all confer a certain form of authority and power.

Note, however, that just because the rise of modern states was built on a rational-legal legitimacy, that does not mean that traditional or charismatic legitimacy has disappeared. In almost any country, all three forms of legitimacy can be found, to varying degrees. Political leaders in many countries throughout modern history have wielded a great deal of charismatic power and become the centers of large "cults of personality," which we will explore further in Chapter 5. These cults portray the leader as the father (or occasionally, the mother) of the nation, and imbue him or her with almost superhuman powers. Charismatic leadership, and the power that it places in the hands of one individual, can corrupt, but some charismatic figures have dramatically changed the course of politics for the better—Mohandas K. Gandhi in India, or Nelson Mandela in South Africa, for instance.

Traditional power can similarly be found in a wide variety of circumstances. The United Kingdom, Japan, Sweden, and more than twenty other countries still have monarchs. Although the powers of most of these monarchs are now quite limited, they remain important symbols and attract national and sometimes even international attention—think of the international obsession with the British royal family. Even rules and regulations can over time take on a kind of traditional legitimacy, if they function for so long that people can't imagine doing things any other way. The U.S. Constitution, for example, is simply a set of rules for conducting politics, but it is also considered to be a sacred symbol of what makes the United States unique and powerful. Is the difficulty in modifying the U.S. Constitution due to the procedures involved, or has there developed over time a resistance to tinkering with this "sacred" document? If the latter is true, then it is not simply rational-legal but also traditional legitimacy that binds American politics together.

To summarize, all states seek authority and power through some form of legitimacy. Traditional legitimacy stresses ritual and continuity; charismatic legitimacy, the force of ideas as embodied in a leader; rational-legal legitimacy, laws and rules. Whatever the form or mixture, legitimacy makes it possible for the state to carry out its basic functions. Without it, a state will find carrying out these tasks very difficult. The public, having little faith in the state, will frequently ignore political responsibilities, such as paying taxes, abiding by regulations, or serving in the armed forces. Under these conditions, the state has really only one tool left to maintain order: the threat of force. Paradoxically, then, states that use the most coercion against their citizens are often the most weakly institutionalized states, for without violence, they cannot get the public to willingly comply with the rules and duties set forth.

Centralization or Decentralization

In addition to varying in the kind and level of political legitimacy they enjoy, states also vary in their distribution of power. Chapter 1 introduced the matrix of freedom and equality with regard to the centralization of power. Individual freedom is typically associated with the decentralization of power, whereas collective equality is typically associated with a greater centralization of power.

State power can be centralized or decentralized in a couple of different ways, the first of which is the dispersal of power within the state itself. Under **federalism**, significant powers, such as taxation, lawmaking, and security, are devolved to regional bodies (such as states in the United States, *Länder* in Germany, republics in Russia, or provinces in Canada) that control specific territory within the country. These powers are defined within the national constitution and therefore are not easily constricted or eliminated by any government. In contrast, **unitary states** invest most political power at the national level, with limited local authority. The central government is responsible for most areas of policy. Territorial divisions within unitary states, such as the United Kingdom, Japan, or Sweden, are not very important in terms of political power.

Another way in which power may be dispersed is between the state and nonstate actors, such as the public or organized rivals. In this regard political scientists often make a distinction between **strong states** and **weak states**. Strong states are those that are able to fulfill basic tasks: defending their territory, making and enforcing rules, collecting taxes, and managing the economy, to name some of the more important responsibilities. In contrast, weak states cannot execute such tasks very well. Rules are haphazardly applied, if at all; tax evasion and other forms of public noncompliance are widespread; armed rivals to the state, such as rebel movements or organized crime, may control large chunks of territory or of the economy. State officials themselves, having little faith in their office or responsibilities, may use their jobs simply to fill their own pockets through corruption and theft. In turn, economic development is

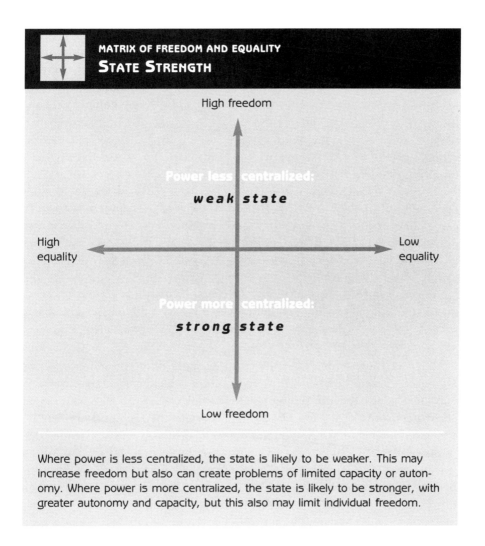

MATRIX OF FREEDOM AND EQUALITY
STATE STRENGTH

High freedom

Power less centralized:
weak state

High
equality

Low
equality

Power more centralized:
strong state

Low freedom

Where power is less centralized, the state is likely to be weaker. This may increase freedom but also can create problems of limited capacity or autonomy. Where power is more centralized, the state is likely to be stronger, with greater autonomy and capacity, but this also may limit individual freedom.

certain to be much lower as a result of this unstable political environment. In general, a weak state is not well institutionalized and lacks authority and legitimacy. At an extreme, the very structures of the state may become so weak that they collapse, resulting in a complete loss of power; anarchy and violence erupt as order breaks down. This situation has been seen in a number of cases in the last decade; they are commonly referred to as **failed states**.[5]

Comparative politics further builds on the categories of weak and strong states through the use of two other terms: capacity and autonomy. **Capacity** refers to the ability of the state to wield power in order to carry out the basic tasks of providing security and reconciling freedom and equality. A state with high capacity is able to formulate and enact fundamental policies and ensure stability and security for both itself and its citizens. A state with low capacity is unable to do these things very effectively. High capacity requires not just money, but also organization, legitimacy, and effective leadership. Roads get paved, schools get built, regulations are created and followed, and those who break the law are punished.

In contrast, **autonomy** is the ability of the state to wield its power independently of the public. In other words, if an autonomous state wishes to carry out a policy or action, it can do so without having to consult the public or worrying about strong public opposition that might force it to reverse its decision. A state with a high degree of autonomy may act *on behalf of* the public, pursuing what it believes are the best interests of the country, irrespective of public opinion. A state with a low degree of autonomy will act largely *at the behest of* private individuals or groups and will be less able to disobey the public will or the demands of well-organized groups.

Each of these concepts helps us to evaluate different states in terms of power. Strong states with a high degree of capacity and autonomy may be able to execute major policies relatively easily. China's current construction of the world's largest dam, despite the technical challenges, enormous cost, and widespread international criticism for its possible environmental impact, is a case in point. But too much power centralized within the state can come at the expense of democracy, as has certainly been the case in China, where little dissent is tolerated. States with a high degree of capacity but low autonomy may have similar powers, but they are subject to greater public control. The United States is a good example of such a system, which is further reinforced by its federal structure. Individual freedom in the United States may be high, but it can sometimes fetter the state and hinder change, as policy becomes captive to special interests. States with high autonomy but low capacity may lack the ability to execute policy. North Korea is a tragic example in this regard, an authoritarian communist country that over the past decade has become incapable of feeding its own people. Finally, states may lack both autonomy and capacity. Since the end of the racist apartheid regime in South Africa in 1994, that country has confronted limits in both autonomy and capacity, as a newly mobilized and active public has sought to expand its political demands on a state with limited resources that were once largely

STATE AUTONOMY AND CAPACITY

		Autonomy	
		High	Low
Capacity	High	State able to fulfill basic tasks, with a minimum of public intervention; power highly centralized: Strong state. **Danger:** Too high a level of capacity and autonomy may prevent or undermine democracy. **Example:** China	State able to fulfill basic tasks, but public plays a direct role in determining policy and is able to limit state power and scope of activity. **Danger:** State may be unable to develop new policies or respond to new challenges due to the power of organized opposition. **Example:** United States
	Low	State is able to function with a minimum amount of public interference or direct control, but its capacity to fulfill basic tasks is limited. **Danger:** State is ineffectual, limiting development that may provoke public unrest. **Example:** North Korea	State lacks both the ability to fulfill basic tasks and is subject to direct public control and interference—power highly decentralized among state and nonstate actors: Weak state. **Danger:** Too low a level of capacity and autonomy may lead to internal state failure. **Examples:** South Africa, Afghanistan (failed state)

reserved for a small white elite. At an extreme, too little capacity and too little autonomy can bring down the state entirely, as occurred in Afghanistan, paving the way for rivals like the terrorist organization Al Qaeda to establish control.

In Sum: Studying States

This chapter began by defining the state as a monopoly of force, but also as the institution charged with transforming freedom and equality from ideas into concrete action. The kinds of decisions made toward this end, however, are shaped by regimes and governments. Regimes are the fundamental rules and norms of politics, providing long-term goals regarding individual freedom and collective equality, and the location and use of power toward those goals. Governments, in contrast, are those political elites in charge of running the state. Influenced by the existing regime, they attempt to formulate policy regarding freedom and equality that may then be executed by the state. These represent the most basic facets of states everywhere—and indeed, states *are* everywhere. Although similar political organizations have existed for thousands of years, only within the past few centuries did states arise in Europe and quickly come to dominate the globe. States are the main political players in the world today.

The universal presence of states compels comparativists to find some way to study and evaluate them. One way is by assessing their legitimacy; different kinds of legitimacy—traditional, charismatic, and rational-legal—all create their own kinds of authority and power. The other is by assessing the actual dispersal of power itself; states may be weaker or stronger, with more or less capacity and autonomy, depending on how power is distributed within the state and between the state and the public. Too much power in the hands of the state risks tyranny; too little power risks chaos. Finding the right mix is not simply a technical question, but one shaped by a people's views regarding freedom and equality. This debate over freedom and equality, then, ranges far beyond the boundaries of the state itself. As we shall see in the chapters that follow, it is influenced by society, through ethnic and national identity, culture, and ideology; by economic institutions and the interaction between states and markets; and by democratic practices and authoritarian ones.

Since the dawn of human civilization people have relied on some form of political organization to strike a balance between individual freedom and collective equality. For the past few centuries, states have been that form of organization. Do states now represent an end point in human intellectual evolution, or at some point in the future will new forms of political organization displace states, just as states displaced empires? Might civilization at some point reconcile or even transcend the notions of freedom and equality, so that political organization—at least as we understand it now—will cease to exist? These questions may seem unanswerable, more amenable to fortune-telling than to research. But as we shall see, they lie at the heart of conflicts that have transformed the world in the past and will continue to confront us in the future.

NOTES

1 In the United States, the word "state" refers to the federal structure of regional government. As a result, for Americans the word "state" conjures up the idea of local government, whereas for political scientists (and most people around the world) the word "state" refers to national, not local, organization. This confusion stems from U.S. history. During the period of revolutionary struggle and the creation of a federal system, the former British colonies in America viewed themselves as independent political units—in other words, as *states*. With the creation of a federal system of government, however, their individual powers were subordinated to central authority. The United States of America, in other words, eventually became a system of national government, with the term "state" left as a remnant of that brief period when they acted as largely independent entities.

2 Charles Tilly, *Coercion, Capital, and European States: 990–1990* (Oxford, U.K.: Blackwell, 1990).

3 Jared Diamond, *Guns, Germs, and Steel: The Fates of Human Societies* (New York: W. W. Norton, 1997).

4 Max Weber, "Politics as a Vocation," in H. H. Gerth and C. Wright Mills, trans. and eds., *From Max Weber: Essays in Sociology* (New York: Oxford University Press, 1958), 77–128.

5 For a discussion of state failure see Robert Kaplan, *The Ends of the Earth: From Togo to Turkmenistan, from Iran to Cambodia, a Journey to the Frontiers of Anarchy* (New York: Vintage, 1997).

3 NATIONS AND SOCIETY

Society is a broad term that refers to complex human organization, a collection of people bound by shared institutions that define how human relations should be conducted. From country to country and place to place, societies differ in how individuals define themselves and their relationships to one another, as well as their relationships to government and the state. These relationships are unique; for all the surface similarities that may exist between societies, each country views itself and the wider world around it in distinct way. These differences make comparative politics a rich field of study, but also a frustrating one, as social scientists seek to find similarities that are often few and far between.

In this chapter we will look at the ways in which people identify themselves and are identified, both as individuals and in groups, and how these identifications relate to politics and the state. Human beings are often defined by such basic identities as "left" or "right," "us" or "them." These identities shape politics and influence the debate over freedom and equality by generating diversity, cooperation, and conflict. How these identities differ from place to place has profound implications for comparative politics.

We will start with the concepts of ethnic and national identity, two of the most basic ways in which individuals and groups define themselves politically. What does it mean to be part of an ethnic group? How is such a group defined? What is the difference between an ethnic group and a nation? We will also make a distinction between ethnicity, nationality, and citizenship. What does it mean, for example, to say that someone is a "Chinese citizen" as opposed to saying that they are "ethnically Chinese" or just "Chinese"? A related question arises in the distinction between nationalism and patriotism: What is the difference between being patriotic and nationalistic? We will answer these questions by looking at some examples of each and tracing their historical origins. Throughout recent history the world has witnessed violent domestic and international conflicts connected to national and ethnic identities. Why do such conflicts occur? Are they a natural or inevitable part of human organization, or something manufactured by political leaders to serve their own purposes? In this chapter we will also look at some of the effects of these different identities when they conflict with one another.

From there we will move on to a discussion of political attitudes and ideologies. Whereas ethnicity, nationality, and citizenship are group identities, political attitudes and ideologies are the values and positions that individuals take with regard to freedom and equality. To what extent can each of these "goods" be achieved through politics? What compromises must be made? And how fast should change be enacted to achieve the proper balance? Ideologies attempt to answer these vital questions. One thing we will see is that although basic political attitudes and ideologies can be compared around the world, their relative strength or influence differs dramatically from country to country. What is considered conservative in one place may be radical in another. One possible explanation for this difference may be cultural. Politics may be more than a freewheeling contest between different values; it may be fundamentally shaped by how each society views and defines itself.

ETHNIC IDENTITY

One term that we often use to identify individuals in society is through ethnicity, as when we speak of people as German or Irish, Kurdish or Zulu, Latino or Ukrainian Canadian. When we use the terms "ethnic identity" or "ethnicity" we emphasize a person's relationship to other members of society. **Ethnicity** refers to any specific attributes and societal institutions that make one group of people culturally different from others. These attributes can include language, religion, geographic location, customs, and history, among other things. As these distinct attributes are

IN FOCUS
ETHNIC IDENTITY IS . . .

- Specific attributes and societal institutions that make one group of people culturally different from others.

- Often based on customs, language, religion, or other factors.

- Ascriptive, generally assigned at birth.

- Not inherently political.

institutionalized, they provide a people with a particular identity that is passed down over time from generation to generation. This process is called "ascription"—the assigning of a particular quality at birth. People do not choose their ethnicities; they are born into them, and their ethnic identity remains largely fixed throughout life.

These differences are not mere curiosities, but vital components of how people view themselves and their relationship to the wider world. Each ethnic group is characterized by its own set of institutions that embody norms and standards of behavior, and a single society can be broken up into numerous ethnic groups. For example, Singaporean society is made up of ethnic Chinese, Malays, and Indians. In the United States there are also numerous ethnic groups, such as African Americans, Japanese Americans, and Native Americans, who further classify themselves as Hopi or Makah, for instance. In both Singapore and the United States there exists a broader society, made up of many different ethnic groups. In fact, the majority of countries in the world are not ethnically homogeneous; in this world of immigration and globalization, rarely are society and ethnicity one and the same. Societies are made up of various ethnic groups, in some cases only a few, in other cases tens or even hundreds, each with its own particular identity. It is important to note that ethnicity is a social, not a political identity; people may identify themselves with an ethnic group without drawing any particular conclusions about politics on that basis. Ethnicity in itself is not inherently political.

Although we have listed a number of common attributes that often define ethnic differences, it is important to stress that there is no "master list" of differences that automatically defines one group as ethnically different from another. In Bosnia, for example, the main ethnic groups—Croats, Serbs, and Muslims—speak the same language and are similar in numerous other ways. What divides Bosnians is primarily religion: Croats are mostly Roman Catholic, Serbs are Eastern Orthodox, and Muslims practice Islam. Yet we speak of Germans as a single ethnic group, even though some are Catholic and some are Protestant. Why are ethnic groups in Bosnia divided by religion, while in Germany such divisions don't produce different ethnic groups? In an even more confusing case, that of Rwanda (where some of the most horrific ethnic killing since World War II took place in 1994), the Hutu and Tutsi ethnic groups cannot be easily distinguished by any of the factors listed above. Both speak the same language, practice the same religions, live in the same geographic regions, and share the same customs. For most outside observers, there is no real ethnic difference between the two, and even Hutus and Tutsis cannot easily distinguish between one another—they rely on such vague distinctions as height, facial features, and diet.

Ethnicity, then can be called a "social construction," built not out of a uniform set of factors but in each case a unique combination of attributes. Ethnicity exists where people acknowledge and are acknowledged by outsiders as belonging to a distinct group. Even though such distinctions may be difficult to observe, these ascriptive identities exist.

NATIONAL IDENTITY

In contrast to ethnicity, which may be constructed in a unique manner from group to group and is not an inherently political concept, the idea of a nation or national identity is much more consistent across various cases. It is also a much more inherently political concept. Rather than being connected through social institutions, **nations** are bound together by a common set of political aspirations, among which the most important is self-government. **National identity** is a sense of belonging to a nation and a belief in its political aspirations. Returning again to the concepts of freedom and equality, national identity implies a demand for greater freedom from another's political system, as in a colony's revolt against its colonial master. National identity may also involve issues of equality, as it may stem from the belief that one's own group is subject to unequal treatment at the hands of an existing political system, and that this situation can be solved by creating a separate country for one's own group.

IN FOCUS

NATIONAL IDENTITY IS . . .

Based on the concept of a *nation:* a group of people bound together by a common set of political aspirations, especially self-government and sovereignty.

Often (but not always) derived from ethnic identity.

Inherently political.

The basis for *nationalism:* pride in one's people and belief that they have a unique political destiny.

As you might suspect, national identity often—but not always—develops from ethnic identity. For example, an ethnic group may chafe against the political system under which it lives; its members may feel that they lack certain rights or freedoms. Often this dissatisfaction arises because the ethnic group represents a minority within the current political system. As a result, some leaders may argue that the ethnic group should have greater political control and that the group's own interests would be better served if it controlled its own political destiny. Self-government can transform a minority into a majority in a new country and give a group the control it desires.

The interaction between ethnicity and national identity can be seen in recent developments in Canada. There, the French-speaking population of the province of Québec constitutes its own ethnic group, quite distinct from the English-speaking citizens of the rest of Canada (as well as from their own French ancestors). By the 1960s, this ethnicity began to develop into a sense of national identity, as some in Québec argued for separation from Canada, where they saw themselves as a minority whose unique concerns were not taken into consideration. Such arguments actually led to national referenda on the issue of secession in 1980 and in 1995. In the latter case the proposal that Québec secede failed by little more than 1 percent of the vote. Thus ethnic identity has also fostered a national identity among many—although not all—Québecois.

National identity can thus create **nationalism**, a pride in one's people and the belief that they have their own unique political destiny that is separate from those of others. In Québec, for example, we find a people uncertain of whether they are just an ethnic group or also a nation—a group that desires self-government through an independent state. This lack of clarity between ethnicity and national identity is also evident in some of the other cases listed below, such as the Basque minority in Spain and the Scots

ETHNONATIONAL INDEPENDENCE MOVEMENTS IN THE 1990s

Country	Ethnic group
Canada	Québecois
Spain	Basques
Indonesia	East Timorese (gained independent state, 2002)
Ethiopia	Eritreans (gained independent state, 1993)
Russia	Chechens
United Kingdom	Scots
Sri Lanka	Tamils
India	Kashmiris
Syria, Iraq, Iran, Turkey	Kurds

in the United Kingdom. In both of these cases, some, but not all, members of the ethnic group support the nationalist cause of independence. In other words, although ethnic identity often leads to a political identity built on nationalism, this is not always the case. A minority ethnic group may feel itself to be part of a larger nation, especially where such minorities have been given a great deal of local autonomy, as in Spain. Under these conditions, people may have a strong ethnic identity yet remain content to belong to a larger nation. A 2001 public opinion survey in the Basque region of Spain showed that more than 40 percent of those surveyed considered themselves equally Basque and Spanish, while only 23 percent considered themselves purely Basque. Consider Native Americans in the United States: If reservations were given the opportunity to secede and become independent states, would many choose to do so?

In short, ethnicity can lead to nationalism if a distinct group develops political aspirations as a way to assert or defend its own uniqueness. But ethnicity does not always lead to national identity. Groups may have a distinct ethnic identity without translating it into a national consciousness and demand for independence. This leads us to a new question: If one can have ethnicity without it leading to national identity, can one have national identity without ethnicity? In other words, must ethnicity always be the source of nationalism? This is hard to answer, and political scientists have not reached any consensus on this question. At first glance it would seem logical that without ethnicity, there is no foundation for national identity; people would lack a common identity and set of institu-

WHAT'S IN A NAME? THE NATION OF ISLAM

The Nation of Islam is a U.S.-based Muslim religious group whose members are primarily African Americans; it counts among its past and present members Malcolm X and Muhammad Ali. In politics, the concept of a "nation" implies sovereignty and self-determination, and this is true in the case of the Nation of Islam as well. According to one of the Nation of Islam's documents, titled *The Muslim Program*, the group wants its members "in America whose parents or grandparents were descendants from slaves, to be allowed to establish a separate state or territory of their own—either on this continent or elsewhere." The use of the term "nation" in the name of the religious group is therefore not an arbitrary one; the Nation of Islam views its goals as not simply those of spiritual redemption, but as concrete political goals that require the establishment of a separate state.

tions on which to build national pride and a desire for independence. But like ethnicity, nationality lacks a "master list" to define it. In the case of the United States, it is easy to conclude that there is no single American ethnic group. But is there an American nation? Some might say no, because nationalism is often assumed to require an ethnicity on which political aspirations can be built. Yet Americans are bound by certain common historical symbols such as the flag, the Declaration of Independence, and the Statue of Liberty. One could thus argue that even in the face of great ethnic diversity the United States is indeed a nation, bound together by a sense of pride in certain democratic and individualistic ideals, and by belief in a unique political destiny. Just as some in Spain may consider themselves ethnically Basque and nationally Spanish, or some in the United Kingdom ethnically Scottish but nationally British, so too do many Americans see themselves as Black or Korean or Hispanic or Indian but also as American. Thus national identity *can* be constructed even when a common or dominant ethnic identity is absent.[1]

Many cultures in one nation

CITIZENSHIP AND PATRIOTISM

Our final form of identification is citizenship. So far we have noted that ethnicity is not inherently political, although it may develop a political aspect through nationalism. At the other end of this spectrum, citizenship is a purely political identity, developed not out of some unique set of circumstances or ascripted by birth but rather developed explicitly by states and accepted or rejected by individuals. **Citizenship** can be defined as an individual's or a group's relationship to the state; those who are citizens swear allegiance to that state, and that state in return is obligated to provide rights to those individuals or the members of that group. In a democracy citizenship includes the right to vote and other civil liberties, whereas in authoritarian systems, one's rights may include little more than the ability to reside in that country. Citizenship can also convey certain obligations, such as the duty to serve in the armed forces or to pay taxes. Citizens are therefore defined by their

IN FOCUS
CITIZENSHIP IS . . .

An individual's relationship to the state; the individual swears allegiance to state, and the state in turn provides certain benefits or rights.

Purely political, and thus more easily changed than ethnic identity or national identity.

The basis for *patriotism*: pride in one's state and citizenship.

particular relationship to one state rather than to one another. Although citizenship is often gained at birth, like ethnicity, citizenship has qualities quite separate from those of ethnic or national identity. Birth is no guarantee of citizenship (a state may not necessarily grant citizenship to all those born on its territory), and individuals may in theory change their citizenship from one state to another.

Citizenship is thus a potentially more inclusive concept than is national identity or ethnicity, though like the other two, its boundaries are rather clear—you are either a citizen or you are not. Some people change their citizenship when they move from one country to another, while others maintain the citizenship of their home country even if they spend decades living in another part of the world. But even with citizenship, ethnicity and nationality can play an important, often limiting, role. In many countries, these three identities are strongly interconnected, and citizenship is restricted to members of a certain ethnic group that views itself, and itself alone, as the nation. Yet because citizenship is a purely political identity, it is much more open to redefinition and change than is ethnicity or national identity. A state may choose suddenly to grant citizenship to immigrants or to extend to all citizens rights that had formerly been restricted to a particular ethnic group.

Citizenship, in turn, can give rise to **patriotism**, or pride in one's state. People are patriotic when they have pride in their political system and seek to defend and promote it. When we think of patriotism, some of the things that may come to mind are our flag, important historical events, wars, anthems—all images that people associate with politics and the state. States that are weak or illegitimate often have difficulty instilling patriotism among their citizens, which makes tasks like defending the state in times of war very difficult. Being a citizen does not automatically make you patriotic.

To sum up, ethnicity, nationality, and citizenship are identities that define groups in different ways and that carry different political implications. Ethnic identity is built on unique social attributes among people, such as language or culture, with no inherent political meaning, whereas national identity implies political aspirations, specifically the desire for self-government. Although an ethnic identity often leads to a national identity and nationalism, it does not always do so, nor does the absence of a single dominant ethnicity prevent nationalism from developing. Finally, citizenship is a purely political identity built on a relationship to the state. As should be clear, none of these identities is exclusive; all of us possess different combinations of ethnicity, national identity, and citizenship, with each contributing to how we see the world and our role within it.

ETHNIC IDENTITY, NATIONAL IDENTITY, AND CITIZENSHIP: ORIGINS AND PERSISTENCE

Now that we have distinguished between these three identities, it is worth considering the origins of each—where did they come from and why do they exist? Contrary to most people's assumptions, ethnic and national identities are relatively recent concepts that emerged in Europe toward the end of the eighteenth century. Citizenship, too, has relatively recent origins: although the concept can be traced back to ancient Athens and to the Roman Empire, the notion of citizenship disappeared with the fall of Rome, only to resurface centuries later.

The emergence (or re-emergence, in the case of citizenship) of these identities had much to do with the formation of the modern state.[2] As states took form in Europe in the fifteenth and sixteenth centuries, asserting sovereign control over people and territory, their subjects experienced increased interaction. People could travel greater distances within their own country's borders, enjoying the security provided by the state. This mobility in turn increased commerce, which was often centered around the city where the state leadership was based. These fortified capitals served as centers for trade, information, and new social relationships. Such interaction in turn fostered increased homogeneity. The variety of different languages and dialects that existed within countries began to merge into a common tongue; language was further standardized by the state through written laws and other documents. Varied customs were shared and adapted into common norms or activities recognized across villages and regions. Common religious practices also developed, often created or supported by the state (as during the Protestant Reformation). In other words, new social institutions began to take shape that were meaningful to a majority of a country's population. People could now identify themselves not by village or profession, but by the institutions they shared with many thousands of other people they had never met. These institutions formed the foundation for ethnic identity. As states helped codify the norms, habits, and values of people within their territory, the people in turn slowly began to identify with each other primarily on this basis—as German, or French, or English.

Growing ethnic identity was thus in some ways the unintended consequence of state development. As states became more powerful in Europe, they facilitated the development of social institutions that laid the foundation for ethnic identity. However, state leaders also came to recognize this development as something that could serve their own interests. By encouraging the formation of a single ethnic identity, the state could in turn claim that it existed to defend and promote the unique interests and values of its people. The state came to be portrayed as the embodiment of the people. Within this logic we can see the seeds of the next major step, the concept of national identity, which became a potent force by the eighteenth century. National identity when added to ethnic identity creates a powerful political force by asserting that the state is legitimate because it maintains national values, and that the people and the state are united in the quest to chart an independent political future. This change occurred in Europe as part of a transformation of political authority. In contrast to earlier political systems founded on tradition or charismatic authority, the modern state claims authority on the basis of its rational pursuit of the national interest.

The development and fusion of ethnic and national identities radically transformed states. On the basis of the idea that the people and their state were bound together, states could mobilize the public in ways never before possible. Most importantly, countries with a strong sense of nationalism could raise mass armies, comprising people fighting not for spoils or pay, but for the glory and destiny of their nation. The very thought that individuals would fight and die for some abstract political concept was a radical change in human history. In Europe, Napoleonic France became the first country able to use such nationalist sentiment to its own advantage; Napoleon created a huge volunteer army that would conquer much of Europe. Both threatened and inspired by such nationalist fervor, other European peoples and states in turn forged their own national identities. Across Europe different peoples began to view themselves as nations with unique political identities and destinies, and in turn sought national independence and self-government. This transformation gave rise to the nation-state, a state encompassing one dominant nation that it claims to embody and represent. Within a hundred years most of the multiethnic empires that dominated Europe would be destroyed, replaced by nation-states that embodied distinct ethnic groups and political identities.

Finally, the development of ethnic and national identities paved the way for the re-emergence of the concept of citizenship in the eighteenth and nineteenth centuries. As societies viewed themselves first in ethnic and then in national terms, their relationship to the state began to change. If the state was the instrument of national will, some extended this logic to conclude that not only were the people subjects of the state, but the reverse was true as well. State and people were bound by a set of mutual responsibilities and obligations in the form of a social contract, as we discussed in Chapter 2. How far this citizenship should be extended and what rights it should entail have come to be central concerns for all societies, democratic or authoritarian.

The concepts of ethnic and national identity that developed in Europe during the past 500 years spread around the world with the rise of European power, and they transformed the way in which peoples everywhere defined themselves in relation to one another and the state. Yet over the past half-century many political scientists and other scholars began to argue that national and ethnic identities were things of the past. As people became more economically developed, more literate, and more exposed to the world around them, these scholars asserted, they would lose interest in such narrow, "local" identities. Ethnicity would fade away as new ideas and values transformed societies everywhere, and nationalism would be rejected as an outdated and narrow view of the world. Citizenship, too, would be eroded by new global ties and connections, these scholars asserted. Most observers looked on these changes with optimism, for exclusionary forms of membership were presumed to be hostile to progress.

Many scholars have retreated from these earlier arguments, however, primarily because such identities have been much more resilient than expected. In the aftermath of the Cold War, ethnic and national identities have intensified in many countries. In fact, it would appear that in many cases these identities have resurfaced in response to such factors as development and globalization. As the world grows ever closer together, as borders become more transparent, people may feel themselves increasingly lost in a chaotic global environment. Local identities provide some sense of stability in this period of rapid change. Paradoxically, then, the closer people grow together, the more they may come to rely on ethnic or national identity to define themselves.

SOURCES OF ETHNIC AND NATIONAL CONFLICT

Political scientists are particularly interested in the way in which national identity and ethnicity can lead to cooperation or conflict between people. Why are some countries able to build on differences between people, whereas in other countries such differences lead to seemingly irreconcilable conflict? Why do some very different identities peacefully coexist for decades and then suddenly flare into violence? Political scientists have different and often contending explanations for such forms of conflict.[3]

At its most basic level, the very process of defining oneself in terms of nation and ethnicity excludes others. Moreover, emphasizing the unique qualities and goals of one's own group can lead to the conclusion that difference equals superiority, that one's own group is somehow better than others. The quest for freedom and equality may well involve achieving it at the expense of others.

Just as national identity and ethnic identity are strongly linked, though one can exist without the other, one can similarly find ethnic or national conflict, as well as situations in which both forces are at work. In **ethnic conflict**, different ethnic groups struggle to achieve certain political or economic goals at each other's expense. However, this struggle does not imply nationalism. Neither side may seek to separate and form an independent country; instead each may hope to increase its own position within the existing state, regime, or government. By contrast, in **national conflict** one or more groups do develop clear aspirations for political independence, clashing with others as a result.

Around the world we can find examples of both ethnic and nationalist conflict. Afghanistan, for example, has seen frequent ethnic conflict. This conflict is not nationalist, however; the different Afghan groups are seeking not independence but greater power over each other within the country. In contrast, the American Revolution can be seen as a nationalist rather than an ethnic conflict. The American colonies broke away from Great Britain to form a separate country, but this separation was not based on ethnic differences. Rather, it was based on conflicts over political rights and the desire for sovereignty. Finally, there are cases where both ethnic and national conflict are at work. During the 1980s, a number of ethnic groups within the Soviet Union began to actively seek independence, clashing with one another and contributing to the breakup of that country in 1991. In short, countries may exhibit ethnic conflict, national conflict, or a combination of both. Each leads to different kinds of problems and possible solutions.

In addition to arising out of different objectives, conflict can emerge in different ways. Political scientists disagree about whether ethnic and nationalist conflict originates primarily from the top down or from the bottom up—in other words, whether conflict begins among political leaders and then spreads down to society, or whether conflict begins among the people and spreads up to the government and the state. In reality, both paths have been evident in cases of ethnic and nationalist conflict, sometimes simultaneously.

Top-down conflicts often result from the policies of states, regimes, or governments that intentionally pit different groups against one another, either by giving preferential treatment to one group (thus generating resentment among others) or by actually inciting violence as a way to create scapegoats, divide the population, and rally support around the leadership in the face of a supposed threat. For example, in Zimbabwe on the eve of the 1999 parliamentary elections government leaders bused black supporters into the countryside to seize land owned by white farmers (whites make up about 1 percent of the population but own more than 30 percent of the country's farmland, a remnant of the country's former colonial status), harassing and sometimes killing the farmers in the process. The government hoped that the land seizures would garner public support by portraying the whites, rather than the government itself, as the source of all economic problems in the country. It also hoped to deepen divisions between blacks and whites in order to prevent the formation of a strong opposition to those in power. In the case of Zimbabwe, as in many other countries, economic and ethnic conflicts are closely connected when one ethnic group is economically advantaged over others. In spite of its unpredictable and destructive tendencies, conflict can sometimes be exactly what a government wants, especially if it directs the people's anger away from those in power and weakens opposition in the process.

Bottom-up ethnic conflict results from long-standing friction, competition, or grievances between different groups vying for power. Often bottom-up conflicts are built on a long historical pattern of hostility or violence between groups. Although political development may suppress these divisions, dramatic social events, such as economic decline, war, or political change, can unleash deep-seated hostilities. Conflict in such situations is much more institutionalized and can persist long after the original participants and victims have passed from the scene. In the search for reasons for the 1991 breakup of the Soviet Union, many would point to long-standing hostilities between various ethnic groups, fueled by sudden political and economic changes. The fact that Americans still argue over the flying of the Confederate flag, nearly 140 years after the end of the Civil War, shows how tenacious group rivalries can be.

It is difficult to know which type of ethnic and nationalist conflict—top-down, generated by political elites, or bottom-up, a product of historical patterns—is more common, since in many conflicts both factors are present,

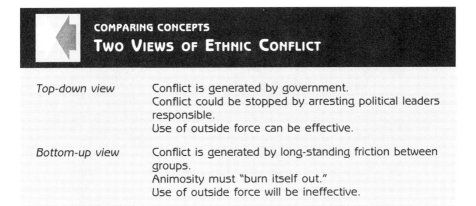

COMPARING CONCEPTS
Two Views of Ethnic Conflict

Top-down view	Conflict is generated by government.
	Conflict could be stopped by arresting political leaders responsible.
	Use of outside force can be effective.
Bottom-up view	Conflict is generated by long-standing friction between groups.
	Animosity must "burn itself out."
	Use of outside force will be ineffective.

each feeding off the other. Pointing to one source, moreover, can have profound implications. An observer convinced that ethnic or national conflict is generated by a government or regime may well conclude that political change—ousting those in power, or rewriting the constitution—could bring an end to the conflict. On the other hand, an observer convinced that such conflicts are a function of broader societal relationships would be much less optimistic that a leadership or policy change could end such strife.

These different views could be seen at work in the case of the Bosnian civil war in the 1990s. Bosnia, part of the former communist country of Yugoslavia, in 1992 collapsed into civil war between Croats, Serbs, and Muslims. Academics and foreign governments came to very different conclusions as to how the international community should respond. Those who believed that the conflict was primarily top-down argued that the use of force and the arrest of those political leaders responsible for the violence could lead to peace. Meanwhile, those who believed that the conflict was primarily bottom-up rejected such a view, seeing the violence as part of a long-standing historical animosity that could be extinguished only through either an outright victory by one side or mutual exhaustion among the rival groups. In the United States, believers in the bottom-up view of ethnic conflict helped persuade the Clinton administration that it should not intervene militarily. Only in 1995, after several years of bloodshed, did the United States and its allies in the North Atlantic Treaty Organization (NATO) use force to bring an end to the conflict.[4] Although this result would appear to have vindicated the top-down view, the continued need to post peacekeeping troops in the region could be seen as evidence that intervention alone did not alleviate ethnic animosity.

In addition to disagreements about how ethnic and national conflicts erupt, the issue is complicated by the way in which states have spread around the world. Often Western observers see ethnic conflict through their own eyes of relatively homogeneous states, wondering why other countries are so divided and conflictual. But as we saw earlier, ethnic identity and national identity developed first in Europe and over a long period of time. The creation of the homogeneous Western states was no peaceful process. Ethnic and national conflicts took millions of lives over centuries in Europe; now such conflicts are causing bloodshed in places such as the former Yugoslavia, Russia, and the Basque region of Spain.

Outside of Europe, moreover, the state is a relatively recent development, imported or imposed from the outside. There states were not wrought slowly over the centuries but arrived in the wake of European imperialism. These states were largely the creation of European rule, and their territories were delineated as a result of political negotiations between rival European empires. Although the end of colonialism in the second half of the twentieth century brought independence to these peoples, their states remained defined by borders that had been generated from without, not within.

Imperialism contributed to ethnic and national conflicts around the world in other ways, too. The Western powers that once ruled much of the world brought their conceptions of ethnicity, nationality, and race to areas where such ideas were largely unknown. European imperialism, fueled in part by ethnic and national pride and a belief in the inferiority of non-Europeans, imposed these values on the populations of the areas they ruled. Moreover, these concepts were often used specifically to create a hierarchy of ethnicity where none had existed before, in order to serve the needs of imperial rule.

These points are well illustrated by the case of Rwanda. Long before European imperialism, Rwandans had divided themselves into two groups, Hutus and Tutsis. These were not ethnic groups, but rather something akin to castes or social classes. Hutus were the agricultural segment of society, whereas Tutsis were cattle herders and tended to be the politically dominant group. Neither identification was fixed; an individual could change from Hutu to Tutsi, in the same way that you might go from being an impoverished college student to a wealthy entrepreneur.

When Belgium took control of Rwanda in the late 1890s, however, Belgian officials viewed the Rwandan population through their own preconceptions, seeing fixed ethnic groups where none really existed. Believing that the Tutsis, who represented about 17 percent of the population, were a "superior race" of people, they used Tutsi elites to rule the country on behalf of Belgium. Under Belgian influence, identities began to become rigid, and the label "Hutu" or "Tutsi" became part of each individual's identification papers and relationship to the state. Each Rwandan was now permanently one or the other. These fixed ethnic identities, when combined with the inequality generated by Belgian preferences for Tutsi administrators, sowed the seeds of ethnic conflict. Once the Belgians departed from its African colonies in the 1960s, Rwanda suffered from frequent outbursts of ethnic conflict, the most recent of which took place in 1994, when perhaps as many as 500,000 Tutsis were killed in a genocidal war provoked by the Hutu-led government.[5]

Given the vast problems that plague much of the postcolonial world, political scientists and other observers often conclude that one of the main failures of European empires was to draw "incorrect" borders that discounted realities on the ground. Some ethnic groups were bifurcated by colonial borders and thus wound up in different countries after decolonization, while in other cases different and often hostile groups were forced together in the same country. This arbitrary gathering and dividing of peoples, these observers argue, set the stage for later conflict. But although

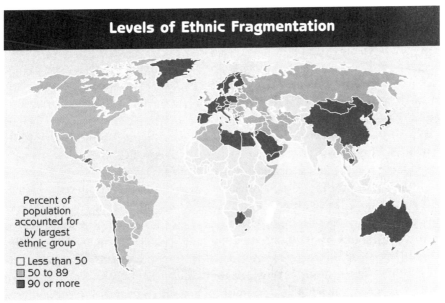

Levels of Ethnic Fragmentation

Percent of
population
accounted for
by largest
ethnic group

☐ Less than 50
▨ 50 to 89
■ 90 or more

Source: www.sciam.com/1998/0998issue/0998numbers.html

Note: Country data are the most recent available as of early 1999.

such borders certainly could have been drawn to more accurately reflect ethnic divisions, there are few cases where simply changing the borders would solve problems. In most countries such divisions could not so easily be drawn, as in the case of Rwanda, where Hutus and Tutsis share the same territory. The level of ethnic fragmentation throughout the postcolonial world can be seen in the map on page 61; in many parts of the world the largest ethnic group makes up less than 50 percent of the population.

Ethnic and national conflict may thus emerge from a number of different forces, operating in either isolation or combination. Conflict may be generated by elites to solidify their own power through conflict or to favor one group over another. Conflict may also result from long-standing friction between groups, catalyzed by economic or political changes. And in some situations, conflict is fueled by both the top and the bottom, locked in a cycle of violence. Each type of conflict presents different challenges in the search for peace and stability. Finally, ethnic and nationalist rivalries are exacerbated by the inherent heterogeneity of much of the world. Clear borders between groups are more the exception than the norm. In much of the world, the territory in which people find themselves, and even the ethnicities they claim, are legacies of imperialism. We will turn to these ideas in more detail in Chapter 9, which looks at less-developed and newly industrializing countries.

PATTERNS OF ETHNIC AND NATIONAL CONFLICT

At their core, ethnic and national conflicts between competing groups constitute battles between rival visions of freedom and equality. Must your group be equal to mine? Is my group's freedom a threat to yours? When such conflicts do occur, they manifest themselves in a number of different ways. Each relies to varying degrees on the state to limit some group's freedom and equality, and each involves varying levels of violence.

One manifestation of such conflict is *exclusion*, whereby certain groups are not granted full political rights by the dominant ethnic group. Recall the earlier point that in many countries there is a strong interconnection between ethnicity, national identity, and citizenship; a single ethnic group may define itself, and itself alone, as the nation, and therefore restrict citizenship for other groups. When Estonia and Latvia broke away from the Soviet Union in 1991, each comprised not only ethnically Estonian and Latvian populations, respectively, but also large numbers of ethnic Russians, who had migrated to Estonia and Latvia in the preceding four decades. Ethnic Latvians and Estonians worried that these people still con-sidered themselves not just ethnically Russian, but nationally Russian as well—that is, loyal to the Russian nation (and, by way of extension, to the Russian state). Estonians and Latvians feared that if ethnic Russians were given the right to vote, they might support the country's reunification with Russia—exactly what ethnic Latvians and Estonians had fought against in their struggle for independence. Many Latvians and Estonians also resented the presence of these Russians within their country; they viewed the Russians as remnants of a colonizing force. As a result, neither state granted automatic citizenship to ethnic Russians unless they could speak Estonian or Latvian (which few of them could). Both countries now are home to large Russian populations with no citizenship of any sort—they are neither citizens of Russia nor of the countries in which they live.

Similar populations can be found among ethnic Turks in Germany, many of whom (and their parents and even grandparents) have lived in the country all of their lives. Moreover, in contrast to the Russians in Esto-nia and Latvia, most Turks not only speak German, but the younger gen-erations may not even speak Turkish. Nevertheless, they are still considered foreigners by the German state and the German nation, since they are not ethnically German. The question of what defines national identity and cit-izenship, and whether either should be more inclusive, is a growing prob-lem in many once-homogeneous countries that are becoming more ethnically diverse as a result of immigration.

A second way in which ethnic and nationalist conflict manifests itself is through *removal* via ethnic cleansing or forced assimilation. In the case of ethnic cleansing, one population seeks to rid itself of another by forcibly driving the target population from their traditional homeland. This strat-egy is common when two or more ethnic groups occupy the same area, each claiming it as a homeland. The term "ethnic cleansing" was coined with reference to events in Bosnia and elsewhere in the former Yugoslavia, but the practice has a long history and has taken place all around the world. The forced migration of many Native American tribes by the U.S. government onto reservations far from their traditional homelands, for example, is a clear example of ethnic cleansing. In many other cases, vio-lent clashes between rival ethnic groups can be seen as an attempt at eth-nic cleansing, at forcing out another group through violence and fear. Race riots often take this form, with one group's neighborhoods and shops being looted and burned by another.

Forced assimilation, in contrast, occurs when a dominant nation or ethnic group seeks to eliminate another by forcibly integrating it and eradicating its differences in the process. Commonly this technique involves the suppression of different languages, religions, customs, or other characteristics that would distinguish the target population from the dominant group. In Bulgaria in the 1980s, for instance, people with last names of Turkish origin were forced to change them to Bulgarian names. Under authoritarian rule in Spain from the late 1930s until the 1960s, the Basque language and culture were actively suppressed, and schools and universities could not teach in the Basque language. Indigenous people in North and South America have for many centuries confronted forced religious conversion and the suppression of their language and customs, and debates rage in much of the world about the degree to which immigrants must surrender their "alien" customs or languages. Does ethnic diversity strengthen a country by widening its values, or weaken it by undermining a single national identity?

The third and most violent type of ethnic and national conflict is genocide, a state-directed war against members of a specific ethnic or national group with the explicit objective of killing all or part of them. This practice, the most horrible form of ethnic conflict, is also much less common. Although the term is sometimes used loosely to imply any killing on a mass scale, true genocide has taken place in recent history only in a few cases, such as in Germany against the Jews during World War II, in Turkey against Armenians in 1915, in Rwanda against the Tutsis in 1994, and in the former Yugoslavia in the 1990s, where thousands of Bosnian Muslims and Kosovar Albanians were killed by Serb forces. In all three cases, the government sought to kill every last "enemy" in its midst.

Each of these forms of conflict—exclusion, assimilation and ethnic cleansing, and genocide—calls on social scientists and governments to

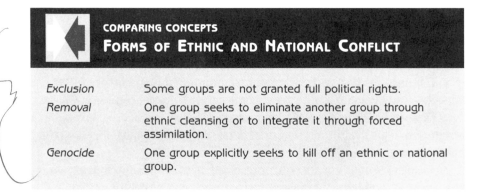

COMPARING CONCEPTS
FORMS OF ETHNIC AND NATIONAL CONFLICT

Exclusion	Some groups are not granted full political rights.
Removal	One group seeks to eliminate another group through ethnic cleansing or to integrate it through forced assimilation.
Genocide	One group explicitly seeks to kill off an ethnic or national group.

develop some response. Creating such conflicts seems to be much easier than solving them, although there are preventative steps that can be taken. Where exclusion is a problem, finding ways in which citizenship can be extended without raising fears in the majority ethnic group is important. How to do this is less clear. Moving away from a concept of citizenship based on one's ethnic origins (*jus sanguinis*) and toward one based on one's birthplace (*jus soli*) is a starting point. Such a shift in defining citizenship recently occurred in Germany, allowing many more individuals who were ethnically non-German to seek citizenship. A greater emphasis on bilingualism may also help—not increasing the use of minority languages, but rather making certain than ethnic minorities are able to communicate not only in their native language but also in the national tongue, so that language divides are not a source of marginalization. By forging such communication, greater trust can be formed between majority and minority, and a wider concept of the nation built. States must be careful, however, to ensure that bilingualism is not seen by the minority as forced assimilation.

Where forced assimilation or ethnic cleansing is a threat, different responses are called for. Constitutional provisions must ensure that ethnic groups have the freedom to practice their own religions and customs without interference, and to be educated in the native tongue of the ethnic group where it represents a significant proportion of the population. One might note, however, that this proposed response seems to clash with the remedy discussed above: Which is more important, to promote bilingualism or to allow a minority language to dominate local life? The answer depends on the situation. In cases of exclusion, minority ethnic groups are often completely unconnected to the dominant ethnic and national identity. Under these circumstances, greater connections must be forged by minorities to the majority. In cases where forced assimilation or ethnic cleansing threatens, however, the minority population has often willingly or unwillingly been tightly connected to the dominant ethnic group. Here what is important is that the minority is able to maintain its identity while still remaining part of a larger nation. Frequently, the extension of greater rights to a minority under these conditions takes the form of *devolution*, in which local bodies are given greater autonomy over education, police, and other important tasks. In Spain, for example, devolution was used to give greater powers to the Basques and other ethnic minorities, helping to rebuild trust and national solidarity after decades of authoritarian rule under which forced assimilation was the norm.

Perhaps the most difficult type of conflict to address is that of genocide. Where genocide has occurred, those responsible must be held accountable, if only to give pause to the next leader who might consider such a policy. One problem with assigning guilt, however, is that genocidal killing involves thousands of individuals at all ranks of society. Who is to be found guilty when so many are complicit? A second problem is that of state sovereignty; when the state has violated the most basic premise of citizenship—to protect its own people—the international community is obligated to intervene. In 1948 the United Nations adopted the International Convention on the Prevention and Punishment of the Crime of Genocide, defining genocide as a violation of international law and empowering the international community to act against responsible states and leaders. The Genocide Convention was not formally involved, however, until the 1990s, when criminal tribunals were set up to investigate and prosecute the genocides in Rwanda and the former Yugoslavia. In 1999, the Yugoslav government and regime, held widely responsible for the killings in Bosnia and Kosova, was overthrown after a NATO bombing campaign, and its former president, Slobodan Milosevic, was extradited to the United Nations International Criminal Tribunal for the former Yugoslavia. Milosevic was subsequently put on trial for genocide. The international community has been less willing, however, to live up to the provisions of the Genocide Convention that oblige states to prevent genocide, as they imply the pre-emptive use of military force. One solution to this dilemma may lie in the creation of a more reliable "early-warning system" that could indicate where genocide may be threatened, allowing international actors to step in and defuse the situation.

POLITICAL ATTITUDES AND POLITICAL IDEOLOGY

We have covered a great deal of ground so far in our discussion of the ways in which societies are organized and the identities they construct. As we have seen, ethnicity, national identity, and citizenship are each ways in which people view themselves in relationship to one another, vis-à-vis other groups, and in their relationship to the state. In addition to these basic forms of group identity, people also hold individual views regarding the relationship between freedom and equality within their own country and in the wider world. These views are not defined by birth or by the state, although they may be influenced by either or both. Nor are the boundaries between such views as clear or evident as they are with ethnicity, national identity, or citizenship; people may freely modify or combine values, in spite of the wider pressures or expectations of state or society.

In the rest of this chapter we will categorize these views into two different types: political attitudes and political ideology. Political attitudes are concerned with the speed and methods with which political changes regarding freedom and equality should take place in a given society. Political ideology comprises the basic values held by an individual about the fundamental goals of politics, or the ideal balance between freedom and equality. Although political attitudes focus on the specific context of political change in a given country (that is to say, they are *particularistic*), political ideology is *universalistic*, for it assumes that there is an ideal balance of freedom and equality for people everywhere. Unfortunately the terms "political attitude" and "political ideology" are often used interchangeably, causing great confusion. Let's look at each in detail and distinguish further between the two.

Political Attitudes

Political attitudes describe views regarding the necessary pace and scope of change between freedom and equality. The attitudes are typically broken up into the categories of radical, liberal, conservative, and reactionary and are often arrayed on a spectrum, from left to right, as shown on page 68.

Radicals are placed on the extreme left. **Radicalism** is usually defined as a belief in dramatic, often revolutionary change of the existing political, social, or economic order. Radicals believe that the current system is broken and cannot simply be improved or repaired but must be scrapped in favor of a new order. As a result, most radicals do not believe in slow, evolutionary change. Politics will only be improved, they believe, when the entire political structure has been fundamentally transformed, remaking the

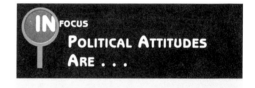

POLITICAL ATTITUDES ARE . . .

Concerned with the speed and methods of political change.

Generally classified as radical, liberal, conservative, or reactionary.

Particularistic: relative to the specific context of a given country. A view that is "radical" in one country may be "conservative" in another.

Distinct from political ideologies.

political institutions of government, regime, and state. As a result, radicals may be more inclined to favor violence as a necessary or unavoidable part of politics. The institutions of the old order, in some radicals' view, are maintained through inertia and will not change willingly; they will have to be destroyed, if necessary through force. These views are not held by all radicals, however. Some may argue that radical change can be achieved

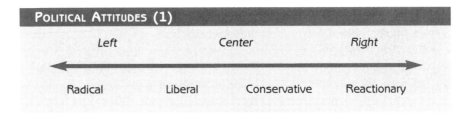

POLITICAL ATTITUDES (1)

Left	Center	Right
Radical	Liberal Conservative	Reactionary

through peaceful means, by raising public consciousness and mobilizing mass support for wide-ranging change.

Liberals, like radicals, believe that there is much that can be changed for the better in the current political, social, and economic institutions, and liberals too support widespread change. However, instead of revolutionary transformation, **liberalism** favors evolutionary transformation. In the liberal view, progressive change can happen through changes within the system; it does not require an overthrow of the system itself. Liberals believe that although there may be a need for change, the system is not fundamentally unjust or broken, and change can be pursued through the political process. Liberals may favor a change in government or even in regime, but they do not demand sudden transformation. Moreover, liberals part from radicals in their belief that the state can be an instrument of positive change. Liberals also believe that change can, and sometimes must, occur over a long period of time; they are skeptical that institutions can be replaced or transformed within a short period of time, and believe that only constant effort can create fundamental change.

Conservatives break with both radicals and liberals in this view of the necessity of change. Whereas radicalism and liberalism both advocate change, disagreeing only on the degree of change and the tactics to achieve it, **conservatism** questions whether any significant or profound change in existing institutions is necessary. Conservatives are skeptical of the view that change is necessarily good in itself, and view instead it as disruptive and leading to unforeseen outcomes. Conservatives see the state and the regime as important structures that provide basic order and continuity to politics, economics, and society, and they view unnecessary tinkering with this system as dangerous. Should too much change take place, conservatives argue, the very legitimacy of the system might be undermined, destroying the basic values and norms that hold society together. Conservatives also question the extent to which the problems that radicals and liberals point to can ever really be solved. At best, they believe, change will simply replace one set of problems with another, and at worst, it will actually create more problems than it solves.

Reactionaries are similar to conservatives in their opposition to further evolutionary or revolutionary change, yet unlike conservatives and similar to radicals, they view the current order as fundamentally unacceptable. Rather than a transformation of the system into something new, however, **reaction** seeks to restore political, social, and economic institutions that once existed. Reactionaries advocate a restoration of older values, a change back to a previous regime or state that they believe was superior to the current order. Some reactionaries do not even look back to a specific period in history, but instead seek to "return" to an envisioned past ideal that never really existed. Reactionaries, like radicals, are more willing to use violence to advance their cause.

The left-right continuum on which these attitudes are typically illustrated gives the impression that the further one travels from the center, the more polarized politics become. By this logic, then, radicals and reactionaries are miles apart from one another, with nothing in common. But our discussion above indicates that in many ways this interpretation is incorrect. Thus some political scientists believe that viewing left and right as a single continuum is misleading, for the closer one moves toward the extremes, the closer the attitudes become. These political scientists have devised an alternative way to envision the spectrum of political attitudes. They bend the straight continuum into a circle, bringing the two ends, radical and reactionary, close

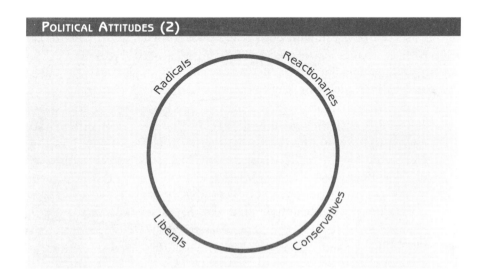

POLITICAL ATTITUDES (2)

together, as shown on page 69. And in fact, radicalism and reaction share much in common. Both believe in dramatic change, though in different directions, and both contemplate the use of violence to achieve this change. Although their ends may be quite different, the means of both groups can often be similar. In fact, just as liberals sometimes become conservatives and vice versa, radicals and reactionaries often cross over into each other's camps. For example, many reactionary fascists in Europe became supporters of radical communism after World War II.

One thing you might have noticed by this time is that our discussion of the political spectrum of attitudes has not provided any specific examples, such as welfare policies, economies, or defense—common sources of political division that separate right from left in the United States and in most industrialized democracies. But these specific policy areas belong instead to the concept of political ideology, those basic beliefs about how politics should be constructed. It is important to emphasize that ideology and political attitudes are *not* interchangeable. The attitudes of radicalism, liberalism, conservatism, and reaction often take on different ideological content in different societies.

Consider some examples. In the United States, Canada, or western Europe, radicals are viewed as those who seek to fundamentally transform or overthrow the current capitalist democratic order, replacing it with a system of greater economic and social equality. Radicals believe that by ending economic injustice and inequality, blights such as racism, sexism, and war would disappear, deprived as they would be of their financial underpinnings. Liberals in these countries are sympathetic to some of these ideas but believe in pursuing gradual changes within the current system. Rather than believing that politics is part of the problem, they believe that existing government, regime, and state institutions can be part of the solution. Income inequality or discrimination, for example, can be solved through income redistribution, affirmative action, and laws against discrimination. Conservatives believe that the current economic and social structures are fine as they are and do not wish to tamper with the political order. In their mind, discrimination and inequality, although unfortunate, will always exist; governments cannot make these problems go away, so it is up to individuals to overcome these obstacles themselves. Reactionaries, meanwhile, reject the very idea that discrimination or inequality is bad, viewing as natural the hierarchy between people and advocating that it should be restored, through violence if necessary. The foregoing is a simplified but accurate description of how political attitudes are manifested in the United States and much of the West.

These same political attitudes would manifest themselves quite differently in a country such as China, however. China is an authoritarian country still controlled by a communist party, even though dramatic economic
(if not political) reforms have taken place in China over the past twenty
years, creating a system with some elements of capitalism. Given this context, a Chinese radical, defined as someone who seeks the destruction of
the current system, would advocate the overthrow of communist rule and
its replacement by a democracy like those found in the West. Students
who were active in the Tiananmen Square protests for democracy in 1989
were frequently described or condemned by observers and the Chinese
government as "radicals" for their demands for sweeping change in the
communist system. Chinese liberals are also likely to favor many of the
changes that were advocated in Tiananmen Square, although they would
approach these reforms much more slowly and in a less confrontational
manner, favoring a process of gradual change within the existing political
system. In 2000, secret Chinese government documents concerning the
crackdown against the Tiananmen Square protesters were leaked to the
international media by someone presumed to be an inside government
source. Many assumed that this was the work of liberals within the Communist Party who hoped that the documents would discredit their conservative and reactionary opponents, who had directed the massacre of the
protesters. Chinese conservatives, those individuals suspicious of change,
continue to resist calls for democratic reform or for an admission that the
use of violence in 1989 against nonviolent protesters was a mistake. They
may support or tolerate some market reforms, but they do not view these
steps as leading down an inevitable path to democracy or capitalism.
Finally, Chinese reactionaries strongly oppose any reforms that might jeop-
ardize communist rule, viewing the Tiananmen Square events as proof that
communism had been undermined by reforms carried out over preceding
decades. These "hard-liners" favor a return to earlier, "purer" communist
values and policies, bringing reforms to an end and rolling back changes
that have already taken place.

As a result, American or Western European radicals would have little
to say to Chinese radicals; both are united by their attitudes toward the
scope and speed of political change, but in terms of their political values
and goals—their ideologies—they are dramatically different. Indeed, Chinese radicals might have more in common with American or European
conservatives in terms of their support for democracy and capitalism. Chinese reactionaries, on the other hand, might have more in common with
American or European radicals: the former wish to return to communism

as it existed before recent reforms, and many of the latter seek to achieve the same kind of outcome in their own countries.

Political Ideology

The preceding discussion of the importance of context in understanding political attitudes might lead one to conclude that making any meaningful attitudinal comparisons between countries would be difficult—what is considered radical in one country might be conservative in another. In order to move past these particularistic differences between countries, political scientists also speak about political ideologies. **Political ideologies** are sets of political values held by individuals regarding the fundamental goals of politics. Rather than being concerned with the pace and scope of change in a given context, as political attitudes are, ideologies are concerned with describing the ideal relationship between freedom and equality for all individuals, and the proper role of political institutions in achieving or maintaining this relationship. Supporters of each ideology work to ensure that their values become institutionalized as the basic regime, or rules of the political game. In the modern world there are five primary ideologies.

INFOCUS
POLITICAL IDEOLOGIES ARE . . .

- Sets of political values regarding the fundamental goals of politics.

- Exemplified by five dominant modern ideologies: liberalism, social democracy, communism, fascism, and anarchy.

- *Universalistic:* not specific to one country or time.

- Distinct from political attitudes.

Liberalism as an ideology (rather than as a political attitude) places a high priority on individual political and economic freedom. Adherents of a liberal ideology believe that politics should seek to create the maximum degree of liberty for all people, including free speech, the right of association, and other basic political rights. This goal requires a state with a low degree of autonomy, so that it can be easily controlled or checked by the public should it begin encroaching on individual rights. For liberals, the lower the ability of the state to intervene in the public's affairs, the greater the scope and promise of human activity and prosperity. As Thomas Jefferson said, "the legitimate powers of government extend to such acts only as are injurious to others. But it does me no injury for my neighbor to say there are twenty gods, or no God. It neither picks my pocket nor breaks my leg."[6]

It is from these ideas of liberalism that we take our current definition of democracy, which is often defined as *liberal democracy*—a system of political, social, and economic liberties, supported by competition, partic-ipation, and contestation (such as voting). To be sure, liberals do recog-nize that not all individuals will succeed if left to their own devices, and that there will inevitably be great economic inequality between the wealth-iest and the poorest. In spite of this shortcoming, liberals argue that a high degree of freedom will produce the greatest amount of general prosperity for the majority.

As a final point, we should note that liberalism as an ideology and lib-eralism as a political attitude are very different things; in China, the ide-ology of liberalism would be considered a radical political attitude; in the United States, the ideology of liberalism is essentially a conservative polit-ical attitude, since it represents the current status of the U.S. regime. Ide-ologically the United States is a liberal country, founded on free markets, individualism, and a state with relatively low autonomy.

Communism differs greatly from liberalism in its view of freedom and equality. Whereas liberalism enshrines individual freedom over equality, com-munism rejects the idea that personal freedom will ensure prosperity for the majority. Rather, it holds that in the inevitable struggle over economic resources, a small group will eventually come to dominate both the market and the state, using its wealth to control and exploit society as a whole. Pros-perity will not be spread throughout society but will be monopolized by a few for their own benefit. The gap between rich and poor will widen and poverty will increase. For communists, liberal democracy is "bourgeois democracy"—of the rich, by the rich, and for the rich. Such institutions as free speech and voting are meaningless when a few control the wealth of society.

To eliminate exploitation, communism advocates that the state control all economic resources in order to produce true economic equality for the community as a whole. This goal requires a powerful state in terms of both autonomy and capacity, able to restrict those individual rights (such as owning property or opposing the current regime) that would hinder the pur-suit of economic equality. Individual liberties must give way to the needs of society as a whole, creating what communists would see as a true democ-racy. The Soviet Union from 1917 to 1991 and China since 1949 are examples of countries where this communist ideology has been installed as the political regime through revolution, creating what these countries call (or called) "people's democracies." Thus democracy can be a slippery concept, defined differently depending a person's ideology. We will turn to this problem in greater detail in Chapter 6.

A much more restricted version of communist ideology is known as **social democracy** (sometimes also called "socialism"). Social democracy has its origins in communism but over time has been influenced by liberal values. Unlike communism, social democracy accepts a strong role for private ownership and market forces while still maintaining an emphasis on economic equality. A state with strong capacity and autonomy is considered important to social democrats to ensure greater economic equality through specific policies, but this commitment to equality, while limiting freedom to a greater extent than under liberalism, recognizes the importance of individual liberty. In much of Europe, social democracy, rather than liberalism, is the guiding political regime.

Fascism, like communism, is antiliberal in its focus and hostile to the idea of individual freedom. However, although it favors a collective approach to human organization, fascism rejects the notion of equality. Instead, fascism rests on the idea that people and groups can be classified in terms of inferiority and superiority. Particular nations and ethnic groups are deemed superior to others, thus justifying a hierarchy among them. Neither freedom nor equality is possible or desirable under fascism; individual freedom must submit to the collective will, and the superior must rise above the inferior. Whereas liberals and communists both see inherent potential in every person (although they disagree on the best means to unleash this potential), fascists do not. The metaphor of fascism is one of the society as an organic whole, a single living body, with a few leaders as serving as its brain and controlling its actions. Fascists view the state as a vital instrument for molding society and the economy to best strengthen the nation against inferior people within and without. State autonomy and capacity must therefore be high, and democracy, no matter how defined, is rejected as anathema, just as freedom and equality are rejected. No fascist regimes currently exist in the world, although fascism is well remembered from the Nazi system that ruled Germany from 1933 to 1945. Fascist political parties and movements still do exist, however, ranging from white supremacist groups in North America and Europe to formal organizations such as the German People's Union or the National Association of Patriotic Organizations in Japan. Some observers worry that economic turmoil in Russia and other postcommunist countries might eventually lead to fascist regimes there.

Anarchism departs from these other ideologies quite drastically. If liberalism, communism, and fascism differ over how powerful the state should be, anarchism rejects the notion of the state altogether. Anarchists share with communists the belief that private property leads to inequality, but they are opposed to the idea that the state can solve this problem; power in the hands of the state, in the anarchist view, would not necessarily eliminate inequality and would certainly eliminate freedom. As the Russian

COMPARING CONCEPTS
IDEOLOGY AND POLITICAL ATTITUDES

Ideology	Tenets	Corresponding Political Attitude in North America
Liberalism	Favors a limited state role in society and economic activity; emphasizes a high degree of personal freedom over social equality.	Conservative
Social democracy	Supports private property and markets but believes that state has a strong role to play in regulating the economy and providing benefits to the public; seeks to balance freedom and equality.	Liberal
Fascism	Stresses a low degree of both personal freedom and equality in order to achieve a powerful state.	Reactionary
Communism	Emphasizes limited personal freedom and a strong state in order to achieve social equality; property is wholly owned by the state and market forces are eliminated; state takes on task of production and other economic decisions.	Radical
Anarchy	Stresses the elimination of the state and private property as a way to achieve both freedom and equality for all; believes that a high degree of personal freedom and social equality is possible.	Radical

anarchist Mikhail Bakunin (1814–76) once stated, "I am not a communist, because communism unites all the forces of society in the state and
becomes absorbed in it; because it inevitably leads to the concentration of
all property in the hands of the state, while I seek the complete elimination of the principles of authority and governmental guardianship, which

under the pretence of making men moral and civilizing them, has up to now always enslaved, oppressed, exploited, and ruined them."[7]

Thus, like liberals, anarchists view the state as a threat to freedom and equality rather than as their champion. Accordingly, anarchists believe that both individual freedom and equality can be achieved only if the state is eliminated entirely. Without a state to reinforce inequality or limit personal freedom, argue anarchists, people would be able to freely cooperate as true equals. Moreover, without the state to reinforce private property

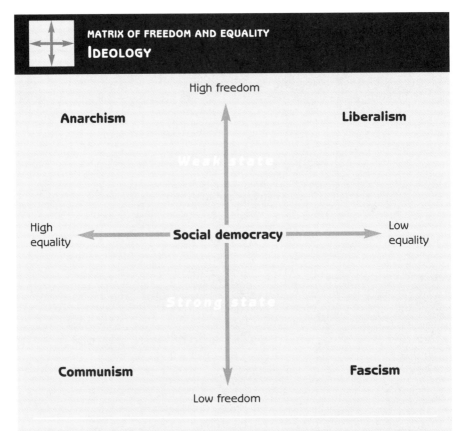

MATRIX OF FREEDOM AND EQUALITY

IDEOLOGY

High freedom

Anarchism

Liberalism

Weak state

High
equality

Social democracy

Low
equality

Strong state

Communism

Fascism

Low freedom

Fundamental political ideologies vary according to the balance they strike between freedom and equality. Liberals and anarchists favor decentralized power and weaker (or non-existent) states, as well as high levels of individual freedom; communists and fascists favor the concentration of state power at the expense of individual freedom; social democrats prefer a balance between state power and individual freedom.

and economic exploitation, these would also disappear. Economic activity would instead take place in a society of relative equality. In short, anarchism believes that in the absence of a state and a capitalist economy, people would be free to pursue their own lives and individual desires.

Given that we live in a world of states, anarchism is the one ideology of the five primary ideologies that has never been realized. No society has ever adopted anarchism as a political regime and dispensed with the state, although anarchist groups, movements, and collectives have appeared in many societies throughout modern history. Anarchist ideas played a role in the Russian Revolution (1917) and in the Spanish Civil War (1936–39). Some point to new technological innovations such as the Internet as potential sources of anarchist politics in the future.

In essence, political ideologies differ according to where they believe the proper balance between freedom and equality lies and what role the state should have in achieving that balance. Building on the preceding chapters' discussion of freedom and equality and state strength, the matrix on page 76 shows how liberalism, social democracy, communism, fascism, and anarchism each try to reconcile freedom and equality with state power. These ideologies do not prescribe a solution or ideal simply for one country or one point in time, but for all people, everywhere, and for the future if not forever. These values are not particularistic, like political attitudes, but are universal in their outlook. And although ethnic and national identities and citizenship may form the lines of conflict between groups, ideologies and attitudes shape the arena of political conflict within groups. How much change should there be? How fast? How peaceful or violent? And to what end? This is the essence of political life, as ideologies rise and fall in prominence, clash peacefully or violently, and pass from the scene as new ones take their place. In 200 years, the ideas of liberalism or communism or fascism may make no more sense than the idea of a powerful monarchy does today.

POLITICAL CULTURE

So far we have discussed how the ways in which societies identify themselves can have important implications for politics. Ethnicity, nationality, and citizenship provide collective identities with relatively clear boundaries, categorizing people and generating questions about the nature of freedom and equality between different groups. In contrast, political attitudes and ideologies shape debates over the pace and scope of political change and ultimately about the ideal relationship between freedom and equality for all groups. These differences in turn create political conflict, competition, and cooperation within societies and help us to understand how societal differences can profoundly shape politics within countries.

But a final question remains. All of these forms of identification help set the arena for political struggles over freedom and equality. But what explains why countries differ so dramatically in their ideological outcomes? Why, for example, in the United States is the regime based on liberalism, with communist ideas considered radical by the public, whereas in China communism forms the ideological core of the regime and liberalism is considered a radical notion? There are a number of possible explanations for these differences; some of these explanations look to such factors as the level of economic development in society or the power of particular individuals or groups to spread or impose their political values. But a societal explanation also exists, embodied in a concept known as "political culture."

Before we discuss this concept any further, however, we clearly understand what is meant by "culture" in general. If society is a complex collection of people bound by shared institutions, as it was defined at the start of this chapter, then *culture* comprises those basic institutions that help define a society. Culture acts as a kind of social road map, telling people what is and is not acceptable, and providing guidelines and priorities for how people organize their lives. In some societies, for example, alcohol may be viewed as a normal part of cultural activities, whereas in other societies it may be frowned upon or taboo. Cultures can differ profoundly in their attitudes toward work, leisure, sex, and politics. Interestingly, culture stands somewhere between the group identities of ethnicity, national identity, and citizenship on the one hand, and individual political attitudes and ideologies on the other. Culture binds groups together, serving as part of the fundamental content of a society—of what makes the French different from Peruvians or Cambodians—yet at the same time it is a personal set of norms that people may choose to accept or reject.

In short, if ethnicity or nationality or citizenship is the definition of what group an individual belongs to, then culture is the activity that group considers proper and normal for its members. **Political culture**, in turn, refers specifically to the basic norms for political activity in a society.[8]

Initially, it might be hard to believe that any society shares one specific set of political views that are somehow distinct from other countries. In fact, the discussion of political attitudes and ideologies so far in this chapter would seem to have taught us exactly the opposite—that people within countries differ widely in their views. Some political scientists in fact agree with this view, believing that political culture is not a useful concept. In their view, people everywhere are essentially rational and respond toward politics in roughly similar and predictable ways. Others, however, argue that in each society fundamental political views and values are shaped by cultural institutions, and observers cannot accurately understand politics in a country if they do not grasp its political culture. In this view, ideologies and political attitudes rest on a foundation of political culture that gives meaning to political debates.

A few examples may make these ideas clearer. In the United States there has long been a heated debate over whether the government should provide health care to all its citizens. Many other countries around the world, for example, have long had national health-care systems; in these countries there is little debate about the merits of such a program. Some political scientists would hypothesize that this puzzling difference arises from the American political culture of individualism and mistrust of government (consistent with the ideology of liberalism). Others have argued that political culture can be used to explain the rise of fascism in Germany or communism in Russia; these arguments assert that in both cases, authoritarian and anti-individualist elements of German and Russian political culture allowed fascist and communist movements to take root when they were failing in most other countries. Some political scientists and political leaders even go so far as to say that there is in fact a culture of democracy, and that certain cultural systems (Islam or Confucianism are frequently cited) are inherently incompatible with democracy as it has developed in the West. This is a hotly debated topic, however, and many strongly disagree with such a notion. We will discuss this in greater detail in the coming chapters on authoritarianism and democracy. For our purposes here it is enough to say that which ideological debates take priority, and which kinds of ideologies dominate a country's political regime, may be shaped by that country's political culture.

IN FOCUS

POLITICAL CULTURE Is . . .

- The basic norms for political activity in a society.
- A determining factor in what ideologies will dominate a country's political regime.
- Unique to a given country or group.
- Distinct from political attitudes and ideologies.

Assuming that this argument is correct, how resilient is political culture? Political culture, like culture in general, is subject to change over time. Some political scientists, while they believe that political culture is an important factor in comparative politics, expect that in the future different cultures will merge into a common global culture. In this view, as societies modernize and interact as a result of economic globalization and technological innovation, their cultures will grow closer together, exchanging ideas, values, habits, and preferences, eventually leading to a fusion of cultures. They hypothesize that "postmodern" values, such as environmentalism, individualism, human rights, and tolerance, will form as a result of greater global awareness and a rising consensus regarding the balance of freedom and equality. (We will return to this idea in Chapter 7 in our discussion of the advanced democracies.)

Others are more skeptical. Culture, political or otherwise, does not easily change, they argue, and even the most developed countries around the world still remain distinct in how they approach and view politics. Indeed, some argue that in the aftermath of the Cold War and the rise of dramatic technological changes, basic cultural identities will in fact supplant political ideologies as the main dividing lines of global politics. Countries will struggle not over alternative visions of freedom and equality that transcend societies, these scholars believe, but over basic religious and cultural differences that are viewed by many as incompatible and irreconcilable. These identities, they argue, will grow increasingly important as human change increases.[9] The terrorist attacks of September 11, 2001, are often cited as horrible proof of this growing "clash of civilizations."

IN SUM: SOCIETY AND POLITICS

Societies are complex and often difficult to unravel, but in this chapter, we have unraveled them somewhat. In looking at how societal organization shapes politics, we have found that individuals have a number of identities that they hold simultaneously: ethnicity, national identity, citizenship, political attitude, ideology, and political culture. Ethnicity provides a group identity, binding individuals to a group and separating them from others. National identity provides a political aspiration for that group, a desire for self-government, while citizenship establishes a relationship between that group and a state. Although each of these identities is distinct, they are often strongly connected to the point where some see the three as almost interchangeable. Such identities may bind people together; they also can be the source of conflict when different groups see each other as threats to their freedom and equality.

Whereas group identities establish differences between groups, political attitudes, ideologies, and culture all help position an individual within a group. These three identities help clarify an individual's view of the ideal relationship between freedom and equality for society, and of how fast and through what means change, if any, should be achieved.

Society's role in politics is clearly complicated, shaped by an array of factors that affect the ongoing debate over freedom and equality. Not long ago many social scientists dismissed social identities as outdated forms of identification that were giving way in the face of modernization and individualism. However, there is a growing belief that collective identities are more resilient that was once thought, and that they may in fact sharpen in the face of new societal challenges. More broadly, politics is not simply the sum of individual actions but the product of a rich array of institutions that overlap one another, providing meaning to our lives and informing the ideas, viewpoints, and values that we carry within us. We will consider this idea further in the next chapter, as we turn to a new set of institutions and ideas that shape the struggle over freedom and equality: those concerned with economic life.

NOTES

1 For more on nationalism see Benedict Anderson, *Imagined Communities* (London: Verso, 1983).

2 Charles Tilly, ed., *The Formation of National States in Western Europe* (Princeton: Princeton University Press, 1975). See also Reinhard Bendix, *Nation-Building and Citizenship* (Berkeley: University of California Press, 1964), and Douglass C. North and R. P. Thomas, *Rise of the Western World: A New Economic History* (Cambridge: Cambridge University Press, 1997).

3 For an excellent overview see David Horowitz, *Ethnic Groups in Conflict* (Berkeley: University of California Press, 2000).

4 For two views of the conflict see David Rieff, *Slaughterhouse: Bosnia and the Failure of the West* (New York: Simon & Schuster, 1995), and Robert Kaplan, *Balkan Ghosts: A Journey through History* (New York: Vintage, 1994).

5 This is covered in Philip Gourevitch, *We Wish to Inform You That Tomorrow We Will Be Killed with Our Families: Stories from Rwanda* (New York: Farrar, Straus & Giroux, 1998).

6 *Notes on the State of Virginia*, chap. 17, available at xroads.virginia.edu.

7 Quoted in George Plechanoff, *Anarchism and Socialism* (Chicago: C. H. Kerr, 1909), 80.

8 Gabriel A. Almond, "The Study of Political Culture," in *A Discipline Divided: Schools and Sects in Political Science* (Newbury Park: Sage, 1990), 138–56.

9 Samuel P. Huntington, *The Clash of Civilizations and the Remaking of World Order* (Simon & Schuster, 1996).

4 POLITICAL ECONOMY

Like politics, economies are made up of many different institutions—rules, norms, and values—that strongly influence how the economic system is constructed. People often think about economic systems as somehow "natural," with functions akin to the law of gravity. In reality, an economy relies on an array of institutions that enable individuals to exchange goods and resources with one another. Moreover, economic institutions, like political ones, are not easy to replace or change once they have been constructed. They become self-perpetuating, and people have a hard time imagining life without them.

Economic institutions directly influence politics, and vice-versa. The economy is one of the major arenas in which the struggle over freedom and equality takes place. Some view the economy as the central means by which people can achieve individual freedom, whereas others view the economy as the central means by which people can achieve collective equality. These values clash when each ideology has different expectations about how the economy should function and what kinds of societal goals should be pursued. Inevitably, this struggle involves the government, the state, and the regime. How this balance between freedom and equality is struck directly influences such things as the distribution of wealth, the kinds of economic activity and trade that citizens may conduct, and the overall degree of security, insecurity, and prosperity that people enjoy. In short, the interactions between political institutions and economic institutions in any country will have a profound impact on the standard of living of each and every citizen. The study of how politics and economics are related, and how their relationship shapes the balance of freedom and equality is commonly known as **political economy**.

In this chapter we will address these questions through an investigation of the relationship between freedom and equality. We will start by asking what role states play in managing an economy. There are a number of different areas in which states commonly involve themselves in economic life; depending on the dominant ideology and regime, the scope and impact of these actions can vary dramatically. Just as there are different ideologies concerning the ideal relationship between the state and society, as we saw in Chapter 3, there are different ideological views regarding the ideal relationship between the state and the market, each of which leads to a different political-economic system. We will explore each of these political-economic systems and their ideological origins. Once we have compared these differing views, we will consider how we might measure and compare their relative outcomes. Of the several ways in which we might do this, we will look at some of the most common standards by which to measure wealth and its distribution. Finally, with those concepts in hand, we will conclude with a consideration of the future of the relationship between state and market and how their interaction shapes the balance between freedom and equality.

THE COMPONENTS OF POLITICAL ECONOMY

Before we compare the different types of relationships between states and economies around the world, we should first familiarize ourselves with the basic components of political economy. All modern states are strongly involved in the day-to-day affairs of their economies, at both the domestic and the global level. In shaping the economy in order to achieve their stated ideological goals, states and regimes use a variety of economic institutions.

Markets and Property

The most fundamental place to begin is with markets and property. These are terms that we come across all the time. When people speak of markets, one of the first things that may come to mind is a physical place where individuals buy and sell goods. As long as human beings have existed in settled communities that were able to produce a surplus of goods there have been markets. Markets are closely connected with the rise of cities; people would settle around markets, and markets would often spring up around fortifications where commerce could be conducted with some sense of security. Such places still exist around the world. In Istanbul, Turkey, for instance, the Grand Bazaar, which dates back to the fifteenth century, is an enormous covered market comprising thousands of shops that sell everything from gold jewelry and carpets to T-shirts and postcards. No prices are fixed—everything must be negotiated between buyer and seller. Interestingly, the emergence of Internet auctions such as eBay has reintroduced the notion of the bazaar to the Western world, albeit in a "virtual" location.

IN FOCUS

MARKETS

- Sellers seek to create products that will be in demand.
- Buyers seek to buy the best or most goods at the lowest price.
- Markets are the medium through which buyers and sellers exchange goods.
- Markets emerge spontaneously and are not easily controlled by the state.

When social scientists speak of a market they are speaking of these same forces at work, though without a specific location. Markets are the interaction between the forces of supply and demand, and they allocate resources through the process of that interaction. As these two forces interact, they create values for goods and services by arriving at specific prices. What is amazing about markets is the way in which they can be so decentralized. Who decides how many cars should be built this year? Or what colors they should be? Who knows that the price of a candy bar should be? Or the cost of this textbook? These decisions are made not by any one person or government, but by millions of individuals, each making decisions about what he will buy and what she will sell. If I produce a good and set its price at more than people are willing to pay, I will not be able to sell it and turn a profit. This will force me either to lower my price or to go out of business. Similarly, if I produce a good that no one wants, I must either change it or face economic ruin. Sellers seek to create products that people will desire or need, and buyers seek to buy the best or the most goods at the lowest price. Since more than one seller or producer typically exists for a product, this tends to generate competition and innovation. Sellers seek to dominate a market by offering their goods at the cheapest price, or by offering a good that is innovative and therefore superior to any alternative.

In short, markets emerge spontaneously as a community of buyers and sellers in constant interaction through the economic choices that they make. Where there is demand, a market will emerge, whether people like it or not. Because of this spontaneity, states must determine how and if they wish to regulate the market by controlling the supply or demand of certain goods and services. For example, by setting a minimum wage a state is controlling to some extent the price of labor. By making certain drugs or prostitution illegal, the state is attempting to stamp out a certain part of the market altogether, for social or political reasons. Yet these goals are not always easily achieved. Minimum wages can be subverted by illegal immigrants, and "black" markets appear where drugs and prostitution are illegal. Markets have a life of their own, and each state must decide in what way, and to what extent, it will involve itself in them.

Property is a second element critical to any economy. As markets are the medium through which goods and services are exchanged, **property** refers to the ownership of those goods and services. Property can refer to land, buildings, businesses, or personal items, to name some of the most common forms. In addition, a certain set of *property rights* are assumed to go along with ownership, such as the right to buy and sell property, or the right not to have it taken away by the state or other citizens without a good reason (just cause) and compensation. These rights, a core component of individual freedom, require the state to create and enforce them.

In many people's minds, property, unlike markets, has a physical presence. I can see a car, buy it, own it, and sell it when I want a new one. However, property is not always tangible. *Intellectual property*, for example, refers to ownership of a specific type of knowledge or content—a song, a piece of software code, or a treatment for diabetes. As economic developments center more and more on such intangible forms of information and knowledge, the concept of property becomes just as fuzzy as that of markets, with no physical entity to speak of.

States vary in how they construct and enforce property rights, both between people and between the state and society. States may not strongly enforce the rights of individuals to protect their own property from other individuals—by failing, for example, to enact or enforce laws against counterfeiting or theft. States may also assume certain property rights for themselves, claiming ownership over property such as airwaves, oil, land, or businesses. Airlines, for example, are a common form of state-owned business in many countries.

Public Goods

Property as just described typically refers to goods that individuals obtain in a market and own and benefit from themselves. Yet some desirable goods cannot be easily created and traded in this manner. Take, for example,

PUBLIC GOODS

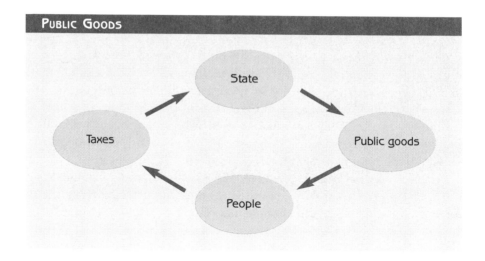

roads or military defense. Although both of these goods can exist in the private realm—in the form of toll roads, and mercenaries or bodyguards—some societies question the moral and practical implications of allowing these goods to belong only to a narrow few. The limitation of such goods may limit economic development; a system of privately held roads might impede trade, a system of private protection may leave many with a sense of insecurity. Because of these concerns, all states provide some level of **public goods**—goods that are used by most or all in society and which no private person can own. Unlike private goods, with their inherent link to individual freedom, public goods generate collective equality, as the public is able to share broadly in their benefits.[1]

In many countries, roads, national defense, health care, and primary education are public goods, since everyone within a country may use them or benefit from their existence. But states do differ greatly in the extent to which they provide public goods, in large part because of the role of ideology in the relationship between states and markets. In the United States, health care is not a public good; it remains in private hands and not everyone has equal access to it. In Canada, however, health care is a public good, provided by the state in the form of publicly owned hospitals and equal, universal benefits for all citizen. In Saudi Arabia, oil is a public good, owned by the state; revenue from its sale is spread (although not equally) among society. In Cuba, most businesses are owned by the state, making them public goods as well. The goods and profits of these firms belong not to a private owner, but to the state, to be distributed as the government sees fit.

Social Expenditures: Who Benefits?

This discussion of public goods leads us into the broader subject of **social expenditures**—the state's provision of public benefits such as education, health care, transportation, etc., or what is commonly called "welfare" or the "welfare state." For many people, the very word "welfare," like "taxes," has an inherently negative connotation: it calls up images of freeloaders living off the hard work of others. To be certain, the redistribution of wealth in this manner is controversial and has become more so in many advanced industrial democracies over the past two decades. Often critics assert that social expenditures lead to counterproductive behavior. High unemployment benefits, for example, may discourage people from seeking work. Moreover, alternative forms of social security that people have relied on in the past, such as the family, the community, or churches, may be weakened by too broad a welfare system.[2] These critics charge that the quest for collective equality has trumped individual freedom.

Even if we reject these arguments, one practical problem that does remain for many countries is that social expenditures can be very costly and particularly hard to fund in countries with an aging population—something common in many parts of the world. (Because many countries fund social expenditures through income taxes, an aging population means that a greater proportion of a country's workers have retired and are no longer paying income taxes while still collecting pension and health-care benefits.) As a result, many countries have in recent years sought to reduce their level of social expenditures, or at least to reduce the rate by which those expenditures increase over time. We will explore this issue further in Chapters 7 and 8, as we consider the advanced democracies and the postcommunist countries.

Who benefits from social expenditures? If we use a strict definition, social expenditures are provided by the state to those who due to various circumstances have been adversely affected: the unemployed, the elderly, the poor, and the disabled. Such expenditures on individuals include health care, job training, income replacement, and housing. However, many of these and other social expenditures can also be defined as public goods. For example, a national health-care system treats employed and unemployed, wealthy and poor alike. Highways, public higher education, and cultural institutions such as museums may primarily benefit the well-off. In fact, if we define social expenditures to include all of those public goods that the state provides, we find that in many countries the majority of funds spent benefit the middle class, not the poor. In this sense, the modern welfare state is less a structure whereby the middle class and the rich are taxed to benefit the poor, than one in which the middle class and the rich are taxed for services that benefit themselves.

Taxation

Over the past fifty years public goods and social expenditures have become major and increasing responsibilities for states. How do states pay for these expenses? One of the major sources of funds is taxation. As with social expenditures, taxation generates passionate opinions: some view it as the means by which a greedy state takes the hard-earned revenues of its citizens, whereas others see it as a critical tool for generating a basic level of collective equality. Regardless of one's opinion of taxation, states are expected by societies to provide a number of public goods and services.

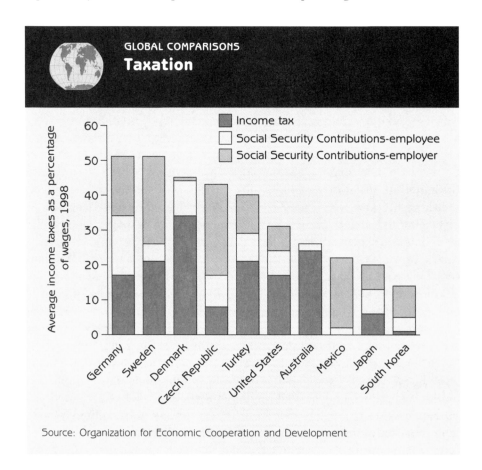

GLOBAL COMPARISONS
Taxation

Source: Organization for Economic Cooperation and Development

Roads, health care, defense, schools, police, and welfare or social security (benefits for retirement, old age, unemployment, and other social needs) all cost money. Taxation is the means by which the state collects the funds to pay for public goods and services—which, in the end, benefit the public directly.

How, and how much, tax is collected varies from country to country. The figure on page 88 illustrates this variation, although it deals only with taxes on wages (as opposed to taxes on business profits). The figure shows that both the level and the sources of those taxes differ from country to country. In some countries individuals pay relatively high income taxes and social security contributions compared to the contributions of their employers. In these cases, such as Australia, the tax burden rests primarily on the average citizen. In other countries, such as France, employers contribute a relatively large amount to social security, while citizens have a much lower tax burden. Some countries have a relatively high tax burden on both citizens and employers, as in Sweden and Belgium. The figure also indicates that total tax rates differ dramatically between countries. Many European countries with large social expenditures tend to have high overall tax rates in order to fund those expenses. All countries struggle with finding the right mix and level of taxation, aiming to extract needed funds without stunting economic growth by taking too much.[3]

Money, Inflation, and Unemployment

It should be getting clearer that many political-economic processes are tightly interlinked. States must form a relationship with markets and property, deciding which goods should remain in private hands and which should be public. They must also determine which goods and services should become publicly distributed to ensure a basic standard of living and security for all citizens. This distribution requires funds, for which states must draw on the public's resources through taxation. But a successful and productive tax base needs a dynamic and growing economy, which is also necessary to meet the public's needs and demands. So the state is also charged with fostering economic growth.

One basic way the state does this is through the creation and management of money. Money is nothing more than a medium of exchange; unlike wealth, which consists of property that has value, money is an instrument through which people conduct economic transactions. Money represents only a tiny fraction of the wealth in the world, most of which is tied up in houses, factories, land, and other property. But without money, economic transactions are difficult. States thus play a critical role in providing money as a means to secure and stimulate economic transactions.

Long ago, money did not exist. People had few goods that they wished to exchange, and what transactions did take place would occur through barter. As goods became more specialized and market forces spread over a greater distance through trade, barter began to be conducted through a limited number of goods that were widely desired, portable, or durable—in other words, products that themselves had some inherent value. Goods such as gold, silver, beads, salt, and tea, to name just a few, gradually replaced other forms of barter. These items were the first forms of money—a basic unit for economic transactions. Money in turn allowed for a system of prices to emerge, as one could gauge the value of various items against a single standard—how many beads is one pig worth?

These forms of money were not created by states. Their value existed only in the worth of the items themselves. As complex political systems began to take shape, however, states began to take responsibility for the creation of money. Initially such money took the form of promissory notes, whereby the state printed bills as a form of IOU, promising to redeem them later for gold or silver. By the early twentieth century, however, states began to abandon such outright promises. In the modern world, people place faith in a state's currency on the basis of their trust in that state. A person accepts payments in dollars or euros or yen because he or she knows others will accept them in turn. The society functioning under that currency trusts that money only so long as it also trusts its state.

As a result of their control over money, states have a great deal of influence over their domestic economies. Part of this power comes through what is known as a **central bank**, an institution that controls how much money is flowing through the economy, as well as how much it costs to borrow money in that economy.[4] One of the main ways a central bank affects these two areas is by changing a national interest rate, that is, the rate charged to private banks when they need to borrow funds from the central bank or one another. When the central bank lowers the interest rate charged to banks, those banks in turn lower their own interest rates for businesses and individuals. Loans become less expensive and saving

IN FOCUS

A CENTRAL BANK . . .

- Controls the amount of money in the economy.
- Controls the cost of borrowing money.
- Lowers interest rates to stimulate the economy.
- Raises interest rates to check inflation.

becomes less lucrative, prompting people to borrow more and spend more. This in turn increases the amount of money active in the economy and thereby stimulates economic growth. If the central bank raises interest rates, on the other hand, people are likely to borrow less and save more, to take advantage of the higher interest their savings can earn. The money supply in the economy contracts as a result, and economic growth is likely to slow. Thus in 2001, when the U.S. Federal Reserve (the U.S. central bank) cut interest rates eleven times, lowering the national rate from 6 percent to less than 2 percent, it was trying to stimulate the economy in the face of an economic downturn.

The actions of a central bank are also closely tied to two other important factors in any economy, inflation and unemployment. Given the discussion above, you might be wondering, if low interest rates stimulate development, why not just keep interest rates low? When the money supply is increased through inexpensive credit, an economy can wind up with too much money chasing after too few goods—an imbalance of supply and demand. In such circumstances, prices begin to rise and money loses its value—a problem known as **inflation**. Although small levels of inflation are not a problem, inflation can become problematic when it is too high. Savings rapidly lose their value, and workers and those on fixed incomes, such as the retired, find that their salaries or pensions buy less and less. People then press for higher wages or benefits to offset higher prices, and this in turn feeds inflation further.

In extreme cases, countries can experience what is known as **hyperinflation**, defined as inflation that is more than 50 percent a month for more than two months in a row. (By comparison, the U.S. inflation rate in 2001 was about 3 percent per year, while that of the European Union was around 2 percent.) Hyperinflation usually occurs when governments find themselves lacking the tax revenues needed to carry out basic tasks, such as paying state employees or funding public goods—in other words, the government has produced a budget deficit. Under these conditions many governments go into debt, borrowing from the public, from international private banks, or from institutions such as the International Monetary Fund. For wealthy countries such as the United States or Germany, lenders are not hard to find. But for poorer or more unstable countries, people and institutions may be unwilling to loan funds. The government in question may therefore decide to simply print money to pay for its own expenditures. When large amounts of money are printed and dumped into the economy, however, that money's value quickly erodes. This in turn leads people to spend their money as quickly as possible, driving inflation

HYPERINFLATION AND WAR IN YUGOSLAVIA

In Yugoslavia in the 1990s the government, suffering from war and an international embargo against it, printed huge amounts of money in order to cover state expenses. As a result, between 1993 and 1995 prices increased by 5,000,000,000,000,000 (5 quadrillion) percent—a phenomenon known as hyperinflation. The Yugoslav currency actually lost value by the hour, creating bizarre outcomes. For example, one individual living in Yugoslavia at the time noted that his expensive long-distance phone calls cost him virtually nothing by the time he actually got the bill, given the rapidly eroding value of his money. Under these conditions, most people relied instead on barter or stable foreign currencies for financial transactions, and many economic transactions stopped altogether.

even higher. As you can imagine, under such conditions normal economic processes quickly become impossible: Why accept money for any transaction when it will be virtually worthless tomorrow?

Given that discussion, you might now conclude that a high interest rate is best; after all, it fends off inflation. Indeed, some countries that have experienced hyperinflation have since kept fairly tight control over their money supply. Yet the trade-off of high interest rates can be higher rates of unemployment and low rates of economic growth. If money becomes too expensive to borrow, businesses may be unable to create new jobs because their supply of credit for additional investment is limited. Individuals may also avoid borrowing and spending, leaving their money in the bank to earn interest at attractive rates. States thus walk a very fine line in managing the money supply, trying to create an economy with low inflation and low unemployment, yet knowing that these two factors may work against one another.

Given the difficulty of this balance and the temptation for governments to use the central bank for their own political ends (such as printing money to cover expenses or lowering interest rates around election time), many countries have insulated central banks from the government by making it difficult for elected leaders to dismiss the directors of the central bank. This is typically done by guaranteeing the head of the central bank a fixed term of office. For example, in Japan the central bank's head serves for five years; in the United States and South Korea, the term is four years.

Regulation

So far our discussion has dealt with the state's role in fostering the development of markets and property—what is to be provided, by whom, at what cost. But states must concern themselves not only with economic output, but also with the means by which that output is created. As with public goods, moral and technical issues often affect a state's approach in this area. Are some economic processes inherently counterproductive in creating goods and services? Are there economic processes that generate "public bads," problems that affect all of society? Whose rights are most important in these cases—the individual's or the group's? These concerns draw states into the realm of economic regulation.

Regulations—rules or orders that set the boundaries of a given procedure—may take a number of different forms. Many regulations are indirect, such as safety or environmental regulations that affect the way in which a business may operate. Other regulations may be more specific, such as those in the area of competition and innovation. One problem encountered in modern economies is the emergence of a single producer of a good or service that is able to dominate the market—otherwise known as a **monopoly**. With the rise of capitalism in the nineteenth century, large corporations came to control national and even international markets for some goods; new technological developments had suddenly made such economic reach possible. States and societies began to fear that domestic economies would soon become dominated by a few huge monopolies, unfettered by competition and able to charge whatever prices they pleased for their goods. Another similar arrangement that emerged to dominate markets is what is known as a **cartel**, which is a grouping of producers that, although individually unable to dominate a market, try to do so in collaboration with a small number of other firms. Microsoft is often viewed by its critics as a monopoly that controls the computer software market, while the Organization of Petroleum Exporting Countries (OPEC), whose members control some 40 percent of the world's oil supply, is an example of an international cartel. The South African firm DeBeers is another example of a cartel; it controls around 60 percent of the world's diamond sales through its own production as well as through agreements with other diamond producers to strictly limit supplies.[5]

Because monopolies and cartels can control prices by limiting supply, some states believe that such entities stifle competition, increase prices, and limit innovation. As a result, states often try to break up such entities when possible. But there is no consensus that this is a proper activity for the state. Many argue against such regulation, believing that if monopolies do emerge, they will grow complacent, fail to innovate, and eventually be unseated by some new upstart rival. Cartels, many believe, will similarly fail due to internal disagreements and the temptation for members to cheat and produce more than the cartel wishes. Others believe that monopolies and cartels are able to crush competition even before it emerges, keeping rivals and new technology out of the market. Finally, some may advocate the creation of domestic monopolies or international cartels, for the very reason that others decry them: they are powerful businesses and can dominate international markets. Each of these views is consistent with a different ideological perspective on the relationship between states and markets, which we will explore later in this chapter in our discussion of political-economic systems.

Trade

States must grapple with the challenge of regulating economic production not just within their country, but between their citizens and the outside world. In most economies, markets are no longer only local; goods and services come from all over the world. States can influence the degree of competition and access to goods within their own country by determining what foreign goods and services may enter the domestic market.

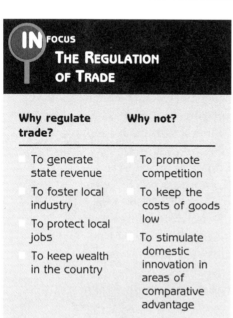

IN FOCUS

THE REGULATION OF TRADE

Why regulate trade?	Why not?
To generate state revenue	To promote competition
To foster local industry	To keep the costs of goods low
To protect local jobs	To stimulate domestic innovation in areas of comparative advantage
To keep wealth in the country	

The way in which a state structures its trade can have a profound impact on its own economic development. States have a number of tools to use to influence trade: **tariffs**, which are basically taxes on imported goods; **quotas** are ways to limit the quantity of a good coming into the country; other **nontariff barriers** may create health, packaging, or other restrictions, whose ostensible purpose is to protect its citizens but which in reality make it difficult or expensive for foreign goods to be sold in the local market. For example, in India and other countries of Asia, "screen quota" laws mandate that a certain percentage of the films shown each year be of domestic origin.

Why regulate trade? States may favor tariffs as a way to generate revenue, and they and local manufacturers may see such barriers against foreign competitors as a way to reduce the competitiveness of foreign goods by increasing their prices, thereby stimulating local production as a result. As in the case of regulating competition, limiting trade is a matter of hot debate. Those in favor of tariffs and other trade barriers argue that the jobs of those producing local goods are at stake, and that the profits from the sales of imported goods will go to foreign producers, transferring national wealth in the process. Those who oppose trade barriers counter that a few jobs do not justify higher costs for the public as a whole. In fact, they believe that greater competition drives weaker firms out of business, stimulating domestic innovation in new areas in which the country can gain a **comparative advantage**[6]—the ability to produce a particular good or service more efficiently relative to other countries' efficiency in producing the same good or service.

We've covered a great deal of ground in this section, so let's quickly review what we have discussed. The most basic "building blocks" of political economy are markets and property; states oversee how goods and services are produced, delineating basic economic rights and limitations. States step into the market when the private sector cannot or should not provide or control certain products, creating public goods and other social expenditures. To fund such expenses, states must not only develop a system of taxation but also help stimulate and secure the economy. Expanding and contracting the money supply helps increase economic development and provide jobs, but states must be careful not to overstimulate the economy, which can generate inflation. In order to prevent such mishaps, many states insulate their central banks from government interference. In addition to overseeing and drawing revenue from the creation of private and public goods, states must also concern themselves with regulating the means of their production. Managing competition, both within the country and between countries, is a contentious task. All of these responsibilities are part of a complex web of cause and effect that can shape freedom, equality, and the generation of wealth. Which mixture of policies across these areas will result in economic prosperity and state power? As we shall see in the next section, there is no easy answer to this question, either. States have taken radically different approaches to the ideal relationship between state and market, leading to a variety of distinct political-economic systems around the world.

POLITICAL-ECONOMIC SYSTEMS

A **political-economic system** can be defined as the actual relationship between political and economic institutions in a particular country, as well as the policies and outcomes they create. Various types of political-economic systems view the ideal relationship between state and market, and between freedom and equality, in a different way. Political-economic systems are commonly classified as either liberalism, mercantilism, social democracy or communism; these four types are shown

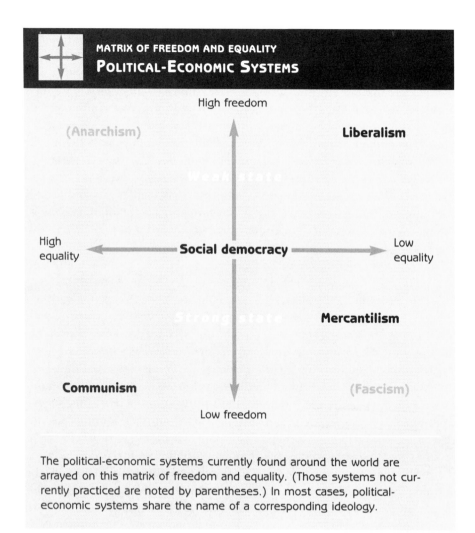

The political-economic systems currently found around the world are arrayed on this matrix of freedom and equality. (Those systems not currently practiced are noted by parentheses.) In most cases, political-economic systems share the name of a corresponding ideology.

in the figure on page 96, placed on our familiar axes of freedom and equality.

As the figure shows, the majority of these political-economic systems match the political ideologies we discussed in Chapter 3. This should not be too surprising: political-economic systems can be seen as the attempt to realize an abstract ideology in the form of real economic institutions and policies. There is always a disjuncture, however, between theory and practice. For example, some subscribers to a liberal ideology would say that existing "liberal" political-economic systems around the world do not live up to liberal ideals. Many communists similarly condemned the communist political-economic system that was practiced in the Soviet Union as a betrayal of "true" communist thought. In addition, you have probably noticed that the ideologies of fascism and anarchism are shown on the figure in parentheses; neither of them has a political-economic counterpart. In the case of fascism, this is because the fascist political-economic systems that arose in the 1930s were destroyed by World War II. Anarchism, meanwhile, has never been realized in politics or economics. The absence of fascism and anarchism from current political economies does not mean, however, that they could not reappear at some point in the future.

These four basic typologies simplify the complexity of political economy. In reality, of course, there are many different variations within and among these four categories. Each of these categories strikes a different balance between state power and the economy, thereby shaping markets and property, public goods and social expenditures, taxation, regulation, and trade.

Liberalism

Recall from Chapter 3 that, as a political ideology, liberalism places a high priority on individual political and economic freedom; it advocates limiting state power in favor of greater freedoms for the individual and the market. Liberalism assumes that individuals are best suited to take responsibility for their own behavior and well-being. Liberal scholars such as Adam Smith put their faith in the market and in private property: if people are allowed to harness their own energies, sense of entrepreneurialism, and, yes, greed, they will generate more prosperity than any government could produce through "top-down" policy-making and legislation.

For liberals, then, the best state is a weak one, constrained in its autonomy and capacity. Markets and property should be regulated as little as possible, they believe, to encourage competition and innovation and produce **capitalism**—a system of production based on private ownership and free markets. The state should provide public goods only in such critical areas as defense or education; social expenditures, like most public goods, should be dramatically restricted to prevent freeriding and to encourage individual responsibility. Regulations and taxation should be kept to a minimum, and property rights protected. Central banks should have a limited ability to intervene in the market, and unemployment should be accepted as an inevitable outcome that cannot be eliminated. Free trade should be promoted to encourage global competition and innovation. Taxation should be kept to a minimum so that wealth will remain in the hands of the public and be reinvested into the economy. Overall, the state should by and large act as a sort of night watchman, intervening to defend the public only when crises arise.

LIBERAL: A CONFUSING TERM

The ideology and political-economic system of liberalism favors a high degree of individual freedom and a weak state in order to ensure the greatest prosperity, even if this means tolerating inequality. Yet this definition flies in the face of the term "liberal" as used in the United States and Canada, as it typically implies a stronger state and greater state involvement in economic affairs. This confusion stems in large part from historical developments: over time, liberals who once placed their faith in the market to expand freedom and equality came to believe more and more that state intervention was necessary. Liberals in North America essentially became what many other countries would refer to as "social democrats."

This kind of ideological transformation did not occur in many other countries, however. Outside of North America, liberalism has retained its original meaning. Some political scientists therefore use the term "classical liberalism" to refer to the original tenets of the ideology. Others, particularly critics of the ideology, often use the term "neoliberalism" instead, indicating that the original ideas of liberalism (free markets and greater individualism along with a tolerance for inequality) are resurgent around the world.

So the term "liberal" can have many different meanings:

1. As a political attitude: favoring slow, evolutionary change (see Chapter 3);
2. As a political ideology in North America: favoring a greater state role in limiting inequality, or what many outside of the region would call "social democracy";
3. As a political ideology outside of North America: favoring free markets and individualism, accepting greater inequality; and
4. As a political economy: favoring a limited state role in the economy.

These conditions describe the liberal tenet of **laissez-faire**, which holds that the economy should be "allowed to do" what it wishes.

Under these minimalist conditions, liberals believe, economic growth will be maximized. Moreover, under such conditions people will enjoy the greatest amount of personal and political freedom. Liberals would in fact stress that democracy *requires* a free market. If too much economic and political power is concentrated in the hands of the state, they believe, this monopoly would endanger democracy. In their view, private, individual economic power must act as a check on the political power of the state. As Adam Smith, one of the scions of liberal ideology, argued in 1755, "little else is requisite to carry a state to the highest degree of opulence from the lowest barbarism but peace, easy taxes, and a tolerable administration of justice: all the rest being brought about by the natural course of things."[7]

Liberalism as a political-economic system, then, is defined by its emphasis on individual freedoms over collective equality, and on the power of markets over the state. The political economies of many countries around the world are founded on these essential liberal values. If we stretch the definition, we might even argue that any capitalist democracy is an example of liberalism at work. However, to remain true to the essential values of liberalism, this book will confine its definition to those countries where state involvement in the economy and society is relatively low.

As you might imagine, the United States is typically touted as a paragon of liberal values. The U.S. Constitution, for instance, explicitly attempts to separate and weaken state power as a check on the possible growth of tyrannical government. Regulations are often much weaker and social expenditures and taxation tend to be lower in the United States than in other industrialized democracies, and the American public is largely skeptical of state power. For many critics of American liberalism, however, this emphasis on individual rights over the needs of society appears amoral and irresponsible, a celebration of selfishness over community that only increases the gap between the rich and the poor.[8]

But the United States is not the only country in the liberalism camp. The United Kingdom, the intellectual wellspring for much of liberal thought, is also viewed as a liberal country, as are Canada, Australia, and New Zealand (all, like the United States, former British colonies). Other countries around the world, ranging from Chile to Estonia, have over the past twenty years embraced the "neoliberal" economic model and are noted for their low levels of government regulation, taxation, and social expenditures, and for their protection of property rights. (For an explanation of the term "neoliberal," see the box on page 98.) Yet even though liberal ideology would argue that a free market and democracy are inseparable, we do find countries with liberal political-economic systems that nevertheless restrict democratic rights. Singapore, for example, is regularly noted for having one of the freest economic systems in the world, yet individual political and civil rights in Singapore are sharply limited. Critics of liberalism often highlight this contradiction, pointing out this free market that sits easily with political repression. We will discuss this contradiction further when we turn to authoritarianism in Chapter 5.

Social Democracy

In Chapter 3 we noted that social democracy combines elements of liberalism and communism in an attempt to temper the extremes of too much freedom or too much equality. Like liberalism, social democracy functions on a foundation of private property and open markets, but it has come to accept this system rather slowly. Most political parties and ideas that we would define as social democratic today have their ideological origins in communism. Social democrats broke with communists by rejecting the radical call for revolution and state appropriation of private property and wealth. Most notable among early social democratic thinkers was Edward Bernstein (1850–1932). In his 1898 work *Evolutionary Socialism,* Bernstein rejected Karl Marx's belief in inevitable revolution, concluding instead that democracy could evolve into socialism through the ballot box rather than through the gun.[9]

Based on this rejection of revolution and embrace of democracy, over time social democracy has come to accept a role for private property and market forces, but it remains ambivalent about their ultimate benefits to society. Unchecked economic development produces great inequality, social democrats argue, by concentrating wealth in the hands of a very few. This in turn can polarize society, pitting owners against laborers, rich against poor, city against countryside. In this way of thinking, the state is seen less as a threat to society (as liberals tend to view it) than as a creator of certain positive social rights, basic foundations of collective equality that social democrats feel are lost in the vicissitudes of the market. The manifesto of the Party of European Socialists explains,

> For socialists and social democrats, a modern economy can only be developed in close cooperation with social partners. We know that economies are stronger when societies are just. The poverty of some diminishes the lives of all who live in a divided society. . . . That is why we say "yes" to a market economy, but "no" to a market society.[10]

These problems of economic injustice and instability can be amelio-rated by the state, say social democrats, in a number of different ways. Markets and property should be encouraged by the state but controlled in order to prevent individual profit at the expense of society as a whole. A wide array of public goods, such as health care and transportation, should be made available by the state. Money and inflation should be actively managed by a central bank that responds to the government's need to combat and eliminate unemploy-ment. The need for competition should not stand in the way of state regulation or even ownership of certain sectors of the econ-omy, and trade should similarly be promoted in such a way that it does not endanger domestic businesses and jobs. Finally, the goal of equality requires a higher level of social expenditures to ensure basic benefits for all. Taxes make these social expenditures possible while also redistributing wealth from the rich to the poor. Thus taxes tend to be higher in a social-democratic system.

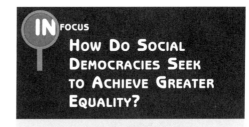

IN FOCUS

HOW DO SOCIAL DEMOCRACIES SEEK TO ACHIEVE GREATER EQUALITY?

- Through taxes, which make high levels of social expenditure possible while redistributing wealth from rich to poor.

- Through trade, which is promoted but balanced with preserving domestic industry and jobs.

- Through government regulation and even ownership of important sectors of the economy.

In addition to these policies, another element common in social dem-ocratic systems is the use of **neocorporatism**, a system of policy-making involving the state, labor, and businesses. In the liberal model, economic decisions are made through the competitive interaction of business and labor; workers demand higher wages or better safety conditions, striking or quitting their jobs when necessary, and employers hire, fire, and nego-tiate with workers as they see fit. In some cases this relationship can be quite antagonistic, leading to conflict that can hurt businesses and result in violence. Thus even in liberal societies a certain level of business and labor regulation exists to protect both workers and businesses from each other. But overall, this conflict is seen by liberals as a necessary and pos-itive part of human economic relations.

In contrast, a neocorporatist system as used by social democrats rejects this combative relationship and the limited role played by the state. Instead, neocorporatism uses policy in order to build consensus over competition, by creating a limited number of associations that represent a large seg-ment of business and labor. Good examples of such associations can be found in Germany, where the German Federation of Trade Unions comprises eleven different trade unions and more than eight million workers. The Confederation of German Employers' Associations includes nearly every large or medium-sized employer in the country. These associations are in turn recognized by the state as legitimate representatives of their members, and together these associations and the state decide on such important economic policy issues as wages, unemployment compensation, or taxation.

In other words, many decisions that under liberalism are left to the state alone or that result from the interaction of business and labor are decided under neocorporatism in a cooperative and organized fashion. The result, supporters argue, is a system that is much less prone to conflict and that provides a greater role for both business and labor in state economic policies. Liberals would retort that such structures harm the economy in the long run by hindering the flexibility of business and labor,

CONTRIBUTORS TO THE THEORIES OF POLITICAL ECONOMY

System	Thinker	Contribution
Liberalism	Adam Smith	*The Wealth of Nations* (1776), considered one of the first texts on modern economics. Articulated the idea that economic development requires limited government interference.
Communism	Karl Marx	*Das Kapital* (1867). Asserted that human history is driven by economic relations and inequality, and that revolution will eventually replace capitalism with a system of total equality between people.
Social democracy	Edward Bernstein	*Evolutionary Socialism* (1898). Rejected Marx's belief in the inevitability of revolution, arguing that economic equality can be achieved through democratic participation.
Mercantilism	Friedrich List	*National System of Political Economy* (1841). Rejected free-trade theories of liberalism, arguing that states must play a strong role in protecting and developing the national economy against foreign competitors.

making it difficult to fire employees, to close unprofitable factories, or to hire additional workers.

Finally, social-democratic systems often involve themselves in the economic system through state ownership of firms. Even liberal countries have some basic services under public ownership, such as mail services or public transportation, but social-democratic states may own part or all of a much wider set of businesses that provide what they view as public goods. These can range from extractors of natural resources such as oil, timber, and the like, to various large industries, including steel, banking, or automobile production, which are seen as too large or economically important to be left in the hands of a few private owners. As a result, the social-democratic state assumes control, believing that it can better serve society by directly owning and managing the firms. In France, for example, the state owns more than 40 percent of the auto manufacturer Renault; in Sweden, all iron mines are owned by the state, having been purchased from private businesses decades ago.

Social-democratic systems are most common in Europe; they include France, Germany, Sweden, and Denmark. These states generally have more autonomy and capacity than do liberal states, since they are able (and expected) to actively intervene in the economy in order to guide it toward certain social goals. Social democrats laud these systems for their attempt to balance market forces with societal needs; liberals view them as overly regulated, inflexible, and thus a drag on economic growth.

Communism

Whereas social democracy departs from liberalism in its attempt to balance individual freedom and collective equality, the political-economic system of communism chooses to effectively eliminate the former in order to fully achieve the latter. We will discuss communism in much greater detail in Chapter 8, as we look at communist and postcommunist countries; for now we will focus on its basic institutions. Communist thinkers such as Karl Marx began with the premise that private property and a free market cannot truly serve the needs of society as a whole. Communists view private property as a form of power that inevitably leads to control over others. Economic competition between people creates exploitation and a development of social classes in which a narrow group of the wealthy dominate and benefit from the labor of the poor majority. Both domestically and internationally, this exploitation opens an ever-wider gap between those who control the economy and those who merely labor in it. Such inequalities, Marx argued, will inevitably lead to a revolution, during which a single communist party will take control of the state on behalf of all people.

Given this interpretation of the nature of markets and property, communist systems choose to transform both. Private property is fully nationalized, placed in the hands of the state on behalf of the people. Through nationalization, communism seeks to eliminate the economic differences between people and the instruments of exploitation. In other words, the entire economy becomes a public good, existing for the benefit of all. In addition, market forces are eliminated by the state; almost all private transactions are considered to be black markets. In stark contrast to the "invisible hand" of liberalism's market and the guided economies of social democracy, under communism economic decision-making is entrusted entirely to the state, which is assumed to make the most rational economic decisions that produce the greatest benefits for the whole of society.

Since all economic decision-making and ownership are centralized under state control, many of the essential tasks of states in other political-economic systems are fundamentally different under communism. Taxation, for example, takes an indirect form through fixed prices and wages; any profit produced by a worker or a firm goes to the state for public expenditures (which include guaranteed employment). Since all firms are owned by the state, competition is also eliminated, and regulations, although present, may be much weaker—since the state winds up regulating itself. Finally, trade is highly restricted; the only imports are those the state deems necessary that cannot be produced domestically. State capacity and autonomy are extremely high; the state can operate without the interference of either the public or private economic actors.[11]

As you would expect, supporters of private property and market forces argue that states lack the ability to make the kinds of economic decisions made by a decentralized market. Inefficiency and waste are likely in such a state-dominated system. Moreover, supporters of democracy argue that so much power in the hands of the state would guarantee authoritarian rule. If there are no property rights left with the people, and if all economic decisions are made by the state, there is no separation between public and private. States wind up controlling the fates of people—where they live and work, what they earn, what they may buy. In response, communists would say that what they offer is total equality for all; their system emphasizes equality and sacrifices individual freedom, just as liberalism does the opposite. And even if such a system is inefficient, its supporters might argue, better that economic resources are wasted in the attempt to

COMPARING CONCEPTS
POLITICAL ECONOMIC SYSTEMS

	Liberalism	Social Democracy	Mercantilism	Communism
Role of the state in the economy	Little; minimal welfare state	Some state ownership, regulation; large welfare state	Much state ownership or direction; small welfare state	Total state ownership; extensive welfare state
Role of the market	Paramount	Important but not sacrosanct	Limited	None
State capacity and autonomy	Low	Moderate	High	Very high
Importance of equality	Low	High	Low	High
How is policy made?	Pluralism	Corporatism	State	State/Party
Possible flaws	Inequality, monopolies	Expense of welfare state, inefficiency	Can tend toward authoritarianism; can distort market.	Authoritarianism and inefficiency
Examples	US, UK, former British colonies	Western Europe (Germany, Sweden)	Japan, South Korea, India	Cuba, Soviet Union, China

provide for all than squandered on luxuries for a wealthy few, as is common in market economies.

Mercantilism

The final political-economic system, **mercantilism**, stands quite apart in the debate over freedom and equality that separates liberalism, social democracy, and communism. Whereas all three systems we have studied so far theoretically emphasize the needs of society, albeit in different ways, mercantilism focuses on the needs of the state; it is much less concerned with either individual freedom or collective equality. Instead, national economic power is paramount. As a result, mercantilism views the domestic economy as an instrument that exists to serve not the public but rather the needs of the state, by generating wealth that can be used for national power. Mercantilist states focus in particular on their position in the international system, for they believe that economic weakness undermines national sovereignty. Political power must be backed by wealth, in the mercantilist view, and that wealth should be directed toward national ends.[12]

Although this system may seem a strange outlier in the debate between freedom and equality, as it seems to emphasize neither, as a political-economic system mercantilism is the oldest of the four we have covered. At the advent of modern economies in Europe centuries ago, most countries engaged in mercantilist practices. The building of empires, in particular, was an outgrowth of mercantilism, a way in which a state could use its political power to gain control over resources and markets, shutting out its rivals. The creation of British colonies in North America and elsewhere, and the requirement that they trade only with the home country are good examples of mercantilist practices at work. And in spite of the challenges posed by other political-economic alternatives, mercantilism continues to be an attractive system for countries around the world, some of which have used it to great effect.

One way that mercantilist states attempt to achieve state economic power is through an active industrial policy. Economic ministries seek to direct the economy toward certain industries and away from others through such policies as taxation and subsidies. In some cases mercantilist states, like social democracies, may rely on partial or full state ownership of specific industries, by attempting to create certain businesses that are viewed as critical for international competitiveness. Capitalism is guided by the state toward goals set by the government.

Another complementary method to boost the domestic economy under mercantilism is the strong use of tariffs, nontariff barriers, and other trade regulations. Mercantilists often believe that goods that are not locally produced lead to a loss of national profits and an increased dependency on foreign economies. High tariff barriers are a common way to shield and promote domestic industry. For example, in Japan after World War II, the Japanese government relied on its Ministry of International Trade and Industry to steer the economy toward exports such as electronics and automobiles. High tariff barriers kept foreign competition at bay, and subsidies were provided to certain industrial sectors, such as semiconductors. South Korea subsequently followed a similar set of policies.

In its emphasis on state power mercantilism does not typically focus on social expenditures in the way that social democracy does. Welfare benefits tend to be much lower in mercantilist states. Indeed, there may be a certain logic to this policy: if benefits are low, the public knows that it must bear the burden for retirement and health care. This can encourage higher public savings, providing more capital that can be borrowed by the state or businesses. Lower levels of expenditure are also likely to translate into lower taxes. Finally, the central bank is a critical mercantilist tool: it promotes industrialization through such policies as low interest rates to encourage borrowing. State capacity and autonomy are much higher in mercantilist political economics than in liberal or social-democratic systems. However, unlike under communism, markets and private property remain powerful under mercantilism, even though they are administered by state policy.

Supporters of mercantilism cite its ability to direct an economy toward areas of industrial development and international competitiveness that the market, left on its own, might not pursue. For developing countries, such direction is particularly attractive, and Japan and South Korea are cited as exemplars of mercantilism's strengths. Critics of mercantilism respond that states are not well suited to decide what kinds of industries are likely to be successful in the long run, and that putting so much economic power into states' hands while limiting competition is a recipe for waste and corruption. Even though Japan and South Korea are examples of successful mercantilism, some critics argue, the economic downturns in both countries during the 1990s were the inevitable result of overly tight connections between the economy and the state. Using many other examples, such as India, critics assert that mercantilist policies have failed to reap significant rewards. Finally, critics note that, in its most extreme form, mercantilism is connected to the ideology of fascism, with the state directing the economic in the same way in which it seeks to direct society. Fascist Germany and imperial Japan both employed extreme forms of mercantilism and used war as a means to conquer and control important economic resources such as land, food, and

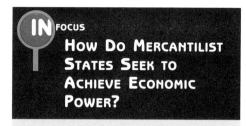

IN FOCUS

HOW DO MERCANTILIST STATES SEEK TO ACHIEVE ECONOMIC POWER?

- By directing the economy toward certain industries and away from others through the use of subsidies and taxation.

- Through partial or full state ownership of industries that are considered critical.

- With the strong use of tariffs, nontariff barriers, and other regulations.

- By limiting social expenditures and therefore keeping taxation to a minimum.

- With low interest rates set by the central bank to encourage borrowing and investment.

oil. Mercantilism is not inherently incompatible with democracy, however; postwar Japan and India are examples of democratic countries that have industrialized using mercantilist methods. Overall, though, mercantilism is more commonly correlated with authoritarian systems than with democracies.

POLITICAL-ECONOMIC SYSTEMS AND THE STATE: COMPARING OUTCOMES

Having gained an understanding of the different political-economic systems used around the world and the different ways they approach their tasks, we next should consider how to compare them. Since each system is founded on a different ideological approach to the paradox of freedom and equality and a different set of institutions to achieve that outcome, it might seem that trying to compare them would be difficult, like comparing apples and oranges. However, there are criteria we can use to compare these systems. These criteria are by no means the "correct" or only ways in which to make comparisons and draw conclusions, but they are useful tools for our purposes.

One basic criterion for comparison we can use is the level of economic development. The most common tool with which economists measure this is **gross domestic product (GDP)**, defined as the total market value of all goods and services produced within a country over a period of one year.* GDP provides a basic benchmark for the average per capita income in a country. However, GDP statistics can be quite misleading. For one thing, a given amount of money will buy more in certain parts of a country than in others. A salary of $30,000 a year will go a lot further in Boise, Idaho, than in it will in New York City, where a home on average costs four times as much as in Boise. The same problem arises when one compares countries: people may earn far more in some countries than they do in others,

---

*Another common measure of a country's wealth is **gross national product (GNP)**, which is similar to GDP, except that it counts the value of goods and services produced by the residents of a country, including income from abroad. For example, if a French company earns profits from producing goods in China, those profits would be included in France's GNP but not in its GDP. Conversely, those profits would be included in China's GDP but not in its GNP. As international trade has become more important, many countries have switched from GNP to GDP as the primary way of measuring output. For that reason, and in the interests of consistency, GDP is used throughout this text.

GDP vs. PPP

but those raw figures do not take into account the relative costs of living in those countries. To address these difficulties, economists often calculate national GDP data on the basis of what is known as purchasing power parity (PPP). **Purchasing-power parity** attempts to estimate the buying power of income in each country by comparing similar costs, such as food and housing, using prices in the United States as a benchmark. When these data are factored in, comparative incomes change rather dramatically, as shown in the box below. For example, without PPP, Japan's national income appears to be much higher than that of Canada, but when

GLOBAL COMPARISONS
MEASURING THE SIZE OF ECONOMIES

	GDP Per Capita (in U.S. $)	GDP Per Capita (PPP, in U.S. $)
Japan	36,900	24,900
United States	36,200	36,200
Germany	22,500	23,400
Sweden	25,600	22,200
Canada	21,800	24,800
Ireland	24,600	21,600
Greece	10,500	17,200
South Korea	9,500	16,100
Poland	4,100	8,500
Mexico	5,600	9,100
South Africa	2,900	8,500
Russia	1,700	7,700
China	800	3,600
India	500	2,200
Cambodia	200	1,300
Nigeria	300	950

Sources: Central Intelligence Agency, World Bank

Note: Figures are for 2000.

the cost of living in each country is factored in through PPP, the two are nearly equal. Incomes in poorer countries such as China and India also rise quite dramatically when PPP is taken into account.

While GDP can be a useful way to measure wealth, it has its limitations. For example, since these figures capture economic transactions, a country that suffers a natural disaster may see its GDP go up due to increased activity to rebuild the damage. High crime might also increase GDP if more police are hired and prisons built. Nor does GDP take into

GDP takes into effect negative issues too, like war, disaster, etc.

GLOBAL COMPARISONS

DISTRIBUTION OF INCOME IN THE 1990S

	Percentage of Total National Income Held by Segment of Population		
	Poorest 10% of population	Richest 10% of population	Gini Index
Japan	4.8	21.7	24.9
Sweden	3.7	20.1	25.0
Germany	3.3	23.7	30.0
Canada	2.8	23.8	31.5
South Korea	2.9	24.3	31.6
Greece	3.0	25.3	32.7
Poland	3.0	26.3	32.9
Ireland	2.5	27.4	35.9
India	3.5	33.5	37.8
China	2.4	30.4	40.3
Cambodia	2.9	33.8	40.4
United States	1.8	30.5	40.8
Russia	1.7	38.7	48.7
Nigeria	1.6	40.8	50.6
Mexico	1.4	42.8	53.7
South Africa	1.1	45.9	59.3

Source: World Bank

consideration the costs of economic growth such as pollution, or other indicators of social development such as life expectancy (though these, too, can be measured, which we will see below). Material transactions alone do not easily capture the overall well-being or happiness of a society.

Perhaps more problematic is the fact that GDP does not tell us how wealth is distributed among a population. A more sophisticated approach that does so is the **Gini index**, a mathematical formula that measures the amount of economic inequality in a society. Perfect equality is given a Gini ranking of zero, and perfect inequality gets a ranking of 100. Thus the greater the Gini index, the greater the inequality within a given economy.

[handwritten margin notes: Gini; equality = 0; inequality = 100]

As the table on page 110 reveals, there is a correlation between the amount of wealth held by the poorest 10 percent of the population and the concentration of wealth in the hands of the richest 10 percent. In countries where those at the bottom hold less wealth, those at the top (as opposed to those in the middle) tend to hold more. These greater inequalities in turn lead to a higher Gini rating. Interestingly, China and the United States, one a relatively poor, communist country and the other a rich, liberal one, have almost the same levels of income inequality. What explains this similarity? For one thing, over the past twenty years China has been rapidly undertaking market reforms that have increased inequality. In 1985, China's Gini index was 29, similar to that of social-democratic Germany. Meanwhile, Japan and Sweden, one mercantilist and the other social democratic, have some of the lowest levels of income inequality in the world: in each the top 10 percent of the population holds approximately 20 percent of the national wealth. This is particularly curious in the case of Japan, where one would expect the mercantilist system, with its lower emphasis on equality, to have generated a more unequal system.

What conclusions can we draw from the Gini index? One is that social-democratic countries tend to have the lowest Gini ratings, which is not surprising given their emphasis on equality. Although some mercantilist countries, such as Japan and South Korea, have similarly low rates of inequality, others, such as India, are highly unequal. One can see a high level of inequality in liberal countries such as the United States, but other liberal countries, such as Canada and Ireland, exhibit much more equal income distributions. Less-developed countries tend to have the worst levels of inequality.

What are the implications of these differences in income distribution? Does greater inequality imply greater poverty? Not necessarily. If, for example, both the rich and the poor find that their incomes are rising at the same rate, inequality will increase: a 10 percent increase in a $10,000

COMPARING CONCEPTS
MEASURING WEALTH

Measure	Definition
Gross domestic product (GDP)	Total production within a country, regardless of who owns the products.
Gross national product (GNP)	Both production and the flow of wealth into and out of a country, with attention to national versus foreign ownership.
Purchasing power parity (PPP)	Takes cost of living and buying power into account.
Gini index	Assesses inequality.
Human development index (HDI)	Assesses health, education, and wealth of population.

income is only $1,000, whereas a 10 percent increase in a $50,000 income is $5,000. Both segments of society may enjoy the same percentage increase but experience a huge difference in outcome. This will lead to greater inequality, but it is different from a situation in which the average income of the poorest segment is actually declining over time.

Moreover, just as inequality may increase even as both rich and poor become more wealthy, so too can the percentage of global poverty decline even while the total numbers grow. Between 1987 and 1998 the number of the world's poor (defined as those who live on less than one dollar a day) increased as the global population rose. Yet as a percentage of the total world population, the number of people living in poverty declined slightly, from 28 to 24 percent (see the table on page 113).[13]

This interesting lack of correspondence between poverty and inequality may prompt you to risk ask which is worse: Is poverty the main economic and political problem in the world, or is inequality? If for example, poverty could be eliminated worldwide while inequality remained or even grew, would this be a source of concern? Should there be some absolute limit to how much inequality should exist between people, or is inequality unimportant so long as everyone can enjoy a basic standard of living?

There is one measure of the relationship between wealth and poverty that tries to evaluate outcomes to answer that question. The **Human**

Development Index (HDI), developed by the United Nations Development Program, looks not simply at the total amount of wealth in a society, as GDP does, nor even at its distribution, as with the Gini index, but at the overall outcome of that wealth—the health and knowledge of a country's people. The HDI takes into consideration such factors as adult literacy, life expectancy, and educational enrollment, as well as GDP. By looking at such data, we can consider whether the wealth generated in a country is actually used in a way that provides a basic standard of living for all, whether through public or private means. All 162 countries in the world are ranked on the HDI; in 2001, Norway was ranked at number one and Sierra Leone, wracked by civil war, came in at the very bottom.[14]

The HDI does show a strong correlation between standard of living and a country's GDP, as shown in the table on page 114. Those countries with the highest national incomes also show the highest levels of education and life expectancy in the world. Interestingly, the HDI lists social-democratic systems such as Sweden right alongside more liberal countries such as Canada and the United States and mercantilist ones such as Japan and South Korea. Each of these political-economic systems, it would seem, can create its own path to high standards of living. Communist and post-communist states, however, rank further down on the HDI, and their rank-

GLOBAL COMPARISONS
POVERTY RATES BY REGION, 1987 AND 1998

	1987	1998
East Asia and the Pacific	26.6	15.3
Eastern Europe and Central Asia	0.2	5.1
Latin America and the Caribbean	15.3	15.6
Middle East and North Africa	4.3	1.9
South Asia	44.9	40.0
Sub-Saharan Africa	46.6	46.3
Total rate of world poverty	**28.3**	**24.0**

Source: World Bank

Note: Figures show percentage of total population that lives in officially defined poverty.

GLOBAL COMPARISONS
MEASURING WEALTH AND PROSPERITY

Country	GDP (PPP, in U.S. $)	HDI Rank
Canada	24,800	3
Sweden	22,200	4
United States	36,200	6
Japan	24,900	9
Germany	23,400	17
Ireland	21,600	18
Greece	17,200	23
South Korea	16,100	27
Poland	8,500	38
Mexico	9,100	51
Russia	7,700	55
Brazil	6,500	69
China	3,600	87
South Africa	8,500	94
India	2,200	115
Cambodia	1,300	121
Nigeria	950	136

Sources: Central Intelligence Agency, United Nations Development Program
Note: HDI rank is out of a total of 162 countries in 2001. GDP data is for 2000.

ings have changed little over the past twenty years. One might conclude from this that communism does not provide basic human standards that are at the core of its political rationale. Yet although it is true that communist systems rank lower on standards of living in comparison to the wealthiest countries, they also often provide a much higher level of human development relative to their GDPs. For example, once-communist Poland and Russia have per capita GDPs close to that of capitalist Brazil, yet the latter still lags far behind the former two in terms of HDI. This outcome could be viewed as consistent with the goals of a communist political economy that emphasized not wealth but rather a basic standard of living for all.

THE FUTURE OF POLITICAL ECONOMY

For a century these four major models of political economy have rivaled one another as they have sought to strike the ideal relationship between freedom and equality. In the early years of modern capitalism, mercantilism was a dominant force, but by the nineteenth century liberalism had spread alongside democracy across Europe and North America. In the early twentieth century, liberalism too began to falter, challenged by fascism and communism and their alternative forms of political and economic organization. For many observers in that period the extreme mercantilist systems practiced in Germany and Japan under fascism, or the Soviet Union's communism, were attractive alternatives to a liberalism that appeared economically and ideologically bankrupt.

Yet as we stand at the beginning of the twenty-first century the world is a quite different place. The most extreme forms of fascist mercantilism were destroyed by World War II, and even more limited mercantilist policies have in recent years stumbled, hurt by inefficient practices and a changing international economy. Communism has largely vanished; it survives in only a few countries such as North Korea and Cuba. Even those countries that still profess a communist political ideology, such as China, have moved ever closer to open markets and private property. Social democracy, too, is under challenge, struggling with the high costs of the public goods it provides.

For some, then, the twenty-first century represents the triumph of liberalism, a victory for private property and free markets over state regulation of the economy. Freedom, it would seem, has trumped the quest for equality. Some observers see this triumph as nothing less than the "end of history"—liberalism has won, and the great battles of ideology and political economy that once gripped domestic and international politics are over. The world we live in now is one dominated by a liberal political economy.

To what extent are these cries of victory borne out by evidence? One interesting study is summarized in the table on page 116, which compares the level of economic changes around the world consistent with liberalism, taking into account such factors as government expenditures, price

GLOBAL COMPARISONS
INCREASING LEVELS OF ECONOMIC LIBERALIZATION, 1980–99

Country	1980	1999	Change
United States	8.6	9.0	0.4
Ireland	6.6	8.5	1.9
Canada	7.9	8.2	0.3
Germany	7.7	8.0	0.3
Japan	7.5	7.9	0.4
Sweden	6.1	7.9	1.8
South Korea	6.0	7.3	1.3
Greece	5.7	7.3	1.6
South Africa	5.6	7.0	1.4
Mexico	5.1	6.5	1.4
China	4.3	5.8	1.5
Poland	3.6*	5.7	3.5
Nigeria	3.1	4.5	1.3
Russia	1.6	3.9	2.3

Note: 10 = most liberal
*1985 data
Source: Fraser Institute

controls, taxes, individual property rights, and trade. Changes in these areas that limit the power of the state over that of private property and market forces are commonly referred to as **economic liberalization**. The ratings in the table are given on a ten-point scale, with ten being the most liberal and zero being the least. The study (conducted, not surprisingly, by a liberal organization) concluded that from the 1980s to the 1990s almost all countries around the world moved in the direction of greater economic liberalization (although there has been some movement in the opposite direction in the past few years).[15] Even its critics acknowledge that economic liberalization has grown, in some cases dramatically, around the world.

So is liberalism now the only game in town? It may still be too early to write the epitaph for any of the other political-economic systems. Although other forms of political economy may be down, they are not necessarily out. Just as liberalism seemed on the edge of extinction in the 1930s, only to re-emerge, so too might any of these other political-economic arrangements re-emerge—rethought, revamped and re-energized. Moreover, in spite of its victories, liberalism remains burdened with concerns that it has not yet been able to resolve: inequities between rich and poor, boom-and-bust cycles of economic development, and, some believe, an overemphasis on material goods over intangible elements of society, such as community, environment, and leisure. Whether money can buy happiness is an important question for liberalism, since material wealth is liberalism's primary product.

In Sum: The End of Economic History?

As we have seen, states play a large role in the domestic and international economy. They must deal with and manage markets and property, with an eye toward generating societal wealth and revenue so that basic political tasks can be funded. This is no small task, as it goes to the heart of freedom and equality: How should they be reconciled through economic policy, and what mixture of the two will create the greatest degree of wealth? Different political-economic systems give very different answers to those questions. Economic liberalism has weathered various challenges to emerge as the dominant system in much of the world. As we shall see in the next two chapters, this "triumph" of liberalism has occurred alongside political liberalization as well, as many authoritarian regimes around the globe have given way to democracy.

But in spite of these dramatic changes it would be foolish to assume that political economy has reached its endgame. We cannot know what other economic challenges, opportunities, and ideas lie on the horizon. The modern industrial economy and the various political-economic systems that describe and manage it are all relatively new, having formed only in the past few centuries—the blink of an eye in terms of human history. Can we be so certain that in a world of rapid economic change our current assumptions about markets and property, freedom, and equality will remain valid for long? We may be living not at the end of history, but at the end of an era, with further dramatic transformations yet to come.

NOTES

1 For a discussion of the difficulties inherent in providing public goods see Mancur Olson, *The Logic of Collective Action: Public Goods and the Theory of Groups* (Cambridge: Harvard University Press, 1965).

2 For a discussion of this problem as it relates to the United States, see Charles Murray, *Losing Ground: American Social Policy, 1950–1980* (New York: Basic Books, 1984).

3 See Sven Steinmo, *Taxation and Democracy: Swedish, British, and American Approaches to Financing the Modern State* (New Haven: Yale University Press, 1993).

4 A good comparative discussion of central banking can be found in Majorie Deane and Robert Pringle, *The Central Banks* (New York: Viking, 1995).

5 Stefan Kanfer, *The Last Empire: DeBeers, Diamonds and the World* (New York: Farrar Straus & Giroux, 1993).

6 The arguments in favor of free trade and can be found in Jagdish Bhagwati, *Free Trade Today* (Princeton: Princeton University Press, 2002). For a protectionist view see Patrick Buchanan, *The Great Betrayal: How American Sovereignty and Social Justice Are Being Sacrificed to the Gods of the Global Economy* (New York: Little, Brown, 1998).

7 Adam Smith, *Essays on Philosophical Subjects* (Indianapolis: Liberty Classics, 1980), lxxx.

8 See, for example, Robert Kuttner, *Everything for Sale: The Virtues and Limits of Markets* (Chicago: University of Chicago Press, 1999).

9 Edward Bernstein, *Evolutionary Socialism: A Criticism and Affirmation* (New York: Schocken, 1961).

10 Party of European Socialists, *Manifesto for the 1999 European Elections*, 3.

11 For a discussion of communist political economies see Robert W. Campbell, *The Socialist Economies in Transition: A Primer on Semi-Reformed Systems* (Bloomington: Indiana University Press, 1991).

12 The classic work on mercantilism is Friedrich List, *The National System of Political Economy* (New York: A. M. Kelley, 1966).

13 For data and discussion on global poverty see the World Bank Poverty Net Website, www.worldbank.org/poverty/.

14 See the *United Nations Human Development Report 2001*, available at www.undp.org/hdr2001/.

15 Fraser Institute, *Economic Freedom in the World Annual Report 2001*, available at www.fraserinstitute.ca/.

AUTHORITARIANISM 5

"Man is born free but everywhere he is in chains," wrote Jean-Jacques Rousseau in 1762. Since his time, democracy has emerged and flourished in many places throughout the world. However, according to Freedom House, an American nongovernmental organization that monitors and promotes open markets and democratic institutions around the world, approximately 60 percent of the world's population still lives in societies defined as either "partly free," where some personal liberties and democratic rights are limited, or "not free," where the public has little individual freedom.[1] In neither case can these regimes be described as democratic; they are instead authoritarian.

In this chapter we will look at the internal dynamics and origins of authoritarianism and explore the myriad nondemocratic systems that fall under this term. After defining the term and its relationship to freedom and equality, we will look at its sources, addressing the puzzle of why authoritarianism is the dominant regime in some countries but not in others. Behind this puzzle lies the broader question of whether society's natural political state is one of democratic or authoritarian rule. We will specifically look at competing societal and economic explanations for authoritarianism. What circumstances, if any, are more likely to promote authoritarianism? This discussion of the possible sources of authoritarianism will lead us into an examination of how authoritarian rulers maintain their hold on power. The countries of the world display a much greater diversity of authoritarianism than they do of democracy, since the former lacks any universal rules or norms other than the preservation of power. Nevertheless, we can identify a number of common methods that authoritarian rulers use to maintain control; these methods have led political scientists to classify various types of authoritarianism. Finally, we will consider the future of authoritarianism. After 1989 and the end of the Cold War, many assumed that liberal democracy was the wave of the future and that authoritarianism's days were numbered. In recent years, however, some question whether, in the face of tremendous political, social, and economic obstacles, democracy is ever going to spread to all people. Such issues will set the stage for Chapter 6, in which we will look at democracy.

DEFINING AUTHORITARIANISM

Scholars define **authoritarianism** as a political system in which a small group of individuals exercises power over the state without being constitutionally responsible to the public. In authoritarian systems, the public does not play a significant role in selecting or removing leaders from office, and thus political leaders in authoritarian systems have much greater leeway to develop policies that they "dictate" to the people (hence the term "dictator"). As one can imagine, authoritarian systems by their nature are built around the restriction of individual freedom. At a minimum, they eliminate people's right to choose their own leaders, and they also restrict to varying degrees other liberties such as the freedom of speech or of assembly. Authoritarianism's relationship to equality is less clear. Some authoritarian systems, such as communism, limit individual freedom in order to produce greater social equality. Others seek to provide neither freedom nor equality, existing only to enhance the power of those in control.[2]

Various types of regimes and ideologies can be found in authoritarian systems. Authoritarian leaders do not always rule completely arbitrarily; indeed, authoritarianism can have a strong institutional underpinning of ideology. As ideologies, fascism and communism, for instance, explicitly reject democracy as an inferior form of social organization, favoring instead a powerful state and restricted individual freedoms. This ideology provides the set of norms that fascist or communist authoritarian leaders follow. But some other authoritarian systems, however, are not ideological,

IN FOCUS

AUTHORITARIANISM

A small group of individuals exercises power over the state.

Government is not constitutionally responsible to the public.

Public has little or no role in selecting leaders.

Individual freedom is restricted.

Authoritarian regimes may be institutionalized and legitimate.

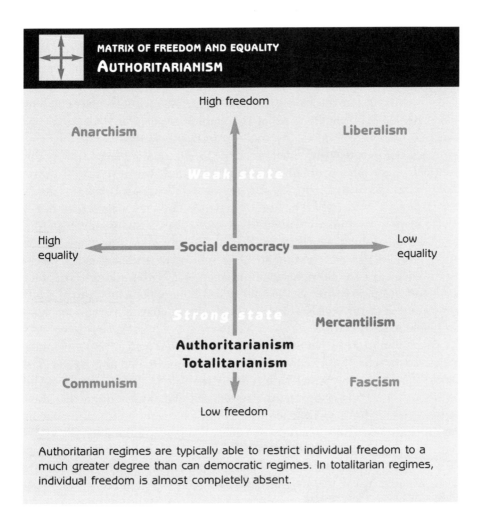

MATRIX OF FREEDOM AND EQUALITY
AUTHORITARIANISM

High freedom

Anarchism   Liberalism

Weak state

High   **Social democracy**   Low
equality   equality

Strong state   Mercantilism

Authoritarianism
Totalitarianism

Communism   Fascism

Low freedom

Authoritarian regimes are typically able to restrict individual freedom to a much greater degree than can democratic regimes. In totalitarian regimes, individual freedom is almost completely absent.

and their politics are often driven entirely by the whims of those in power. In this case it becomes difficult to even speak of a regime. Indeed, under such conditions the term is often used pejoratively by critics, coupled with a leader's name (such as "the Castro regime" in reference to Cuba). This terminology reflects the critics' view that all decisions flow from the ruler, unfettered by political institutions of any sort. The leader, in essence, *is* the regime.

Many people use the terms totalitarian and authoritarian interchangeably to describe political regimes that severely limit individual freedom. But totalitarianism is more accurately used as a subcategory of authoritarianism. **Totalitarianism** is practiced by authoritarian regimes that possess some form of strong ideology that seeks to transform fundamental aspects of state, society, and the economy, using a wide array of organizations and the application of force. In other words, totalitarian systems seek to control and transform the *total* fabric of a country according to some ideological goal. Because of the ambitious goals of totalitarianism, violence becomes a necessary tool to destroy any obstacle to change. Violence not only destroys enemies of the totalitarian ideology, but, as the political philosopher Hannah Arendt pointed out, the very use of terror shatters human will, destroying the ability of individuals to create, much less aspire to, freedom.[3] The use of violence does not necessarily mean that a state is totalitarian. Totalitarianism requires a totalist ideology, the organizations to achieve those goals, and the unbridled use of terror and violence to break down the human spirit in order to remake it in the image of the ideology. Totalitarianism often emerges in cases where those who have come to power profess a radical or reactionary political attitude, both of which reject the status quo and see dramatic change as indispensable and violence as necessary or even positive.

Many countries in history have been controlled by leaders with totalitarian aspirations, but few of these leaders have been able to put their theories to practice. The Soviet Union under the rule of Josef Stalin from the 1930s to the 1950s is commonly viewed as totalitarian; during that time most aspects of Soviet private life were controlled by the state and the Communist Party. Millions who opposed these changes (and millions who did not) were imprisoned and even executed. China during the Cultural Revolution of the 1960s and Cambodia under the Khmer Rouge in the 1970s are other examples of communist totalitarianism. In both cases those in power sought to dramatically remake society through revolutionary change and violence, and in both countries millions were killed in the course of only a few years. Nazi Germany is also commonly viewed as a totalitarian regime, although in some areas, such as the economy, changes were relatively few. Other fascist systems, such as Italy during World War II, cannot be described as totalitarian, even though they openly aspired to be so.

In the modern world, only communist North Korea can still be properly described

IN FOCUS
TOTALITARIAN REGIMES . . .

- Seek to control and transform all aspects of the state, society, and economy.
- Use violence as a tool for remaking institutions.
- Have a strong ideological goal.
- Have arisen relatively rarely.

EXAMPLES OF AUTHORITARIAN AND TOTALITARIAN REGIMES OF THE TWENTIETH CENTURY		
Country	**Ideology**	**Type of Regime**
Soviet Union, 1917–91	Communist	Totalitarian (Stalin), one-party rule
Mexico, 1915–2000	None	Authoritarian, one-party rule
Germany, 1933–45	Fascist	Totalitarian, one-party rule
Zaire, 1965–1997	None	Authoritarian, personalistic

as totalitarian, dominated by a totalist ideology that is backed by violence, widespread fear, and the absence of even small personal freedoms. By way of comparison, a country such as Iraq, although highly oppressive, cannot be described as totalitarian because it lacks a clear ideology. Saddam Hussein's primarily goal as Iraq's leader is simply to maintain and expand his political power as an end in itself. Violence, then, is a means to one end alone—keeping Hussein in control—and not to a transformation of society.

To sum up, authoritarian rule is a political regime in which power is exercised by a few, unbound by any public or constitutional control. The public lacks not only the right to choose its own leaders but also any other personal liberty that those in power may see as a threat, such as freedom of speech or assembly. In some cases, particularly where it is coupled with a radical or reactionary political attitude, authoritarianism may take the form of totalitarianism. Such efforts are always sweeping, violent, and devastating.

SOURCES OF AUTHORITARIAN RULE

Now that we have defined authoritarianism, we might consider its source. What brings authoritarianism about? Naturally, there is no single or simple explanation. The earliest political philosophers debated the nature of human organization and the distribution of power within it; some, such as Karl Marx, believed that society first emerged from coercion, with the few in power limiting the freedoms of others in order to increase their own wealth at the expense of society's. Others, such as Rousseau, stressed that social organization emerged from the desire of individuals to form a society and viewed authoritarianism as a subversion of this natural state. Modern scholars continue to debate the contribution of various forces to authoritarianism. Political scientists do not agree on what factors are most important in explaining authoritarian rule, and this debate is further complicated by their own ideological biases. These issues will become clearer as we look at the most prominent economic and societal explanations for authoritarian rule.

Economic Sources of Authoritarianism

Many observers argue that authoritarianism is essentially an expression of economic forces and institutions. Liberal and communist ideologies have been particularly powerful in this debate, and their views merit some consideration. Liberals, for example, believe that there is a strong connection between markets and authoritarianism. Free markets, liberals argue, generate and distribute wealth to a much greater and wider degree than any other economic form, creating a broad middle class. This leads to two further developments that undermine authoritarian rule. Not only is a middle-class society more educated and able to articulate its own political goals, but because wealth is dispersed the public will seek to limit any individual's or group's ability to gain enough power to threaten the wealth of the middle class. In turn, the middle class inevitably seeks to expand its own economic power into the realm of politics.[4] Where there is no middle class, however, and where poverty and inequality are great, an authoritarian system is much more likely to develop, either to defend the economic wealth of the few who possess it against the majority (producing an authoritarianism that is elite-focused), or to forcibly distribute that wealth among the majority population (producing an authoritarianism that is mass-focused). Liberals thus view laissez-faire capitalism as a powerful defense against authoritarianism.

Communists would agree that there is a strong connection between politics and economics, but in their view, capitalism is often the source of, rather than the solution to, authoritarianism. They are skeptical that capitalism can produce widely distributed economic benefits, since in their view such wealth is produced through the exploitation of others. A middle class may thrive under capitalism, they believe, but only on the back of the poor. Moreover, members of the middle class, whose democratic system really extends only to themselves, will gladly embrace authoritarianism if it means keeping the lower class under control. Even when wealthy countries reject authoritarianism at home, communists argue, they will support its perpetuation overseas so as to better exploit poorer countries. When liberals argue that capitalism inevitably proves lethal to authoritarianism, communists counter that so long as there is inequality, authoritarianism will thrive.[5]

Who is right? As we know, ideologies are built around ideals of how the world should be, but in reality, the circumstances are much more complicated. For example, although free markets may in many countries serve only as engines of wealth and enemies of democracy, we can find examples where the failures of capitalism have ushered in authoritarian rule. Periods of hyperinflation, discussed in Chapter 4, can quickly destroy the wealth of the public, generating widespread insecurity and poverty and leading to calls for drastic action, where the public is willing to see a curtailment of freedom in favor of greater economic security. The rise of Nazi rule in Germany in the 1930s, for example, was preceded by devastating hyperinflation that wiped out the savings of the middle class. When members of the middle class believes that economic insecurity, rather than those who hold political power, is the greatest threat to their wealth, they may become the greatest supporters of authoritarian rule.

Second, many who themselves accept a liberal view of politics and economics question whether a market economy automatically fosters democracy. Many authoritarian systems have been built alongside private property and market forces. Capitalism can be tolerated or even encouraged while political freedoms are restricted or eliminated entirely. In fact, some have argued that in order to build a strong market economy, political rights *must* first be restricted. According to this view, by restricting political rights the government can focus on constructing the necessary environment for a market economy and attract investment by limiting the kind of turmoil that might come about in a new or weak democracy. Many modern authoritarian regimes have used this argument to justify their system, arguing that democracy is a "luxury" that their country cannot yet afford—bread first, ballots later. For example, South Korea, Taiwan, and Singapore experienced long periods of authoritarian rule during which they rapidly industrialized; all three are now fast-growing and powerful economies. Only in the 1980s and 1990s did Taiwan and South Korea democratize (Singapore has yet to do so).

Although these cases are pointed to as proof of the wisdom of restricting freedom for the sake of development, many more cases can be found of authoritarian systems whose economies stagnated or declined. Authoritarianism alone is no recipe for wealth. Nonetheless, in the real world capitalism and economic development can coexist with authoritarianism.

Whether in the long run the former will inevitably erode the latter is still hotly contested.

Communist views of authoritarianism are similarly problematic. Because of their belief that the core problem is one of inequality, communists typically argue that it is vital to increase state power over the economy in order to ensure the equal distribution of wealth. Yet where economic and political power are concentrated in the hands of state, it is unlikely that the people will be able to check state power—paving the way for the restriction of personal freedoms in the name of equality. Under these conditions, not only personal freedom but societal wealth is threatened. Individuals lose the protection of property rights that is the cornerstone of entrepreneurship, and the state takes responsibility for all economic activity, often leading to disastrous outcomes. Communist regimes in the modern world have consistently led to the deaths of tens of millions people through terror and economic miscalculation. Thus communist views of the link between authoritarianism and capitalism must be considered in light of communism's own horrors. Whatever the differences, however, both liberals and communists share a belief that wealth and its distribution are key to understanding the emergence and persistence of authoritarian rule.

Authoritarianism and Society

Economics is not the only possible explanation for authoritarian rule, and many political scientists do not view wealth or inequality as key issues. They believe instead that authoritarianism is somehow connected to culture. (We saw in Chapter 3 that culture in the political context is a set of societal institutions that act as a social roadmap, providing guidelines for how we organize our lives.) According to this argument, culture has the capacity to either encourage or constrain democratic development, depending on whether the existing culture embodies norms and values that are consistent with democratic practices. More specifically, the cultural argument asserts that democracy is a unique product of interconnected historical experiences in Europe, such as Christianity (particularly Protestantism), the emphasis on individualism and secularism, the development of the nation-state, early industrialization, and the development of capitalism, among others. These factors, the argument goes, allowed for the creation of democracy as a system built on liberal values that emphasize freedom—what we typically call "Western" societies. According to some scholars, these liberal values are not universal, and other societies are constructed around norms and institutions that do not fit easily in with West-

---

COMPARING CONCEPTS
SOURCES OF AUTHORITARIANISM

Economic	*Liberal view:* Capitalism undermines authoritarianism by promoting the distribution of wealth and the creation of a middle class that favors democratic rule.
	Communist view: Capitalism inevitably generates inequality, often necessitating authoritarianism to prevent the redistribution of wealth among the people.
Societal	*Cultural view:* Certain cultural institutions are more amenable to authoritarianism because they promote such values as hierarchy, community over individual rights, and deference to authority.

---

ern democratic practices. As evidence, they would note that the further one travels from the "West" (meaning North America, western Europe, and Japan), the fewer democracies one finds, even in societies that over the past few decades have seen a dramatic rise in wealth, such as the oil states of the Middle East.[6]

Some have further asserted that under Islam the relationship among religion, the nation, and the state has profound implications for the likelihood of authoritarian rule. In such societies, political power and religious power are one and the same: laws are seen not as societal institutions to protect or advance individual rights, but as codes handed down by Allah that are to be observed and defended. Similarly, nationality and citizenship are defined not by allegiance to a collective group or state, but by faith. Thus, some would argue, Western ideas of competing political ideologies, of societies divided by ethnicity and citizenship, and of state power separated from religious authority are alien in Islamic society. In this view, Westerners' assumptions that all societies seek to be democratic are not only misguided but dangerous. Other societies may not only view their own authoritarianism as a superior form of politics, but may also view Western liberal democracy as something inherently egocentric, atomized, ungodly, and destructive.

This debate over the relationship between authoritarianism and culture can be seen beyond the case of Islam, as well. It is also illustrated by what is commonly called the "Asian values" debate, which essentially asks to what extent there are particular cultural values in eastern Asia that conflict with "Western" notions of individualism, democracy, and liberty. Pro-

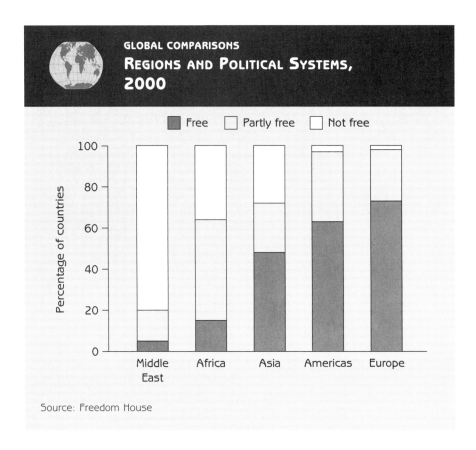

GLOBAL COMPARISONS

REGIONS AND POLITICAL SYSTEMS, 2000

■ Free   □ Partly free   □ Not free

Source: Freedom House

ponents of the idea of Asian values argue that Asia's cultural and religious traditions stress conformity, hierarchy, and obedience, which are more conducive to a political system that limits freedom in order to defend social harmony and consensus. The philosophy of Confucianism is most commonly cited in this regard. Confucianism, they assert, with its emphasis on obedience to hierarchy and its notion of a ruler's "mandate from heaven," promotes authoritarian rule; the ruling elite acts as a parental figure over the people, acting in the public's best interest but not under its control. As Malaysian prime minister Mahathir Mohamad, one of the major proponents of "Asian values," has put it,

> When citizens understand that their right to choose also involves limits and responsibilities, democracy doesn't deteriorate into an excess of freedom. . . . These are the dangers of democracy gone wrong, and in our view it is precisely the sad direction in which the West is heading.[7]

As you might imagine, there are many both inside and outside of Asia that reject the notion of "Asian values" and the supposed natural tendency of Asians toward authoritarianism. Critics point out that Asia, like any other part of the world, is far too diverse to speak of one set of values; differences in history, religion, social structure, and other institutions have led to very different political values from country to country. Asia has no clear set of cultures or civilizations, they assert, but rather an array of different and overlapping ideas that are in a continuous process of interaction and reinterpretation. Confucian thought, just like the Bible in the West or the Koran in Islamic countries, can be interpreted in very different ways by different readers. Thus, the very notion of "Asian values," critics argue, is a misinterpretation by observers who fail to grasp the complexity of Asia or who use the idea simply to justify authoritarian rule. As Kim Dae Jung, president of South Korea, argued, "The biggest obstacle is not [Asia's] cultural heritage but the resistance of authoritarian rulers and their apologists. . . . Culture is not necessarily our destiny. Democracy is."[8] These same criticisms can also be applied to those arguments that view democracy and Islam as incompatible.

A look at history may shed some light on these debates. In the past it was often argued that "Latin" cultures, those strongly influenced by Roman Catholicism, were also inherently authoritarian in nature (as opposed to cultures steeped in Protestant forms of Christianity). The reasons given for this were very similar to those discussed above: an emphasis on hierarchy, a lack of tolerance for other views, and a focus on community versus individual rights. In fact, several decades ago this argument would have had strong empirical support. In Europe, predominantly Catholic, Italy gave birth to fascism, and after World War II in western Europe authoritarian systems persisted only in Catholic Spain and Portugal and in Eastern Orthodox Greece. Latin America, long influenced by Catholicism, also had a strong history of authoritarian rule. However, by the 1970s the last authoritarian systems in western Europe moved to democracy, and similar processes have been under way in Latin America since the 1980s, to such a point that the majority of states there are now democratic. Perhaps culture may be more amenable to change than some think.

AUTHORITARIANISM AND POLITICAL CONTROL

There is clearly no consensus about what brings about authoritarian rule. Economic arguments emphasize wealth and its distribution, whereas cultural arguments emphasize the societal institutions that may foster or hinder the concentration of power. But even if we cannot be certain how authoritarianism comes to power, we can carefully examine how it stays in control. As with all political systems, a number of different state, regime, and government activities and institutions perpetuate authoritarianism. Some of these use fear and violence, others do not. In fact, in this section we will need to answer a difficult question alluded to earlier in the chapter: Do all authoritarian regimes by nature rely on force to intimidate a hostile public, or can authoritarianism be accepted or even embraced by the people? But first we should outline some of the most common features of authoritarian regimes.

Violence and Surveillance

One feature that we may initially associate with authoritarianism (and especially with totalitarianism) is the use of violence and surveillance. Compliance and obedience with authoritarian goals are often enforced through close observation of and the use of force against the population, sending a clear signal that those who oppose the authoritarian regime or government will be identified and dealt with harshly. Authoritarian systems commonly use violence as a mechanism of public control, threatening those who challenge the political order with severe retribution: arbitrary arrest, detention without trial, torture, and even death. In several authoritarian systems in Latin America in the past, "death squads" made up of police or military troops targeted individuals suspected of harboring political views opposed to the authoritarian regime. These individuals were abducted by the death squads and murdered, frequently after torture. In some cases, their bodies were dumped in the open, as a warning to others who dared to question the system; in other cases, the victims became one among thousands of "disappeared," never to be seen again.

In other authoritarian systems, terror has been used even more indiscriminately. When Stalin consolidated his totalitarian rule in the Soviet Union in the 1930s, he carried out what are known as "purges," widespread arrests that decimated the ranks of the Communist Party and the state bureaucracy. Former leaders of the 1917 Revolution, city mayors and local party bosses, high-ranking officers in the army and the navy, university professors, scientists, diplomats, and many others were detained, tortured, coerced into confessing during "show trials," forced to implicate others in their supposed crimes, and either sent to forced labor camps or executed. The targets of the purges were not limited to the party or the state; writers, artists, students, farmers, and workers were also among those accused of political sabotage and anti-Soviet views. It is not known how many died in these purges; estimates range from 5 million to 20 million. Undoubtedly, in the vast majority of these cases the victims were innocent, yet this was unimportant to Stalin's regime. By making everyone fear that they too can be arrested, the public can be controlled and even turned against itself, with everyone fearing that they will be denounced by someone else. Stalin's tactics have not been forgotten; Iraq's Saddam Hussein is apparently a great student of Stalinism and has applied the use of terror to great effect.

Another important means of authoritarian control is the ability to maintain a close watch over the population. Surveillance allows the government to prevent opposition from organizing and also instills uncertainty among the population—are they being watched? Surveillance may be conducted through the use of an internal security force or "secret police," charged with monitoring public activity, spying on individuals, and interrogating members of the public suspected of political activity hostile to the system. In some countries surveillance has included widespread telephone tapping and the creation of a huge network of public informers, where nearly anyone may be the eyes and ears of those in power.

Cooptation

The prevalence of violence and surveillance in some authoritarian systems may give the impression that an authoritarian regime must be ever vigilant against the public, to prevent opposition or revolution that would bring an end to the regime. But not all regimes need or choose to rely on fear or surveillance as a central means of control. Another method they may use involves **cooptation**, or the process by which individuals outside of an organization are brought into a beneficial relationship with it, making them dependent on the system for certain rewards. Although cooptation is not unique to authoritarianism, it tends to be much more widespread under authoritarian than under democratic systems, which are usually more suspicious of such favoritism.

IN FOCUS

AUTHORITARIAN MEANS OF CONTROL

- *Coercion:* public obedience is enforced through violence and surveillance.

- *Cooptation:* members of the public are brought into a beneficial relationship with the state and government, often through corporatism or clientelism.

- *Personality cult:* the public is encouraged to obey the leader based on his or her extraordinary qualities and compelling ideas.

Cooptation can take many forms. The most structured form of cooptation is corporatism. Recall from Chapter 4 the term *neocorporatism*, a system in which business, labor, and the state engage in bargaining over economic policy. In its earliest form, however, modern **corporatism** emerged as a method by which authoritarian systems attempted to solidify their control over the public by creating or sanctioning a limited number of organizations to represent the interests of the public, and restricting those not set up or approved by the state. These organizations are meant to replace independent organizations with a handful that alone have the right to speak for various sectors of society. For example, under a corporatist system one would be likely to find labor unions, agricultural associations, student groups, neighborhood committees, and the like, all approved and funded by the state. Nonsanctioned, alternative organizations would not be allowed.

As opposed to the overlapping memberships, competition, and ever-changing nature of organizations and political parties in a pluralistic society, corporatism arranges society in a hierarchical manner, with each organization empowered by the state to have a monopoly of representation over a given issue or segment of society (meaning that no other organization may act in that area or speak on that issue). State, society, and the market under corporatism are viewed as a single organic body, with each element cooperating and performing its own specific and limited role. This is quite different from a view of politics that is centered on the individual and that values competition and conflict.

Corporatism can be an effective form of control, as it gives the public a limited influence (or at least the pretense of influence) in the policy-making process. Farmers or students have an official organization with elected officers and resources that are meant to serve their interests. In return, the regime is able to better control the public through these institutions, which are funded and managed by the state. For the average individual, a state-sanctioned interest organization is better than none at all, and many willingly participate in the hope that their needs will be met.

Many modern countries around the world have displayed elements of corporatism while under authoritarian rule. These include fascist Italy and Germany, as well as Spain and Portugal up to the 1970s. In Spain, for example, a single political party organized most business and labor interests together into a limited number of "syndicates" that represented both owners and workers in different sectors of the economy. Communist systems are similarly corporatist. In Cuba, for example, all labor is organized under a single union directly controlled by the state, and independent unions are illegal. Although different in form and degree, in all corporatist systems we see the presence of a limited number of organizations used to represent and direct societal interests, bringing the public under organized state control. In a more pluralist system, by contrast, business, labor, and political parties stand apart from, and often in opposition to, one another.

A less structured means by which states may coopt the public is through **clientelism**, whereby the state coopts members of the public by providing specific benefits or favors to a single person or small group in return for public support. Unlike corporatism, clientelism relies on individual patronage rather than organizations that serve a large group of people. In other words, clientelism creates a patron-client relationship between the state and individual members of the public.

The state has a number of perquisites it can use in coopting individuals. Jobs within the state or in state-run sectors of the economy, business contracts or licenses, public goods such as roads or schools, and kickbacks and bribes are a few of the tools in its arsenal. Such largesse often leads to **rent-seeking**, a process in which political leaders essentially rent out parts of the state to their patrons, who as a result control public goods that would otherwise be distributed in a nonpolitical matter. For example,

RENT-SEEKING IN THE MARKETPLACE IN MEXICO

Mexico's economy is based in part on a large number of street vendors who operate in open-air markets around the country. The authoritarian, one-party regime of the Institutional Revolutionary Party (PRI), which controlled the government from 1915 to 2000, recognized the potential value of such a large group of individuals whose ability to function depended entirely on the permission of the government (since the venders did not own land or shops of their own). Starting in the 1950s, the PRI began to pressure street vendors in Mexico City to provide donations to political campaigns or public support at rallies; in return, the state would not crack down on their activities. Local "bosses" acted as intermediaries between the state and the vendors, collecting funds and mobilizing vendors in return for a share of the wealth. Given the failure of the PRI in the 2000 presidential elections and the ongoing democratization of Mexico, this system may be now breaking down. Similar forms of clientelism may also be present in democracies, though clientelism is more likely and more prevalent in systems that are not accountable to the public nor subject to rules that limit corruption.

leaders might turn over control of the national postal system to political supporters, providing them with jobs and the ability to siphon off public funds from that branch of the state.

In general, cooptation may be much more successful at maintaining authoritarianism than coercive methods such as terror and surveillance, since many in the public may actively support the system in return for the benefits they derive. Political opposition can be dealt with not through repression and violence, but by simply buying opponents off. Such a system, however, runs the risk of running out of perks with which to pacify the public. In addition, in a system where economic resources are doled out for political reasons, economic and other problems may emerge as productive resources are siphoned off to secure the temporary support of the public. At its worst, such a system declines into a *kleptocracy* (literally, "rule by theft") where those in power seek only to further fill their own pockets and drain the state of assets and resources. As these resources dry up, clientelism loses its ability to provide the perks it once did and may quickly unravel.

Personality Cults

Authoritarian and totalitarian leaders may also reinforce their rule through what are known as personality cults. First used to describe Stalin's rule in the Soviet Union, a **personality cult** refers to the promotion of the image of an authoritarian leader not merely as a political figure, but as someone who embodies the spirit of the nation, possesses endowments of wisdom and strength far beyond those of the average individual, and is thus portrayed in a quasi-religious manner—all wise, all seeing, all knowing. In other words, personality cults attempt to generate a charismatic form of authority for the political leader from the top down, by convincing the public of the leader's admirable qualities.

The media and culture play a vital role in this regard, promoting the cult of personality through all aspects of daily life—news reports, public rallies, art, music, films, and other imagery of the leader. All successes in the country are attributed to the power of the leader, and mistakes are blamed on the mortal flaws of the public or on external enemies. Whether the public actually believes in the personality cult is, of course, another issue.

Cults of personality may also function largely through terror; the public may not believe the praise, but no one is willing to say so. This is especially the case where charismatic power has faded over time to become

KIM JONG IL AND THE PERSONALITY CULT IN NORTH KOREA

Communist North Korea is probably the only country in the world that remains totalitarian. Kim Il Sung, the Communist Party leader from 1945 until his death in 1994, created an elaborate personality cult while effectively sealing his country off from the rest of the world. Upon his death, his son, Kim Jong Il, succeeded him, and he also constructed an elaborate personality cult around himself. Consider this passage from a North Korean news report:

> The outstanding greatness of Kim Jong Il as a peerless politician lies in the fact that he has scientifically led the revolution and construction to a brilliant victory without a mistake or failure for nearly 40 years. His greatness is expressed in his pursuing the most independent politics, politics of love and trust and leading the revolution and construction with his invincible army-first politics. The might of his independent politics has been fully demonstrated in the most arduous and complicated struggle. The moves of the imperialists and reactionaries to stifle the Democratic People's Republic of Korea have been totally smashed by his bold grit and just politics. Our people are now holding him in high esteem with loyalty, singing the song of infinite worship for the leader: "We live, believing in him as in heaven."*

*KCNA, Pyongyang, 19 June 2000, reported by BBC Worldwide Monitoring, 19 June 2000.

little more than a facade, held up only by force. Under these conditions there is always the chance that the cult will crack and the public will turn against the leadership. This occurred in Romania in 1989, when Nicolae Ceausescu, the self-styled "conductor" of his country, was shown on national television reacting in a stunned and confused manner when attendees at a public rally he was addressing suddenly turned against him. Within hours revolution had swept the country, and within three days Ceausescu and his wife had been executed by firing squad.

Authoritarianism and Legitimacy

Authoritarianism thus relies on a range of tools to maintain power—some are "carrots" and other "sticks." But even without the use of these tools, some people may view authoritarianism as a beneficial system, because they may agree with the regime's ideology, be direct beneficiaries of its rule, venerate its leaders, or simply fear political change. Support in the absence of coercive or cooptive methods implies that authoritarianism may be a legitimate form of rule. The idea may be hard for some to accept. Particularly in Western democracies, there is the assumption that in every authoritarian system the people are simply waiting for the chance to depose their rulers and install democracy. This belief is an exaggeration. Authoritarian regimes may be just as institutionalized—and therefore as stable and legitimate—as any democratic system, enjoying some, or even a great deal of, public support.

Max Weber's discussion of the forms of legitimacy (discussed in Chapter 2) can help explain this idea further. Authoritarian systems may rely on charismatic authority, as the preceding discussion of the cult of personality indicated. The public may strongly support and venerate its leaders, as was seen in the cases of Mao Zedong, Josef Stalin, and Adolf Hitler, and may see their leadership as indispensable. In spite of the violence used by each of these leaders, their publics venerated them as nearly divine figures. Such forms of legitimacy can produce a tremendous personal following and power.

Other systems may be based on traditional authority. In the case of North Korea, Kim Jong Il's legitimacy rests not just on a personality cult meant to protect charismatic power, but on the fact that he is the son of the founder of the country, Kim Il Sung. In fact, this claim to traditional, hereditary authority may be a greater source of power than any charisma that Kim Jong Il hopes to project. That North Korean totalitarianism weathered the death of Kim Il Sung may have much to do with the fact that his son was waiting in the wings, able to establish continuity in the regime. Similar institutions that support the idea of traditional authority are also present in much of the Middle East, where hereditary monarchies are still powerful and command popular support.

Rational authority may also play a role. Authoritarian systems often claim to be "scientific" or "technocratic" (the latter meaning, literally, rule by expertise), claiming that they alone possess the knowledge and skills necessary to guide the country. The institutions that support authoritarianism may stress a "rational" and "objective" approach to rule, implying that democracy is an emotional, inefficient, and thus inferior means of rule. In the past, both communism and fascism laid claim to rational legitimacy, arguing that their rule was based not just on ideology but on the laws of science. In the case of communism, revolution and the downfall of capitalism and liberalism were seen as inevitable laws of development; theories regarding the superiority or inferiority of peoples and races legitimized fascist rule. More recently, political systems in Asia and Latin America used claims of technocratic expertise to legitimize authoritarian rule.

Finally, authoritarianism may be legitimate among much of the population if the public cannot envision another alternative. If the people have a limited understanding of what democracy means, what it would entail, and how or why it would be better than the status quo, authoritarianism may be a more attractive choice.

TYPES OF AUTHORITARIAN RULE

By now it should be clear that authoritarianism may emerge for different reasons and may persist in different ways by using, to different degrees, tools of fear and support. Based on these characteristics, political scientists often classify authoritarianism into a number of specific forms of rule. The most commonly seen forms of authoritarian rule are personal, military, one-party, and quasi-democratic. Personal rule is based on the power of a single strong leader who typically relies on charismatic or traditional authority to maintain power. Under military rule, in contrast, the monopoly of violence that characterizes militaries tends to be the strongest means of control. One-party rule is often more corporatist in nature, creating a broad membership as a source of support and oversight. Finally, in a quasi-democracy the basic structures of democracy exist but they are not fully institutionalized and often not respected. Since these classifications are by necessity somewhat abstract, in many cases authoritarian systems will combine elements of different categories rather than fitting easily into any one. In spite of this limitation, these categories make for useful comparisons.

Personal Rule

Personal rule most commonly comes to mind when people think of authoritarianism, perhaps because long before modern politics, states, or economies came into being, people were ruled by powerful figures—kings and Caesars, emperors and sultans, chiefs and caudillos. Drawing from charismatic or traditional legitimacy, **personal rule** rests on the claim that one person is alone fit to run the country, with no clear regime or roles to constrain that person's rule. Under personal rule, the state and society are commonly taken to be possessions of the leader, to be dispensed with as he (or, occasionally, she) sees fit. The ruler is not a subject of the state; rather, the state and society are subjects of the ruler. Ideology may be weak or absent, as the ruler justifies his control through the logic that he alone is the embodiment of the people and therefore uniquely qualified to act on the people's behalf. This claim often necessitates a strong personality cult, or a reliance on the traditional authority of bloodlines.

In some cases personal rule relies less on charismatic or traditional authority than on what is referred to as **patrimonialism**, under which the ruler depends on a collection of supporters within the state who gain direct benefits in return for enforcing the ruler's will. The state exists not as a body of trained officials but as a close group of supporters of the ruler, who in return for their allegiance seek personal profit (i.e., a kleptocracy). This is a form of cooptation, although under patrimonialism it is only the ruler's own personal followers who benefit. All others in society tend to be held in check by force, and legitimacy does not extend past the leader's own circle.

An example of personal rule based on patrimonialism was found in Zaire (now the Democratic Republic of Congo) under the rule of Mobutu Sese Seko from 1965 until 1997. Although he once commanded a great deal of charismatic legitimacy, over time Mobutu increasingly used patrimonialism as a way to maintain his power. In particular, Mobutu built his patrimonial system around Zaire's abundant natural resources, such as diamonds, gold, copper, and cobalt. These resources were used by the regime not to benefit the country as a whole, but as Mobutu's personal treasury; he siphoned off the profits from these resources to enrich himself and his followers. The result was a coterie of supporters who were willing to defend Mobutu in order to maintain their economic privileges.[9] This system of dependence and economic reward helps explain how Mobutu maintained power for more than three decades while Zaire's per capita GDP dropped from $392 in 1975 to $127 in 1998.

Military Rule

A second form of authoritarianism is **military rule**. Once considered relatively unusual, over the past half-century military rule became much more common, particularly in Latin America and Africa. In conditions where governments and states struggle with legitimacy and stability, and where there are high levels of public unrest or violence, the military may choose to intervene directly in politics, seeing itself as the only organized force able to ensure stability. This view may be combined with a sense among military leaders that the current government or regime threatens the military's or the country's interests and should be removed. Military rule may even have widespread public support, especially if people believe that the

strong arm of the military can bring an end to corruption or political violence, prevent revolution, and restore stability.

Military rule typically emerges through a **coup d'etat**, in which military forces take control of the government by force. In some cases military actors may claim that they have seized control only reluctantly,
promising to return the state and government to civilian rule once stability has been restored. Often, under military rule, political parties and most
civil liberties are restricted, and civilian political leaders or opponents of
military rule are arrested and may be killed or disappear. The use of terror and surveillance is a common aspect of military rule, since by their
nature militaries hold an overwhelming capacity for violence.

Military rule typically lacks a specific ideology, although sometimes
military leaders espouse radical or reactionary political attitudes. Military
rule also tends to lack any charismatic or traditional source of authority,
meaning that if they seek legitimacy in the eyes of the people they often
must fall back on rational authority. One particular variant of military rule
that reflects this logic is known as **bureaucratic authoritarianism**, a system in which the state bureaucracy and the military share a belief that a
technocratic leadership, focused on rational, objective, technical expertise, can solve the problems of the country—as opposed to "emotional" or
"irrational" ideologically based party politics. Public participation, in other
words, is seen as an obstacle to effective and objective policy-making, and
so is done away with. In the 1960s and 1970s bureaucratic authoritarianism emerged in a number of less-developed countries as rapid modernization and industrialization generated a high degree of political conflict.
State and industry, with their plans for rapid economic growth, clashed
with the interests of the working class and peasantry, who sought greater
political power and a larger share of the wealth. This increasing polariza-
tion in politics often led business leaders and the state bureaucracy to
advocate military rule as a way to prevent the working class and the peasantry from gaining power over the government.[10]

Military rule, like any form of authoritarianism, may lead to a variety
of outcomes. Military rule in South Korea, Taiwan, and Chile occurred
alongside high levels of economic growth that in turn helped pave the way
for democracy in the 1990s. However, in many more cases military rule
has simply meant more instability and violence, and little or no improvement over the governments that were replaced. Even in the most successful cases, as in the three listed above, progress occurred alongside great
losses of life. In the first years of military rule in Taiwan, for instance,
tens of thousands of students, intellectuals, political figures, and commu-

nity leaders were executed. In South Korea, protests by labor unions and students in 1980 lead to a military crackdown during which several hundred were killed. And in Chile, debate still rages over the legacy of Augusto Pinochet, the military leader from 1973 to 1990. During his rule thousands were arrested, tortured, killed, or "disappeared." Nor can we know whether military rule can be credited for the economic successes of these countries, since we cannot determine how they might have developed had the military not intervened in the first place.

One-Party Rule

A third authoritarian regime, and one often associated with totalitarianism in particular, is that of **one-party rule**, under which a single political party monopolizes politics and other parties are banned or excluded from power. The ruling party serves several functions. The party helps to incorporate the people into the political system through membership and participation. Typically the party only incorporates a small minority of the population—in most communist countries, for instance, party membership was less than 10 percent—but this still means that hundreds of thousands or millions of people are party members. One-party rule is often also combined with a larger corporatist system of public control.

Through membership, the party can rely on a large segment of the public that is willing to help develop and support the policies of authoritarian or totalitarian rule, as well as to transmit information back to the leadership on developments in all aspects of society. Single-party systems are often broken down into smaller units or "cells" that operate at the university, workplace, or neighborhood level. These units report back to higher levels of the party, help deal with local problems and concerns, and keep tabs on society as a whole. No area is untouched by the presence of the party, and this helps to maintain control over the public.

In return, members of the party often are granted privileges that are otherwise denied to the public at large. They may have access to certain resources (better health care or housing, for instance) that nonmembers do not; positions in government and other important areas of the economy or society may also be restricted to party members. One important result of such membership is that a large group of individuals in society directly benefit from authoritarianism and are therefore willing to defend it. This pragmatic membership, however, can backfire: if a large portion of the party membership belongs only for the personal benefits and not out of any ideological conviction, they may quickly desert the leadership in a time of crisis.

Finally, the party serves as a mechanism of mobilization. The leadership uses the party as an instrument to deliver propaganda that extols the virtues of the current regime and government; it relies on its rank-and-file members, through demonstrations and mass rallies, to give the appearance of widespread public support and enthusiasm for the leadership. If necessary, it also uses party members to control and harass those who do not support the regime. Although such terror or surveillance may be important to one-party rule, cooptation is the primary mechanism that ensures compliance and support.

One-party regimes are commonly associated with communism and fascism and were present in all cases of totalitarianism. However, they also can be found around the world as part of a variety of authoritarian regimes. In some cases other parties may exist, but they typically are highly restricted by the government so that they cannot challenge the current regime. For many years this was the case in Mexico, which was dominated by the Institutional Revolutionary Party, or PRI. In Zimbabwe, the ruling Zimbabwe African People's Union–Patriotic Front (ZANU-PF) has held power since 1980, and its political power has come under challenge by opposition groups only recently. Cuba, North Korea, China, Vietnam, and Laos are other examples of one-party systems, each controlled by an authoritarian communist party.

Quasi Democracies

Finally, some political systems feature a few or many of the familiar aspects of democracy but remain in essence authoritarian systems. In fact, the table on regions and political systems on page 128 included a large group of countries that are categorized as neither "free" nor "not free," but as "partially free," falling somewhere between democracy and authoritarianism. These systems we term **quasi democracies,** which may appear like other established democracies—people are given the right to vote, elections take place, and political parties compete—but whose regimes use procedures of questionable democratic legitimacy.

Most importantly, quasi democracies usually restrict the democratic process to a great degree, and those rights that do exist are often insecure, subject to arbitrary change or sudden withdrawal. For example, the government may control which political organizations may participate in politics, banning any it thinks might threaten the government's hold on power. Access to the media is also often restricted, with the ruling political elites able to dominate the airwaves while opposition forces have little chance

COMPARING CONCEPTS
TYPES OF AUTHORITARIAN RULE

Type	Definition	Primary Tools of Control
Personal rule	Rule by a single leader, with no clear regime or rules constraining that leadership	*Patrimonialism*: supporters within the state benefit directly from their alliance with the ruler (corruption)
Military rule	Rule by one or more military officials, often brought to power through a coup d'état	Control of the armed forces, sometimes also allied with business and state elites (bureaucratic authoritarianism)
One-party rule	Rule by one political party, with other groups banned or excluded from power	Large party membership helps mobilize support and maintain public control, often in return for political or economic benefits
Quasi democracy	Rule by an elected leadership, though through procedures of questionable democratic legitimacy	Manipulation of democratic procedures, such as vote-rigging or harassment of opposition

to make their views known. Important state institutions such as the judiciary, the military, or state-run industries are likely to be under the direct control of the government and used to control political opposition. Under such conditions, open elections can often be tolerated, since the opposition functions at a great disadvantage. However, as a last resort many quasi democracies will commit electoral fraud, such as buying or forging votes, in order to ensure the perpetuation of the existing regime.

Quasi-democratic systems often involve all of our forms of authoritarian rule—force, surveillance, cooptation, personality cults—to a limited degree, degrading the democratic process. Political leaders similarly call on traditional and charismatic legitimacy even as they participate in a system that should be fundamentally rational and bound by rules. This, too, degrades democracy, since elected leaders are tempted to assert that their "special" claims to authority eliminate the need to abide by rules and standards.

In short, quasi democracy in many ways represents a halfway house between authoritarianism and full democracy. Although the mechanisms of democracy may be in place, they remain weakly institutionalized, operating in an uncertain and hostile environment. Such structures, however, do hold out the possibility of becoming institutionalized over time and of forcing political actors to play by the rules of the game and abide by its outcomes.

Explaining Diverse Authoritarianism

Why is there such diversity in authoritarian rule? Explanations might be traced back to our original debate about the sources of authoritarianism. Economic explanations would suggest that certain forms of authoritarianism are a function of wealth and inequality; for example, rapid industrialization may lead to bureaucratic authoritarianism, as the military intervenes in response to a polarized political environment. Cultural explanations would suggest that certain forms of authoritarianism are more likely in some societies than in others. For example, the corporatist tendencies of one-party rule may be more prevalent in societies where a tradition of individualism is weaker. Whatever the explanation, authoritarianism is clearly adaptable to a number of different conditions and environments.

IN SUM: AUTHORITARIANISM IN RETREAT?

Although authoritarianism exhibits an amazing diversity and flexibility in maintaining political control, the global trend over the past half-century has been away from this form of rule. This trend is especially surprising given that historically authoritarianism has been the dominant trend around the world. In the early part of the last century, democratic countries were few and beleaguered, wracked by economic recession, whereas communism and fascism seemed to promise radically new ways to restructure states, markets, and societies. The quest for equality or inequality seemed to be the dominant concern, and freedom appeared to be an endangered species. The German philosopher Oswald Spengler summarized these views in his 1922 work *The Decline of the West*: "The era of individualism, liberalism and democracy, of humanitarianism and freedom, is nearing its end. The masses will accept with resignation the victory of the *Caesars,* the strong men, and will obey them. Life will descend to a level of general uniformity, a new kind of primitivism, and the world will be better for it."[11]

Yet the exact opposite has taken place. Over the past half-century the world has seen authoritarianism decline in numerous countries and regions around the world, from western to eastern Europe, to Latin America, to

Asia. Freedom has not only regained currency, it has become a powerful force for political change. In some cases the rise of freedom has been incomplete or has failed after a few years. In other cases, though, democracy has fully taken root.

Indeed the figure below shows that the number of countries classified as "not free" has declined dramatically over just the past thirty years, from nearly half of the countries in the world to less than a quarter. The number of fully free countries has increased by 15 percent, while those in the partly free category that we associate with quasi democracies has stayed relatively stable. These data can be viewed another way, by looking at total world population rather than the number of countries: 39 percent of the world's population currently lives in free countries, 25 percent lives in partly free countries, and 36 percent lives in not free countries.

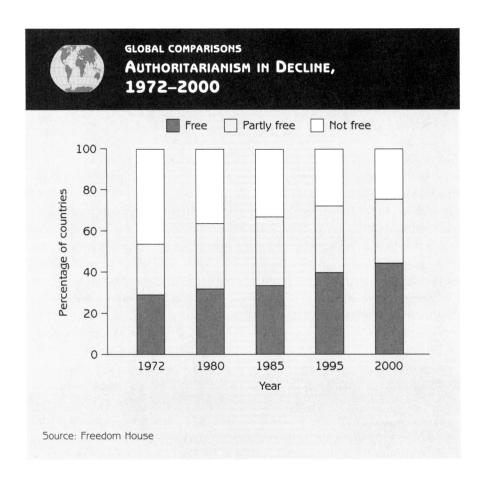

GLOBAL COMPARISONS

AUTHORITARIANISM IN DECLINE, 1972–2000

Source: Freedom House

Why this decline in authoritarianism? An economic argument might point to the fact that the world has become wealthier over the past fifty years. Although this is true in some parts of the world, in regions such as Latin America poverty has increased even as democracy has spread. This is also true of eastern Europe. At the same time, democratization has been occurring even as inequality has increased, both within and between countries. A societal argument is similarly problematic, as democracy has spread to areas previously viewed as hostile to such a system, such as Asia.

Yet there is another, perhaps simpler explanation: authoritarianism has lost much of its appeal. Fifty years ago, ideologies such as fascism and communism could mobilize people with visions of a world to be transformed. Communism promised equality among all people, while fascism promised inequality between a chosen few and their lesser subjects. However, in the aftermath of World War II and the Cold War, there is no longer any strong authoritarian ideology that combines the absence of individual freedom with some broader goal. Authoritarian leaders may claim that limitations on political rights are necessary for stability or economic development, but they no longer offer any real alternative vision for politics. It is increasingly difficult to justify authoritarianism through any universal set of ideas.

Does this mean that authoritarianism's days are numbered? Perhaps. There may in fact come a time when all societies are democratic, and authoritarianism, like slavery, is an aspect of human behavior largely consigned to history and the margins of global society. However, we cannot know what new visions may emerge that again give power and purpose to authoritarian rule. Will rising inequality eventually clash with increased freedom? Will people someday come to see the absence of freedom as a benefit rather than a form of bondage? Might a new religious or secular vision of organizing human life reject democracy as antiquated or profane? Perhaps what we now enjoy is simply a brief aberration in the long human history of authoritarian rule.

NOTES

1 See the Freedom House Website at www.freedomhouse.org.

2 For an excellent discussion of the bewildering variety of authoritarian rule see Juan Linz, *Totalitarian and Authoritarian Regimes* (Boulder: Lynne Rienner, 2000). This work was originally published in Fred I. Greenstein and Nelson W. Polsby, eds., *Handbook of Political Science* (Reading: Addison-Wesley, 1975).

3 Hannah Arendt, *Totalitarianism* (New York: Harcourt, Brace and World, 1951).

4 For a discussion of the role of the relationship between the middle class and democracy, see Barrington Moore, *Social Origins of Dictatorship and Democracy: Lord and Peasant in the Making of the Modern World* (Boston: Beacon, 1966).

5 Giovanni Sartori, *The Theory of Democracy Revisited* (Chatham: Chatham House, 1987), chap. 15. See also Vladimir Lenin, *The State and Revolution* (New York: International Publishers, 1932).

6 Samuel Huntington, *The Clash of Civilizations and the Remaking of World Order* (New York: Simon and Schuster, 1996). See also Francis Fukuyama, "The Primacy of Culture," in Larry Diamond and Mark Plattner, eds., *The Global Resurgence of Democracy* (Baltimore: Johns Hopkins University Press, 1996), 320–27.

7 Mahathir Mohamad and Shintaro Ishihara, *Voice of Asia: Two Leaders Discuss the Coming Century* (Tokyo: Kodansha International, 1996), 82.

8 Kim Dae Jung, "Is Culture Destiny? The Myth of Asia's Anti-Democratic Values," *Foreign Affairs* 73, no. 6 (November–December 1994), 194.

9 For details see Michael Bratton and Nicholas Van de Walle, "Neopatrimonial Regimes and Political Transitions in Africa," *World Politics* 46, no. 4 (1994), 453–89.

10 Guillermo O'Donnell, *Modernization and Bureaucratic Authoritarianism: Studies in South American Politics* (Berkeley: Institute of International Studies, 1973).

11 Oswald Spengler, *Decline of the West* (New York: Knopf, 1928), 347.

DEMOCRACY 6

Democracy is a regime that has both risen and fallen in prominence over time. For most of human history people have not been organized in a way that we would consider democratic; in most political systems few people have been able to exercise power. But in recent centuries democracy has emerged in various parts of the world, especially in the past fifty years. With the collapse of rival, authoritarian ideologies such as fascism and communism, democracy has been on the rise. Around the globe political leaders and publics have sought and gained greater democratic rights, from South Africa to South Korea and from Poland to Chile, pushing aside other ideologies and regimes. From the perspective of those already living in a democratic society, the spread of this political system may appear natural or inevitable—who wouldn't want to live in a democracy? But we must ask ourselves why this should be the case. Why would democracy be an attractive or effective form of government? How does democracy actually work? What sorts of things can democracy provide, and what are its limitations? Does democracy by definition reconcile freedom and equality in a single way, or does democracy allow for different mixtures of the two?

This chapter will speak to these questions in some detail, as we consider the origins, structures, strengths, and weaknesses of democracy. We will begin by defining democracy itself, since different ideologies use the term in very different ways. From there we will investigate democracy's origins in modern politics. Why did it first emerge in the modern world? We will attempt to answer this question by looking at the political development of the United Kingdom, often considered the birthplace of modern democracy. This discussion will lead us into a third question: How or why does democracy spread? Do particular prerequisites, such as economic development or culture, encourage or discourage democracy? After exploring those questions we will consider how democracy actually comes about, and how a country moves away from authoritarianism and toward democracy.

With these issues addressed, we will break down the various institutions that represent democracy itself: participation, competition, and liberty. As we shall see, none of these institutions is ironclad; various democracies construct each institution rather differently, shaping freedom, equality, and the locus of power. Democracies are more diverse than one might expect.

Finally, we shall consider the current limits of, and future challenges to, democracy. What sorts of things can democracy not provide? How might democracy change in the future, and how will this affect politics around the globe? The answers to these questions will help shape the course of individual freedom and collective equality.

WHAT IS DEMOCRACY?

Before we tackle these questions we must nail down our terminology, a particularly difficult task when dealing with the concept of democracy, since the word itself is so loaded with meaning. The word "democracy" has, for many people, an inherently positive connotation: things that are "democratic" are good, whereas things that are "undemocratic" are inherently bad. Of course, in reality this is far from the truth—a university is not a democratic institution, but that does not mean that it is bad or somehow deficient. But because of the word's symbolism many individuals and organizations describe themselves as democratic, although they then define the term in very different ways. For example, in Chapter 3 we noted that for communists, democracy means collective equality and not individual freedom. Countries such as the Soviet Union thus saw themselves as "true" democracies, which they defined as featuring, among other things, full employment, universal education, and the elimination of economic classes. These societies saw democracy in the United States or Europe as little more than the struggle within a small elite over who would dominate the populace. Naturally, capitalist countries viewed communist systems, with their single-party control and lack of civil liberties, as anything but democratic. As you can see, each side is using different criteria to define democracy. For communist systems, collective outcomes are the gauge of democracy, while for the West, the process by which individuals seek particular outcomes is what matters.

How can we make any comparisons if democracy is in the eye of the beholder? One way to begin is to go back to the origins of the word itself. The word "democracy" comes from the Greek words *demos,* meaning "the common people," and *kratia,* meaning "power." Democracy at its most fundamental indicates a system where power resides with the people. Based on this origin, we can begin by defining democracy as a system where political power resides with the people. The people, in turn, may exercise that power either directly or indirectly, and the exercise of power commonly takes three forms: participation, such as through voting and elections; competition, such as that between political parties; and liberty, such as freedom of speech or of assembly. **Democracy**, then, can be fully defined as political power exercised either directly or indirectly through participation, competition, and liberty.

This definition is subjective; it clearly emphasizes individual freedom and is in keeping with the ideology of liberalism. Indeed, many political scientists use the more specific term **liberal democracy** to indicate that when they are speaking of democracy, they are referring specifically to a political system that promotes participation, competition, and liberty. Liberal democracies are rooted in the ideology of liberalism, with its emphasis on individual rights and freedoms.[1]

But liberal democracy is not found only where a liberal ideology and a liberal political-economic system are predominant. Many liberal democracies have social-democratic regimes, which place a much higher emphasis on collective welfare over individual rights, tempering individual freedoms in favor of greater equality. But social democracies nevertheless continue to respect the basic liberal-democratic tenets of participation, competition, and liberty. Having initially been shaped by communist ideology, social democrats over time accepted not just the role of markets and property, but also the importance of the democratic process and individual freedom. Mercantilism, too, emphasizes a strong role for the state and lower personal freedoms as a result, but this has not prevented countries such as Japan, Taiwan, and South Korea from developing liberal-democratic institutions. The matrix of freedom and equality on page 150 shows a line moving away from liberalism and toward mercantilism and social democracy. This can be seen as the trajectory of modern liberal democracy; it surfaced first in societies that embraced liberalism, and came to be adopted later by social-democratic and mercantilist systems as communist and fascist ideological alternatives lost power.

To sum up, liberal democracy presumes a basic set of institutions for participation, competition, and individual liberties. Some democracies go

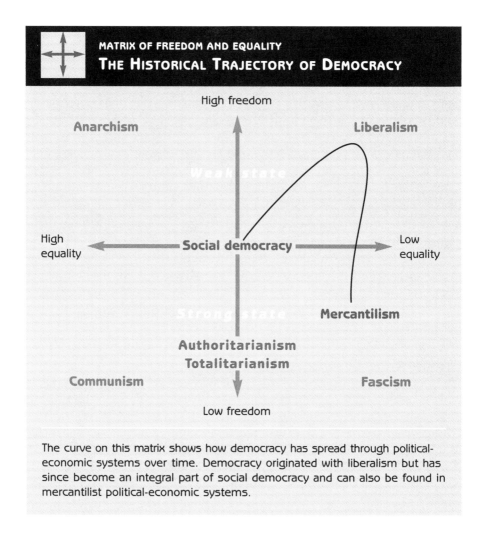

MATRIX OF FREEDOM AND EQUALITY
THE HISTORICAL TRAJECTORY OF DEMOCRACY

High freedom

Anarchism   Liberalism

Weak state

High   Low
equality ←——— Social democracy ———→   equality

Strong state   Mercantilism

Authoritarianism
Totalitarianism

Communism   Fascism

Low freedom

The curve on this matrix shows how democracy has spread through political-economic systems over time. Democracy originated with liberalism but has since become an integral part of social democracy and can also be found in mercantilist political-economic systems.

much further in their emphasis on individual freedoms, whereas others limit freedoms in order to achieve social or national objectives. In all cases, however, the basic conditions of liberal democracy—participation, competition, and liberty—are met. When the term "democracy" is used in the remainder of this chapter, then, it explicitly means liberal democracy. It is also important to remember what is *not* being said here about democracy: this book is not saying that democracy is the only or even the best way to organize politics. All it is saying is that democracy is a particular system of institutions that have developed over time and out of liberal thought. Each person must decide for himself or herself whether the particular goals enshrined in liberal democracy are those that are most important, or whether society is best served by being organized in this manner.

THE ORIGINS OF LIBERAL DEMOCRACY AND THE RULE OF LAW

Where did democracy come from? In the past, when most humans lived in very weakly organized societies in which the issues of freedom and equality were less relevant, many decisions were probably made through some consensus or through the force of a single leader. But as societies became sedentary and developed more complex technologies and human relations, struggles over freedom and equality necessitated political organization and the centralization of power. In many cases this involved coercion, with order imposed from the top down—that is, authoritarianism. But consensus has always been an important element as well, and it eventually sparked democratic development.

Athenian Democracy

Truly complex democratic practices, however, have their roots in ancient Greece, specifically in Athens and its government of public rule. But Athenian and other early Greek democracies were quite different from modern liberal democracies. They were forms of direct democracy. Typically found in small communities, ancient Greek **direct democracy** allowed the public (excluding women, children, and slaves) to participate directly in the affairs of government, choosing policies and making governing decisions. The people were the state. In contrast, in its modern form democracy is one of representative rule, often called **indirect democracy** or "republicanism." Broadly defined, **republicanism** emphasizes the separation of powers within a state and the representation of the public through elected officials (as opposed to the unaccountable powers of a monarchy or the direct participation of the people). Republicanism in its original form did not necessarily mean democracy; many republicans advocated wider control over monarchs (a system of checks and balances) but believed that power should be granted only to the upper classes of society. But as political rights have expanded over the centuries, republicanism and democracy have become intertwined.

THE RISE OF ATHENIAN DEMOCRACY

Athens is commonly viewed as the earliest example of democracy, wherein common people participated in the affairs of politics and voted on specific policies. Why did Athens, originally a small and relatively weak city-state, give birth to democracy? We can see some of the same forces at work in Athenian democracy as we do in the later development of democracy in Great Britain. Initially Athens was controlled by an aristocracy that held much of the city's wealth and made political decisions for society as a whole. By the fifth century B.C.E. the Athenian statesman Solon carried out a series of reforms that benefited the lower classes, encouraging new professions, supporting the export of olive oil, and coining money so as to stimulate commerce. Following Solon, power was seized by the tyrant Peisistratus, who in an effort to strengthen his position against the aristocracy, favored the lower classes by providing loans to develop business and agriculture. Following Peisistratus's death, a period of harsh tyrannical rule returned, but after less than twenty years of such rule, the population rose up and overthrew those in power. Following the revolution the Athenian people created a *demokratia* (rule by the people), in which the public would debate and vote on the essential affairs of politics, unprecedented in world history. As in Great Britain more than a thousand years later, the rise of a middle class in Athens played a critical role in developing a public with the desire and motivation to rule itself.

These modern democracies, like the liberal and republican ideas that gave birth to them, originated in Europe. Why? In short, liberal democracy is closely connected to the rise of the modern state, which as we saw in Chapter 2 first emerged in Europe.

England: The Birthplace of Liberal Democracy

The origins of modern democracy can be traced back to 1215 C.E. in England. At that time, English nobles forced King John to sign the Magna Carta, a document that sought to curb the rights of the king and laid the foundation for an early form of legislature in which the king would consult the barons over such matters as the levying of taxes. The most often noted aspect of the Magna Carta was its assertion that all freemen (at the time, only the aristocracy) should enjoy due process before the law; this assertion set the stage for the idea of civil rights. The Magna Carta states, "No freeman shall be taken, imprisoned, . . . or in any other way destroyed

COMPARING CONCEPTS
TWO FORMS OF DEMOCRACY

Direct democracy	Public participates directly in governance and policy-making. Historically found in small communities such as ancient Athens.
Indirect democracy	Public participates indirectly through its elected representatives. The prevalent form of democracy in the modern age.

. . . except by the lawful judgment of his peers, or by the law of the land. To no one will we sell, to none will we deny or delay, right or justice." Although the Magna Carta was limited in its goals and application, it presented the idea that no individual, not even the king, was above the law—thus it was the first attempt at limiting state autonomy. This concept grew in power in England over the centuries as democratic practices expanded and an ever greater proportion of the public was given political rights. Periodic attempts by the monarchy to expand its power led to violent resistance, most notably in the 1642 English Civil War between King Charles I and Parliament, in which the king eventually lost (and lost his head).

The emergence of democracy in England was thus incremental, developing across centuries. In fact, one notable aspect of British democracy is that as a result of this incremental process, the country still lacks a formal, written constitution. Although various historical documents, such as the Magna Carta or the 1689 Bill of Rights, have helped deepen and define British democracy, there is no single document that lays out the rules of British politics or the rights of British citizens. This often strikes outsiders as amazing: that a country can maintain democracy in the absence of clearly written rules that define the regime.

Was there something special about England that allowed democracy to flourish there in the first place, when it was not emerging elsewhere? Several factors may have been important in this regard, and all are linked to the development of the state. As noted in Chapter 2, there was a strong connection between early political organization and warfare: in Europe, states emerged out of centuries of conflict as rival warlords slowly concentrated their holdings and extended their power. In this regard England enjoyed both

TIMELINE: MILESTONES IN THE RISE OF DEMOCRACY

18th century B.C.E.	Babylonian ruler Hammurabi establishes the earliest known legal code
6th century B.C.E.	Autocratic rule overthrown and first democracy established in Athens
5th century B.C.E.	Democracy collapses in Athens as it is undermined by war and economic crisis
1st century B.C.E.	Roman philosopher Cicero writes of *res publica*, or "affairs of the people," viewing the public as an important source of political power
5th–10th century C.E.	European dark ages: power in Europe is fragmented, fostering intense competition among rulers and setting the stage for the emergence of the nation-state
1215	Writing of the English Magna Carta, an early precedent for establishment of the rule of law
1646	Treaty of Westphalia asserts the right of European states to choose their own religion, enforcing the notion of state sovereignty
1689	Bill of Rights is passed in England, establishing parliamentary supremacy
1690	English philosopher John Locke writes *Two Treatises of Government,* arguing that government's job is to protect "the right to life, liberty, and the ownership of property"
1762	Jean-Jacques Rousseau writes *The Social Contract,* arguing that if a government fails to serve its subjects, the populace has the right to overthrow it
1787	U.S. Constitution and Bill of Rights codify the separation of powers and civil rights
1832–84	Reform Acts in the United Kingdom expand voting rights to much of the male population
1893	New Zealand grants women the right to vote
1945	Defeat of the Axis powers eliminates fascism as a threat to democracy in Europe and Japan
1948	United Nations approves the Universal Declaration of Human Rights, setting the stage for the internationalization of civil rights
1989–91	Soviet Union disintegrates, leading to democratization in Russia and eastern Europe
1994	First democratic elections in South Africa, ending racial restrictions on voting

relatively early unification and the defensive benefits of being an island; the need to maintain a large army to unify and defend the country was much lower for isolated England than for the many other European states that had to defend land borders. This lower need for an army meant that the state did not have to extract great amounts of revenue from the people in the form of high taxes, a fact that further reduced the need for a strong coercive force to take taxes from a less-than-willing public. England's position as an island country also meant that economic development was strongly linked to international trade, which also helped generate state revenues through port taxes. Trade provided an easier means for the state to gain income and lessened the need to forcibly extract taxes from the people.

As a result of these factors, England developed without needing a large, land-based military force to quell threats inside and outside the country, and therefore without the powerful state that would have been necessary to construct and wield such an army. This relative decentralization of power in turn helped foster individual freedom, through the assertion of such notions as civil liberties and economic rights—ideas that would eventually give shape to the ideology of liberalism. It is no accident that an ideology that emphasized individual freedom and private property emerged in a country where the state was historically weak. The public, able to gain the upper hand against the state early on in England's political development, could check attempts by the state to increase its power. This public power paved the way for an expansion of rights over time, culminating in the modern liberal democracy.[2]

Institutionalizing Democracy

We now have an understanding of the origins and basic elements of liberal democracy. But once those elements of democracy emerge, how are they made to last? What are the most effective ways to encourage and safeguard them? How is each reconciled with individual freedom and collective equality? The world's liberal democracies do not answer these questions all in the same way. Each country creates its own unique form of liberal democracy, shaped by state, societal, and economic factors. Through these unique combinations liberal democracies create a **rule of law**—a condition in which the public and those in power respect and abide by the rules and norms of the democratic regime. Democracy is thereby institutionalized. The following section will take us through the institutions of participation, competition, and liberty, showing how each can vary in building a democratic order and the rule of law.

PARTICIPATION: VOTING AND ELECTIONS

Participation is central to liberal democracy; it is hard to imagine a regime as democratic if people have no say in politics. Of the many ways in which democratic participation can be expressed, one of the most basic is voting and elections. Voting and elections allow the public to have control over their public officials and policies through a process of competition in which leaders can be turned out of office. Elections are not the only way in which the public can influence politics (they may also rely on lobbying, letter-writing, or public demonstrations, for instance), but they are an important structure in which people are given a say in the staffing and direction of government, and thereby in the relationship between freedom and equality. Elections also prevent any one individual or group from maintaining its power indefinitely, and as such they limit the possibilities for leaders to abuse their power.

In a true democracy, the right to vote, or **suffrage**, needs to be open to all adult citizens, with few restrictions. In many democracies up until the latter half of the twentieth century, women, individuals from lower classes, and certain ethnic groups were not allowed to vote—something that would no longer be considered as acceptable in a democracy. New Zealand was the first country to give women the right to vote—in 1893—but in the United States women did not gain this right until 1920, and in France not until 1944. In Australia, restrictions on the rights of the indigenous aboriginal people to vote lasted until the 1960s. In the United States literacy tests as a prerequisite to voting rights were used as a mechanism to discriminate against African Americans, who had little access to education. At the opposite end of the spectrum, some countries view suffrage as more than a right—it is a formal responsibility. In Australia, Belgium, Brazil, and a number of other democratic countries, voting is actually compulsory, and those who fail to vote can be fined.

IN FOCUS

PARTICIPATION

- One of the most basic ways in which the public participates in politics is through voting and elections.

- The two main types of electoral systems are first-past-the-post (FPTP) and proportional representation (PR). The majority of democratic countries today use PR. Many use a mix of FPTP and PR.

- Voters may also participate in political decision-making through referenda, initiatives, and plebiscites.

Beyond the basic right to vote is the more complicated question of how votes should be cast and counted. **Electoral systems** are the rules that decide how votes are cast, counted, and translated into seats in a legislature, and these systems vary widely around the world. Such systems matter, for how electoral rules are constructed makes a huge difference in the distribution of political power. Differences in electoral systems affect which individuals or parties gain power and even the degree to which people vote.

All democracies divide their populations up into a number of electoral boundaries or constituencies that are allocated a certain number of legislative seats. The total number of constituencies may vary widely: Norway is broken up into 19 constituencies that correspond to the country's 19 counties, whereas in the United States there are 435 constituencies for elections to the House of Representatives. How these boundaries are drawn matters, too. For example, a small minority group might be concentrated in one region but be divided by electoral boundaries, diluting its voting power. Or different districts may have very different population sizes, but the same number of legislative seats; such circumstances give those in less-populated districts more power. How governments draw electoral boundaries thus can have a huge impact on who gets elected.

Electoral Systems

A second distinction is how votes are counted.[3] A minority of democratic countries around the world, including the United States, Australia, India, France, and the United Kingdom, use a system known as **first past the post** (FPTP). In this electoral system, electoral constituencies function as **single-member districts**, in which several candidates compete to be the sole representative of that constituency. The candidate with the largest number of votes wins the seat. This need not be a majority of votes, only a plurality of votes (the largest share of the total). Those votes cast for other candidates are "wasted"—that is, if the candidate for which a vote is cast does not win, that vote does not count toward anyone getting into office. FPTP can therefore amplify the political power of some parties while weakening the political power of others.

By way of illustration, let's look at the outcome of the 2001 elections for the House of Representatives (the lower legislative house) in Australia. As the table on page 158 shows, although small parties such as Greens and the Democrats each garnered around 5 percent of the vote, they failed to win a single seat. This means that their candidates did not win a plurality of votes in any electoral district. As a result, two strong parties, Labor and the Liberals, wound up winning more seats than their actual shares of the vote would indicate. Finally, the National Party, although it won only 4 percent of the national vote, gained 9 percent of the seats in the

ELECTORAL SYSTEMS AND OUTCOMES: AUSTRALIA AND SOUTH AFRICA

Party	First Past the Post: Australia, House of Representatives, 2001		Party	Proportional Representation: South Africa, National Assembly, 1999	
	Percentage of Votes Won Nationally	Percentage of Votes Won in Legislature		Percentage of Votes Won Nationally	Percentage of Votes Won in Legislature
Australian Labor Party	38	43	African National Congress	66	67
Liberal Party	37	45	Democratic Party	10	10
Australian Democrats	5	0	Inkatha Freedom Party	9	9
Green Party	5	0	New National Party	7	7
One Nation	4	0	United Democratic Movement	3	4
National Party	4	9	African Christian Democratic Party	1	1
			Freedom Front	1	1
			United Christian Democratic Party	1	1
			Pan-African Congress	1	1

House. How could it be possible that they would win so many seats when in fact they received fewer votes than the Greens or the Democrats? As you may have guessed, the National Party was able to gain the largest share of votes in a number of single-member districts in three regions where that party has historically done well. This example shows how FPTP can magnify the power of some parties while marginalizing others.

Not surprisingly, the FPTP system is seen by political scientists as having a profound impact on the number of parties in the legislature. A French political scientist, Maurice Duverger, argued that under FPTP most people are unwilling to vote for smaller parties. Since such parties are unlikely to win first place, voters feel that a vote cast for a small party will be wasted and that they would be better off giving their vote to a stronger party that has a chance of coming in first.[4] As a result, FPTP systems are much more likely to produce a legislature dominated by two parties, as in Australia, the United States, and the United Kingdom, where smaller parties are for the most part unrepresented in the legislature. Even if a smaller party were to win the second-largest share of votes in every electoral district in the country, it would still have failed to gain a single seat.

Quite different from FPTP is a system known as **proportional representation** (PR), which is used in some form by a majority of democracies around the world. In contrast to FPTP, PR generally attempts to decrease the number of votes that are wasted, thus increasing the number of parties in the legislature. Rather than single-member districts, PR relies on electoral boundaries that create **multi-member districts**; in other words, more than one legislative seat is contested in each district. In PR systems, voters cast their ballots for a party rather than for a candidate, and the percentage of votes a party receives in a district determines how many of that district's seats the party will gain. Theoretically, if a party wins 17 percent of the vote in a district, it will receive 17 percent of that district's seats; if it wins 100 percent of the vote in a district, it will receive all of the seats. As opposed to FPTP, where a large proportion, even the majority, of votes cast in an electoral district may not count toward any particular candidate, in PR even small percentages of the vote can result in winning seats. The 1999 elections in South Africa, also detailed in the table on page 158, show how votes under PR can correspond much more closely to the percentage of seats won in the legislature. Small parties that would not have won a single seat under FPTP are in fact represented in the South African National Assembly.

Because PR is based on multi-member districts, elections are not centered on competitions between individuals. Instead, political parties draw up in advance a list of their candidates for each electoral district, usually proposing as many candidates are there are seats. If a district has ten seats, and a party wins 50 percent of the vote in that district, the party will send the first five candidates on its party list to the legislature. As you can imagine, one result of this system is that political parties have tremendous power over who will get on the list and at what rank. A candidate would

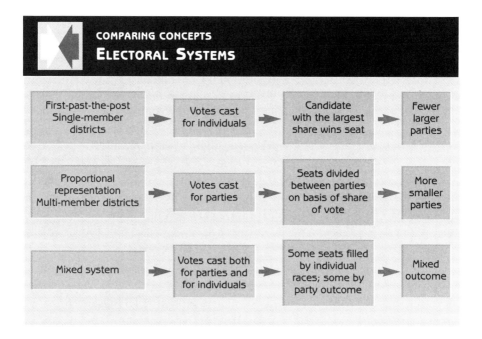

COMPARING CONCEPTS
ELECTORAL SYSTEMS

| First-past-the-post Single-member districts | ➡ | Votes cast for individuals | ➡ | Candidate with the largest share wins seat | ➡ | Fewer larger parties |

| Proportional representation Multi-member districts | ➡ | Votes cast for parties | ➡ | Seats divided between parties on basis of share of vote | ➡ | More smaller parties |

| Mixed system | ➡ | Votes cast both for parties and for individuals | ➡ | Some seats filled by individual races; some by party outcome | ➡ | Mixed outcome |

want to be listed as high up on the list as possible in order to gain a seat even if the party got a small share of the district vote.

PR can have several effects. Most importantly, and in contrast to FPTP, in which voters tend to support only those parties with a chance of winning the largest share of votes in a district, in PR voters are more willing to vote for smaller parties, since they stand a better chance of winning at least some seats in the legislature. Even if a party wins less than 10 percent of the vote, it may well gain seats, as the 1999 South African elections showed. As a result, countries with PR are likely to have many more parties in the legislature than countries with FPTP. Israel's legislature, for example, has more than fifteen parties, some of which are coalitions of several smaller parties.

Which system better serves participation: FPTP or PR? This is a controversial question. Many argue that PR is a more democratic form of electing officials since it wastes votes to a much smaller degree than does FPTP, and in so doing allows for a greater range of political interests to be expressed. PR widens the number of parties able to win seats in the legislature, helping specialized parties concerned with narrow or minority interests to have a greater say in policy-making. Imagine, for example, what kinds of parties there might be in the United States if the U.S. electoral system were PR instead of FPTP: a Pacific Northwest Party? An African

American or Native American Party? In addition, given the lower degree of wasted votes, supporters of PR argue that this system makes more people feel like they have a say in politics.[5]

Those who reject this idea argue that FPTP has particular democratic aspects that are lost under PR. FPTP can make it easier for individuals to connect with their elected representatives than under PR, since voters express their support or rejection of a particular individual in a way not possible under PR. Indeed, in PR a candidate no longer liked by the public can still be elected simply because he or she has the backing of the party and is placed high on the party list. In other words, FPTP supporters argue that it increases accountability. Supporters also note that FPTP eliminates fringe parties from the political scene, allowing for the creation of large parties that are able to muster the majorities needed to govern without being held hostage by smaller ones. Clearly, there is no correct side to this debate, since it turns on differing conceptions of what makes a system more or less democratic.

Given the advantages and disadvantages of both FPTP and PR, some countries have attempted to combine the two. For example, Germany, Hungary, Mexico, and Russia use what is known as a **mixed system** that combines both PR and FPTP. In such systems, voters have two choices on a single ballot, selecting both a political party (PR) and a single candidate (FPTP) for their district. One portion of the seats in the legislature is divided up on the basis of the PR returns for each party, and the other portion is allotted on the basis of which candidate won the largest share of votes in each district. The percentage of the seats allotted by PR and the percentage allotted by FPTP varies from country to country. For example, in Germany the seats in the lower house of the legislature are divided evenly between FPTP and PR, whereas in Japan the breakdown is 60 percent FPTP and 40 percent PR. Under this system voters not only get two votes, but also have the option can split their choice, voting for a candidate from one party in the FPTP portion of their ballot while choosing a different party for their PR vote. For example, in Germany one might vote for the large left-wing Social Democratic Party for the FPTP portion of the ballot (since only a large party is likely to get the plurality of votes needed to win under FPTP), while reserving the PR portion of the ballot for the small environmentalist Green Party.

Referendum, Initiative, Plebiscite

In addition to shaping how one's participation is counted, electoral systems can also affect policy. Although national ballots are typically used to choose parties or candidates for office, many countries also have the option

of allowing a public vote on a particular policy issue. Such a national ballot is commonly known as a **referendum**. In contrast to the more indirect
impact that elections have on politics, referenda allow the public to make
direct decisions about policy itself, by putting certain issues before the
public and allowing them to decide. National referenda are unknown in
the United States and Canada (although they exist in some local and state
governments), but they are used in many other democracies. Recently Italy
and New Zealand used national referenda to dramatically restructure their
electoral and legislative systems, and in Switzerland, where the political
system comes closest to the idea of direct democracy than in any other
country, many of the most important national decisions are regularly
decided by referenda.

Strictly defined, referenda can be called only by the government or
members of the legislature. In some countries the public may have the
power of **initiative**, which is essentially a publicly initiated national referendum. In this process, those organizing the initiative must propose an
issue for a nationwide vote and collect a certain number of supporting sig-
natures from the public; if they are able to do so, the government is obliged
to schedule a ballot. Initiatives and referenda raise the question of whether
the government is obligated to act in accordance with the outcome of a
national ballot. In some cases, governments may call a ballot to consult
public opinion rather than to make a final, binding decision about some
aspect of policy, law, or citizenship. The ballot may provide for a number
of options, rather than a simple yes or no, designed to advise the government on an issue. However, governments are typically not constitutionally
required to act in accordance with the outcome of such ballots. These nonbinding votes are often known as **plebiscites**. In spite of the clear difference, many use the terms "referendum" and "plebiscite" interchangeably.

Initiatives, referenda, and plebiscites are thus all variations on the same
theme, that of a nationwide ballot concerning some particular issue. Does
such a system make a country more democratic? People who favor greater
participation in government policy-making support such direct mechanisms, while others argue that the public is ill qualified to make major
changes to national policy or institutions. In some societies, national referenda or initiatives might help legitimize democracy through direct participation, while in others they might polarize the public and weaken the
commitment to democratic rule.

As you can see, democratic participation is rather complex. When we
speak about the right to vote, we must also consider how that vote is
counted and to what end it is cast. Electoral boundaries and electoral rules

strongly influence the power of one's vote, shaping the number of parties in government and the kinds of interests they may represent. Referenda and initiatives also widen the scope for public participation, by giving the people a direct say in policy. Using these institutions, liberal democracies can secure the participation of their citizens.

COMPETITION: POLITICAL PARTIES AND THE SEPARATION OF POWERS

If participation is a vital part of liberal democracies, it stands to reason that such a right is limited if the public is denied any choice. An election in which there is only one candidate or party to choose from is not a democracy. Therefore, in addition to participation a democracy requires competition between groups, individuals, and ideas, each seeking to realize their own political goals regarding freedom and equality. In this section we shall focus on two important elements in democratic competition: political parties and the separation of powers. Political parties compete against one another to gain control over the government and state, and the separation of powers makes certain that no one party is able to exercise this control completely. Paradoxically, then, liberal democracies must encourage, but also frustrate, the quest for political power.

Political Parties

Among the many political actors engaged in this competition, political parties are the most organized, the most powerful, and seemingly inevitable. As James Madison once wrote, "in every political society, parties are unavoidable."[6] He did not say that political parties are desirable; since the early days of democracy, many people have viewed them as little more than a necessary evil. Why must we have parties at all? Could one have a democracy in which people could choose between candidates but political parties were banned? Isn't political choice, rather than parties *per se,* the most important thing? This is an important question, and one that political scientists often don't consider.

Observers have offered several different reasons for why political parties are vital to liberal democracy. Political scientist John Aldrich in his work *Why Parties?* laid out some of the most common explanations.[7] The first reason for the necessity of political parties in a democracy is that parties are important organizations that bring together diverse groups of people and ideas. These organizations serve two functions. By bringing together different people and ideas into a single group, they help establish the means by which the majority can rule. In other words, without political parties that provide candidates and agendas for politics, the political process would be too fragmented and it would be impossible to enact policy or get much else done. But although political parties bring individuals and ideas together, they remain relatively loose, with differences and factions within them. This relative heterogeneity prevents a tyranny of the majority. No one party can easily impose its will undemocratically on the people, since the very diversity within parties prevents the kind of unanimity necessary for tyranny. Parties in liberal democracies are thus homogeneous enough to create majority rule, but too weak to facilitate a tyranny of the majority.

This leads us to the second reason for the necessity of political parties: political parties create the means by which politicians can be held accountable by the electorate and fellow political elites. By articulating an ideology and a set of goals, parties hold their members responsible for achieving those goals. Voters are able to evaluate a group of politicians on the basis of these goals and promises—did they do what they promised? Lacking parties, the public would have a difficult time evaluating the goals and achievements or failures of each candidate. Parties can thus serve as a political symbol, a shorthand for a set of ideas and objectives, and voters can distill complex decisions into questions of whether to vote for party A or party B. Political parties thus play a key role in encouraging democratic competition. They help articulate broader coalitions while preventing domination by any one group, provide a means to hold elected officials accountable, and thereby encourage democratic debate and the evolution of ideas.

The Separation of Powers

The competition for political power, although vital to democracy, raises that danger that someone might win that competition. More specifically, if too much power rests in any one group's hands, there is the possibility that democracy could be undermined. The loose nature of political parties helps limit this threat, but the problem remains that a particular branch or segment of government may wield too much power and thus be tempted to abuse it. Through the **separation of powers**, democracies diffuse democratic power by giving specific branches the ability to check the political power of other actors within government.[8] Such power may also slow politics by requiring oversight of various branches of government, limiting hasty decision-making that might polarize the public or lead to ill-considered policies. Although it is possible to have democracy without formal checks and balances (the United Kingdom, for example, lacks such structures), they are widely accepted as valuable safeguards. The mere existence of separate branches of government does not ensure an effective separation of powers, however. Each branch must have an independent base of authority, outlined in a constitution, embedded in the regime, and respected by politicians and the public.

IN FOCUS

COMPETITION

- Political parties encourage democratic competition by articulating broader coalitions while simultaneously preventing domination by any one group.

- The separation of power between different branches of government prevents abuses of power by any one branch.

Democracies typically encompass three major branches of government: executives, legislatures, and constitutional courts. As with electoral rules, each of these institutions may be constructed in very different ways in different liberal democracies, reflecting unique conditions and circumstances.

Executives: Heads of State and Heads of Government

We begin with what is the most prominent office in any country, the **executive**, the branch that carries out the laws and policies of a state. When we think of this office what first comes to mind is a single person in charge of leading the country and setting a national agenda—such as a president. But in fact the executive comprises two distinct roles. The first is that of **head of state**, a role that symbolizes and represents the people, both nationally and internationally, embodying and articulating the goals of the regime. In contrast, the role of the **head of government** is to deal with the everyday tasks of running the state, such as formulating and executing policy. This distinction is an old one that goes back to the days when monarchs *reigned* over their subjects, leaving others in charge of *ruling* the country.

In many liberal democracies, this distinction between head of state and head of government still exists in two executive offices. As head of government we find a prime minister, a member of the legislature who has been elected by that body to serve as the executive. Because the prime minister is elected by the legislature, he or she is usually the head of the largest political party, since that party wields the most votes in the legislature. The prime minister and the cabinet (the other chief ministers or officials in government, in charge of such policy areas as defense, agriculture, etc.), are charged with formulating and executing policy. As head of state in such systems, one finds a monarch or a president. In most liberal democracies this position is largely ceremonial. The Japanese emperor, the Israeli president, and the German president have little power, though each serves an important symbolic role, representing the nation and the regime. This type of system, in which the head of state and the head of government are separate individuals, is typically known as a **prime ministerial system**, since the prime minister, a member of parliament, is the chief executive.

In contrast, some liberal democracies fuse the roles of head of state and head of government into a single office in what is known as a **presidential system**. These systems feature a directly elected president who is entrusted with all executive powers and roles in both domestic and international affairs. The president's function is thus symbolic and practical; in many ways the office embodies charismatic legitimacy, albeit within a modern rational-legal framework of elections. The United States is a presidential system, as are many democracies in Latin America. Outside of the Americas, however, such a system is rare.

Political scientists find advantages and flaws in each of these types of system. One important advantage of the prime ministerial system derives from the fact that the prime minister is elected from the legislature. This support reduces the degree of conflict between the executive and the legislature, and in turn increases the possibility that legislation can be passed. Prime ministers thus may make for more effective government. Moreover, if prime ministers do lose the support of the legislature, they often can be removed through a "vote of no confidence" by the legislature; a new prime minister is then chosen or new elections called. In other words, the prime minister and the legislature do not serve fixed terms in a prime ministerial system. Supporters view this as a great source of flexibility should the government lose the people's confidence.

Some critics of prime ministerial systems, however, view the lack of separation between the prime minister and the legislature as a dangerous concentration of power, since both are controlled by the same party. Furthermore, when a single party does not hold a majority in the legislature (a common situation under proportional representation), it is necessary to build a coalition government that involves several parties. Although coalitions may help generate political consensus, they can also create problems. For example, a party with a plurality of seats in the legislature may bring smaller parties into the cabinet in return for their support in elect-ing a prime minister. But such an arrangement can give smaller parties an inordinate amount of power in the government and the ability to stymie politics altogether. In 2002 Israel, with fifteen parties in its legislature, had eight parties represented in the cabinet itself! In short, prime minis-terial government may limit competition between the executive and the legislature but instill too much competition within the executive itself.

In contrast, supporters of a presidential system point first to its direct mandate from the people. This means that presidents serve fixed terms, ensuring stability, as they cannot be removed by the legislature except for

GLOBAL COMPARISONS
EXECUTIVE SYSTEMS IN DEMOCRACIES

Countries	Head of State, How Elected, Powers	Head of Government, How Elected, Powers	Executive System
United States, Mexico	President Directly Strong	President Directly Strong	Presidential
United Kingdom, Japan	Monarch Hereditary Weaker	Prime minister Indirectly Stronger	Prime ministerial
Germany, Italy	President Indirectly Weaker	Prime minister Indirectly Stronger	Prime ministerial
Ireland, Austria	President Directly Weaker	Prime minister Indirectly Stronger	Prime ministerial
France, Russia	President Directly Stronger*	Prime minister Indirectly Weaker*	Semipresidential

*The powers of the president and the prime minister in France are affected by whether or not they belong to the same party.

criminal activity. The fusion of head of state and government gives the office additional legitimacy and may increase executive power. Finally, supporters of the presidential system see it as more democratic, because the head of the country is directly chosen by the people. Critics, of course, are more doubtful of the presidential system's merits.[9] By fusing heads of state and government, too much power is placed in one person's hands, which can limit competition and threaten democracy. This problem is further compounded by an inability to easily remove the president. Finally, because the executive and the legislature are elected separately, divided government (in which the executive is controlled by one party and the legislature by another) is much more likely, leading to deadlock. For these reasons some political scientists have gone so far as to say that presidential systems are more likely to undermine democracy, especially where they are weakly institutionalized. However, the direct role played by the people in choosing their leader still makes it an attractive option for many.

In part because of this dispute some countries have tried to reconcile presidential and prime ministerial systems. In these cases a prime minister coexists alongside a president who is directly elected by the people and who holds a significant degree of power. This power commonly includes control over foreign affairs, the ability to dismiss the prime minister or the legislature under certain conditions, and the ability to call national referenda. Such **semi-presidential systems** can be found in France, Russia, South Korea, and Taiwan, among other countries. Which of the two executives is more powerful under this system depends on the particular issue and the country itself.

A final point about executives is in order: there is no direct connection between the electoral system and the kind of executive system, such as president or prime minister, in any given country. A country may have a directly elected president and use PR for its legislature; it may be prime ministerial and use FPTP; or it may have any other combination of the two systems. What kind of executive system a country has and how its legislature is elected are entirely separate mechanisms.

Legislatures: Bicameral or Unicameral

As with executives, legislatures are an important arena in which people compete for power. Unlike executives, which are charged with carrying out policy, legislatures serve as the main arena in which national politics is debated. The **legislature** is the branch of government charged with making laws. As with all the institutions we have studied so far in this chapter, legislatures vary in their political powers and construction, again reflecting the particular nature of democracy in a country. One major distinction is that between bicameral and unicameral systems. As you might guess from their names, **bicameral systems** have two houses in the legislature, whereas **unicameral systems** have only one. Bicameral systems can be traced back to England and other European states, where two or more chambers were created to serve the interests of different economic classes. The upper house represented the aristocracy; the lower house served the merchant class. In the United Kingdom this distinction is still evident in the names of the two houses, the lower house being the House of Commons, and the upper the House of Lords. Over time, as the powers of the middle class expanded, the powers of the aristocracy in most countries' legislatures were reduced or eliminated.

Yet the idea of upper and lower houses still remains. Why have two chambers if the old class distinctions that gave rise to bicameralism no longer apply? In fact, in the United Kingdom the House of Lords lost the last of its remaining powers nearly a hundred years ago, and in 1999 the House of Commons stripped the House of Lords of most of its aristocratic members as well, yet it chose to maintain the upper house as an institution. It would seem, then, that bicameralism is not like one's appendix, an organ that has lost its function through political evolution. Indeed, bicameralism can play several roles in fostering democratic competition.

First, in many liberal democracies bicameralism is a part of federalism, which was discussed in Chapter 2. Under federalism, bicameralism allows for one house (usually the upper chamber) to represent regional

COMPARING CONCEPTS
BRANCHES OF GOVERNMENT

Branch	Functions, Attributes, and Powers
Executive	Head of state / head of government Prime ministerial, presidential, and semipresidential systems Term length may be fixed (president) or not (prime minister)
Legislative	Lawmaking Unicameral or bicameral
Constitutional court	Determines the relative constitutionality of laws and acts Judicial review (abstract and concrete)

governments and local interests. Local legislatures may appoint the members of that chamber, or those members may be directly elected. In the United States, the Senate was indirectly elected by local legislatures until 1913. Consistent with the idea of federalism, the goal of bicameralism is to strike a balance of power between national and local government, giving the latter the ability to approve or reject national legislation. Bicameralism can also counterbalance disproportionate power in the hands of any regional government. Whereas seats in the lower house are typically allocated by population, in the upper house representation may be uniform. For example, in Brazil each state is given three seats in the Senate, irrespective of the size of each state's population. In the United States each state has two seats in the Senate.

Even where federalism does not exist, bicameralism may use competition between the two houses as a means to slow down the legislative process. When both houses are required to approve legislation, it becomes difficult to quickly pass laws; such systems therefore force consensus-building between the upper and lower houses. In this rationale for bicameralism can be seen echoes of the old aristocratic logic: upper houses are sometimes viewed as a body that must check the passion of the lower house, which may be stirred to sudden and hasty action by members with little political experience. This logic arose in the debates between the Federalists and the Antifederalists during the drafting and ratification of the U.S. Constitution. Many upper houses still reflect this logic through longer terms of office and specific input on changes to the constitution. Different terms of office between the two houses may also serve to increase political stability by preventing a sudden and complete turnover following an election.

Of course, these advantages come at a price. Bicameralism, like any separation of powers, may weaken the legislature by creating too many obstacles to passing legislation, lowering government efficiency. As a result, many countries have opted for relatively weak upper houses, or no upper house at all. Sweden, for example, abandoned its upper house in 1971. But the majority of liberal democracies do retain some form of bicameralism, a trend that may be on the rise as power is further decentralized in many countries. We will talk more about this trend in Chapter 7.

Constitutional Courts

Our discussion of the separation of powers takes us to the last major branch of government in liberal democracies. The **constitutional court** is the highest judicial body that rules on the constitutionality of laws and other government actions. Over the past half-century many democracies have seen the growth of judicial power, and constitutional courts have played an ever greater role in the realm of politics. Whereas at one time the idea of a strong court overseeing the activities of the legislature and the executive would have been seen as unusual, in most liberal democracies constitutional courts are now viewed as important safeguards against abuse. But this development has not been without its share of controversy. Because constitutional courts are not directly elected, some view them as failing to represent and often thwarting the direct will of the people. In addition, members of the court tend to serve long terms in office, meaning that turnover is infrequent and that politicians are unable to influence the court as easily as they might like. Of course, this is precisely the point.

Constitutional courts serve to defend the democratic principles of a country against infringement by public or private actors. The court's powers center on the concept of **judicial review**, the mechanism by which the court can review laws and policies and overturn those that are seen as violations of the constitution. Judicial review may take on two forms. **Concrete review** is the power by which the court can rule on constitutional issues on the basis of disputes brought before it. In other words, the court has power but is reactive and must wait for a legal dispute before it can rule on the constitutionality of any law or state action. **Abstract review**, in contrast, allows a court to decide on questions that do not arise from actual legal cases, sometimes even before legislation actually becomes law. Some constitutional courts have only concrete power, as with the Supreme Court in the United States, whereas others have only abstract power, as with the Constitutional Council in France, meaning that they do not hear specific cases between disputants. Some have both powers at their disposal, as in the case of the Constitutional Court in Hungary.

The growth of judicial power over the past century has been spurred in part by the desire to protect human rights. In the aftermath of World War II, many world leaders and groups realized that democratic electoral systems could nonetheless give rise to authoritarian leaders and that judges who lacked the power to interpret and defend the democratic provisions and spirit of a constitution could not strike down undemocratic laws if they had been promulgated in a technically legal manner. Courts, in other words, have grown in strength as guardians of constitutions and regimes, giving them wider latitude to interpret the law as they see fit. To what extent this growing power interferes with participation and competition by overturning the decisions of elected representatives, however, remains an open question.

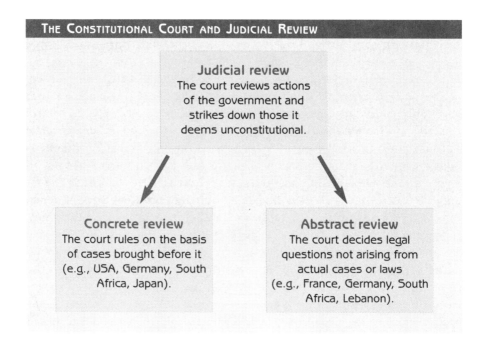

THE CONSTITUTIONAL COURT AND JUDICIAL REVIEW

Judicial review
The court reviews actions of the government and strikes down those it deems unconstitutional.

Concrete review
The court rules on the basis of cases brought before it (e.g., USA, Germany, South Africa, Japan).

Abstract review
The court decides legal questions not arising from actual cases or laws (e.g., France, Germany, South Africa, Lebanon).

LIBERTY: CIVIL RIGHTS

The last component of liberal democracy is liberty itself. Of course, to some extent we have been dealing with liberty throughout this chapter; the rights to participate in elections, to form political parties, and to be protected by constitutional safeguards are all fundamental components of a liberal democracy. Liberty is thus not simply freedom from interference by the state or other actors, but the active creation of rights that otherwise would not exist. These are **civil rights**, enshrined in the law (particularly in the constitution) and the political regime. As with participation and competition, although liberal democracies reach a consensus on those rights intrinsic to liberal democracy, there is a great deal of variation in how these rights are practically defined.

At the core of liberal democracies lie some shared civil rights. These include the rights to free speech and movement, the right to religious belief, the right of public assembly and organization, equal treatment under the law, the prevention of inhuman punishment, the right to a fair trial, the right to privacy, and the right to choose one's own government. Some liberal democracies go beyond these basic rights to include certain social or economic outcomes, such as universal education, health care, or retirement benefits. Such rights are particularly strong in social-democratic regimes. For example, the Swedish constitution states within its section on civil liberties that "it shall be incumbent upon the public administration to secure the right to work, housing and education, and to promote social care and social security and a good living environment." In the Danish constitution, civil rights also include a provision that "efforts should be made to afford work to every able-bodied citizen" and that any person unable to support himself or herself is entitled to public assistance. Critics might question whether such an emphasis on collective outcomes is detrimental to liberty; equality of process, they would argue, should be central.

In addition to differences on how far civil rights should be collectively expanded, liberal democracies also differ in the extent to which individual rights should be limited. For example, all liberal democracies uphold the rights of free speech and association. Yet in some countries, such as Germany, the democratic constitution outlaws antidemocratic activity, meaning that the state can ban political parties that are seen as hostile to democracy. The South African constitution limits freedom of expression by forbidding "advocacy of hatred that is based on race, ethnicity, gender, or religion, and that constitutes incitement to cause harm."[10] While acknowledging these two countries' nondemocratic histories, critics would view such restrictions as more threatening to liberty than any speech or

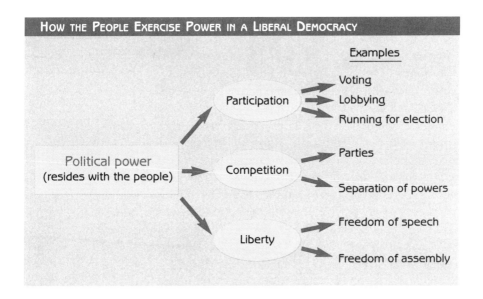

HOW THE PEOPLE EXERCISE POWER IN A LIBERAL DEMOCRACY

Examples

Participation
Voting
Lobbying
Running for election

Political power
(resides with the people)

Competition
Parties
Separation of powers

Liberty
Freedom of speech
Freedom of assembly

organization. A similar debate can be found regarding the right of individuals to possess firearms. What are the limits to liberty? At what point do the rights of the individual threaten democracy itself? No one has a concise answer to this question, and what is the accepted norm at one point in time can change in the future. But that itself is one of the great strengths of democracy—its ability to evolve over time.

IN SUM: FUTURE CHALLENGES TO DEMOCRACY

As we have seen, democracy is one way to manage the dilemma of individual freedom and collective equality, one that this chapter has traced back to ancient Greece and early modern England. In its modern liberal form, democracy emphasizes individual freedom and the need to create rules that place political power in the hands of the people. Liberal democracy does this through three institutions: participation, competition, and liberty. Participation, such as elections, helps provide the public a means of control over the state and the government; competition ensures an open arena of ideas and prevents too great a centralization of power; and liberty creates a basic set of individual rights, freedoms from state interference, and freedoms made possible by the state itself. When these elements are institutionalized—valued for their own sake, considered legitimate by the public—democracy is institutionalized, and we can speak of the existence of a rule of law. No one stands above the democratic regime.

In the next three chapters we will look at the struggle between individual freedom and collective equality in different parts of the world. In Chapter 7, we will see that across the advanced democracies, liberal democracy is the norm. However, the rise of new political systems, such as the European Union; the emergence of new ideas, such as postmodern values; and the return of old ideas, such as nationalism, present a challenge. In Chapter 8 we will compare Western liberal democracy to communist and postcommunist countries. Once the greatest challenge to liberal democracy, communist thought presented an alternative vision of politics based on collective equality—a democracy of outcomes. But this system failed, and postcommunist countries now struggle to create a new relationship between freedom and equality. In some of these countries liberal democracy is now taking form; in others, individual freedom remains fragile and circumscribed. In Chapter 9 we will consider the less-developed and newly industrializing countries, in which liberal democracy is rare and instability and authoritarian rule remain the norm. Will democracy eventually gain ground there, creating a global culture of participation, competition, and liberty? We will consider this question in Chapter 10, which focuses on globalization. Democracy's greatest challenge in the future may lie not in reconciling freedom and equality domestically within a single country, but in finding a mix of the two on a global scale, an optimal blend of the individual rights of people everywhere and the collective needs of a global community.

NOTES

1 C. B. MacPherson, *The Life and Times of Liberal Democracy* (Oxford: Oxford University Press, 1977).

2 For details see Charles Tilly, "War Making and State Making as Organized Crime," in Peter B. Evans, Dietrich Rueschemeyer, and Theda Skocpol, eds., *Bringing the State Back In* (Cambridge: Cambridge University Press, 1985), 165–91.

3 An exhaustive discussion of the different forms of electoral systems and other facets of voting and elections can be found at the Administration and Cost of Elections Web site at www.aceproject.org.

4 Maurice Duverger, *Political Parties: Their Organization and Activity in the Modern State* (New York: Wiley, 1964).

5 An extensive argument in favor of adopting PR in the United States can be found at the Web site of Professor Douglas Amy of Mount Holyoke College: www.mtholyoke.edu/acad/polit/damy/prlib.htm.

6 William T. Hutchinson et al., eds., *The Papers of James Madison*, vol. 14 (Chicago: University of Chicago Press, 1985), 197–98.

7 John Aldrich, *Why Parties? The Origin and Transformation of Political Parties in America* (Chicago: University of Chicago Press, 1995).

8 This idea was first elaborated by Baron de Montesquieu in *The Spirit of the Laws,* trans. Thomas Nugent (New York: Hafner, 1949).

9 See Juan Linz and Arturo Valenzuela, eds., *The Failure of Presidential Democracy* (Baltimore: Johns Hopkins University Press, 1994).

10 The South African and other constitutions of the world can be found online at www.uni-wuerzburg.de/law/home.html.

7 ADVANCED DEMOCRACIES

So far in this book we have moved through various concepts that help us compare politics. With these tools now in hand, we can begin to investigate some specific parts of the world. The areas we will study are not themselves geographic locations, but rather groups of countries that are in some way similar in their political institutions. Recall the discussion in Chapter 1 about the comparative method: by looking at similar countries, we can hope to control our variables so as to better pose questions and test possible answers. Our first group of countries is commonly known as the **advanced democracies**, countries having institutionalized democracy and a high level of economic development.

How is this different from our discussion in Chapter 6? In that chapter we spoke of liberal democracy as a set of institutions through which to exercise political power—a system that may be used in a wide array of countries. In the case of the advanced democracies, however, we are specifically referring to those countries where liberal democracy is institutionalized and, moreover, is coupled with a high level of economic development. This is what is meant by the use of the word "advanced." Some might take issue with the term "advanced democracies," since it seems to imply a value judgment that implies a level of superiority. Indeed, many people would see it as precisely that: a high standard of living and a liberal democratic regime representing the basic aspirations of all humanity. Others would disagree.

In this chapter we will look at the basic institutions and dynamics that characterize the advanced democracies, applying the concepts we have studied so far. We will start by categorizing the advanced democracies: What do they have in common? What differences exist between them?

This comparison will lead us to a discussion of the role of individual freedom and collective equality in the advanced democracies. How do these
countries reconcile the two? Once we have a grasp of these ideas we will
move on to consider political, economic, and societal institutions in the
advanced democracies, particularly the challenges those institutions face
in the new millennium. The forces of integration and devolution—transferring power to international institutions, or down to local ones—
challenge the very notion of state sovereignty that has been at the core of
modern politics. In economics, too, the emergence of "postindustrial" societies is transforming the very nature of wealth and labor, providing new
opportunities to some while marginalizing others. Similar changes can be
seen in societal institutions: new social values may be emerging as a reflec-
tion of political and economic change, reshaping ideology in the advanced
democracies and the debate over freedom and equality.

Are the advanced democracies on the brink of dramatic transformation? If so, is this change a harbinger of things to come around the globe?
This chapter will lay out some of the evidence so that we can consider the
possibilities. To give our discussion focus, we will frequently turn to two
advanced democracies—Sweden and Japan—to illustrate our discussion.

DEFINING ADVANCED DEMOCRACY

What, exactly, are the advanced democracies? In the past, scholars typically spoke of these countries as belonging to the "First World," meaning
that they were economically developed and democratic. They were con-
trasted with the countries of the "Second World," or communist states,
and those of the "Third World," meaning the vast body of less-developed
countries. Categorizing countries into these three "worlds" was always
somewhat problematic, since various factors in various combinations
around the world often confounded these categories. The rise of oil-based
economies in the Middle East, for example, created countries with a great
degree of wealth, but this wealth was based on natural resources controlled
by the state rather than on private property and free markets. The rise in
wealth in these countries also did not coincide with a move toward liberal
democracy—so they did not really fall into the Third World, yet were not
at all part of the advanced First World, either. With the end of the Cold
War and the collapse of communism, the three-worlds approach became
even more confusing, as many industrialized, formerly communist countries embraced capitalism and liberal democracy, while others experienced

economic decline and continued authoritarianism. They had little left in common except history.

Instead of using this problematic three-worlds approach, this book will refer to advanced democracies, communist and postcommunist countries, and developing and less-developed countries. These categories, too, have their limitations, but in contrast to the "worlds" approach, they imply that movement is possible between the categories—that countries can industrialize or democratize, can move to or from communism, can develop or remain less developed. In fact, in some cases we will place countries into more than one category, especially those that may be in transition from one category to another.

So, how do we determine which countries belong to the category of advanced democracies? In the area of democracy, we can rely on the factors discussed in Chapter 6, looking at the degree and institutionalization of participation, competition, and liberty in each. In the area of economic development, we can consider those issues raised in Chapter 4: the presence of private property and open markets and the level of gross domestic product (GDP) at purchasing power parity (PPP). We might also consider the kind of economic output that countries produce. In general, advanced democracies tend to have a relatively small portion of their GDPs arising from agriculture and industrial production. Whereas during the Industrial Revolution and after industry displaced agriculture in many of today's advanced democracies, today that industry itself is increasingly being displaced by the service sector, which includes such things as retail sales, computer programming, and education.

The table on page 179 lists a few countries that can be classified as advanced democracies, with a few non-advanced democracies listed for comparison. The advanced democracies share in common not only liberal-democratic regimes, but also capitalist economic systems (liberal, social democratic, or mercantilist) in which the service sector dominates. This contrasts with countries such as Saudi Arabia, China, India, and Nigeria, which are poorer and lack a strong industrial and service sector or an institutionalized liberal democracy, or both.

Given our definition of "advanced democracies," the countries that we place in this category are rather diverse—a diversity that has grown particularly strong over the past decade. For example, countries such as Poland and South Korea were historically categorized as part of the Second and Third Worlds, respectively. But with economic and political changes in both countries it makes less and less sense to think of them in these terms. Postcommunist Poland now has much more in common economically and

ADVANCED DEMOCRACIES, 2002

North and South America	Europe	Asia	Middle East and Africa
United States	*European Union members:*	Australia	Israel
Canada	Austria	Japan	
Bahamas	Belgium	New Zealand	
Barbados	Denmark		**Recent Democratization:**
Bermuda	Finland		
	France		*South Africa*
	Germany		
Recent Democratization:	Greece	**Recent Democratization:**	
	Ireland		
Argentina	Italy	*South Korea*	
Chile	Luxembourg	*Taiwan*	
Mexico	Netherlands		
Uruguay	Portugal		
	Spain		
	Sweden		
	United Kingdom		

Non-EU members:
Cyprus
Malta
Norway
Switzerland

Postcommunist Democratization:

Czech Republic
Estonia
Hungary
Latvia
Lithuania
Poland
Slovakia
Slovenia

Note: Countries in italics may be in the process of transitioning into advanced democracies.

GLOBAL COMPARISONS
ECONOMIC PORTRAITS

| Country | Percentage of GDP Contributed by | | | GDP (PPP, in U.S. $) | Institutionalized Liberal Democracy? |
	Agriculture	Industry	Services		
Advanced Democracies					
United States	3	22	75	36,200	Yes
Japan	5	31	64	24,900	Yes
Canada	3	22	74	24,800	Yes
Sweden	2	28	70	22,200	Yes
South Korea	6	41	53	16,100	Yes (recent)
Poland	4	37	60	8,500	Yes (recent)
Other Countries (for Comparison)					
Saudi Arabia	6	47	47	10,500	No
China	15	50	35	3,600	No
India	25	24	51	2,200	Yes
Nigeria	40	40	20	950	No

Source: Central Intelligence Agency, U.S. Bureau of Labor Statistics

politically with western European countries such as Germany or France than with many other countries that also were once part of the communist world; South Korea has more in common with Japan than it does with other, less-developed countries around the world.

The countries listed as advanced democracies in this table and in the box above have high levels of economic development (with GDPs of over $7,000), small agricultural sectors, and institutionalized democratic regimes. You will note that within this category are included several recent democratizers and postcommunist countries that also exhibit the hallmarks of economic development and democracy. Scholars continue to debate whether these countries should yet be categorized as advanced democracies, since their economic and political advances are still relatively new and may not be fully institutionalized. Indeed, these countries will be discussed again in the chapters on postcommunist and developing and less-developed countries. In spite of this uncertainty, their presence indicates that as a result of recent global economic and political changes, the camp of advanced democracies appears to be expanding well beyond its traditional provinces of western Europe and North America.

THE PATHS OF ADVANCED DEMOCRACIES

One result of using a broad definition for advanced democracies is the inclusion of countries that have come to this category by very different means—countries that were early industrializers and early democratizers, as well as countries that have moved into both categories more recently. Indeed, the paths to the realm of advanced democracy have been varied. Some countries experienced democratic and economic development early and simultaneously, as did the United States and the United Kingdom in the late eighteen and early nineteenth centuries. In other cases economic development did not lead directly to democratization. For example, in Germany, capitalist industrialization in the nineteenth century occurred under the guidance of a powerful authoritarian regime. This was also the case somewhat later in Japan and subsequently in countries such as South Korea and Taiwan. In these cases, democracy came only in the latter half of the twentieth century. Finally, countries in eastern Europe saw their industrialization carried out primarily by authoritarian communist regimes; their transitions to capitalism and democracy occurred only since the early 1990s.

PATHS TO ADVANCED DEMOCRACY

	Early Democratization	Late Democratization
Early Industrialization	United Kingdom United States	Germany
Late Industrialization		Japan Poland

FREEDOM AND EQUALITY IN ADVANCED DEMOCRACIES

How do advanced democracies reconcile the dilemma of freedom and equality? All countries that fall into this category share in common an institutionalized liberal democracy, private property, free markets, and a high level of economic development based on industry and services. However, this similarity does not mean that these countries' approaches to reconciling freedom and equality are identical. In our familiar matrix of freedom and democracy on page 183 you can see an arc that traces the basic boundaries within which advanced democracies fall. This is not meant to be some definitive border, but rather a way to visualize how advanced democracies can differ in their approaches. As you can see, advanced democracies do range in terms of freedom and equality while remaining capitalist and democratic. Countries with liberal regimes are focused more on individual freedoms than on collective equality, whereas the focus of social-democratic systems tends toward the opposite. Mercantilist systems, meanwhile, have policies that de-emphasize both freedom and equality. In spite of this wide variation, however, these countries are united by common democratic and economic institutions.

First consider the role of freedom: all advanced democracies are institutionalized liberal democracies, sharing in common a belief in participation, competition, and liberty. Yet there are real differences in how countries define each of these categories. For example, civil liberties may be expanded or restricted without calling into question the democratic nature of a country. Take the case of abortion. Some advanced democracies allow abortions during a pregnancy's first trimester with relatively few restrictions, such as Sweden, Japan, the United States, Hungary, Canada, France, and Austria. In others, such as South Korea, Spain, Portugal, and Argentina, abortions are more restricted, and a few countries ban abortions altogether (Chile) or allow them only when a woman's life is threatened (Ireland). We can find similar distinctions in the regulation of prostitution or hate speech, and in the degree to which privacy is protected from state or economic actors.

Advanced democracies also vary in their levels of political participation. The different electoral systems discussed in Chapter 6 can all be found among these countries, alone and in combination. The use of referenda and initiatives differ greatly across these countries; most advanced democracies do use them to some degree, although a few countries allow for such votes only at the local level (the United States, Canada, Germany, and

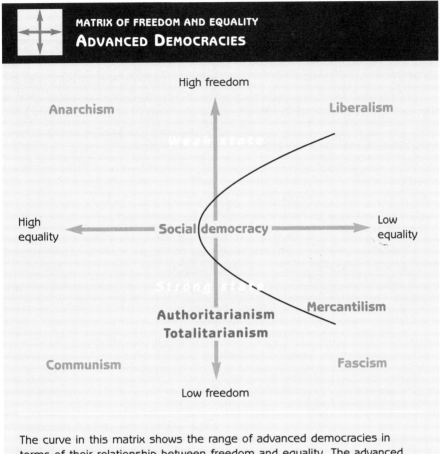

MATRIX OF FREEDOM AND EQUALITY
ADVANCED DEMOCRACIES

High freedom

Anarchism   Liberalism

Weak state

High   Low
equality ←———— Social democracy ————→ equality

Strong state

Mercantilism

Authoritarianism
Totalitarianism

Communism   Fascism

Low freedom

The curve in this matrix shows the range of advanced democracies in terms of their relationship between freedom and equality. The advanced democracies consist of liberal, social-democratic, and mercantilist systems; some embrace stronger or weaker states, some greater or lesser freedom and equality. However, they hold in common the institutions of liberal democracy, private property, and free markets, and their citizens enjoy a high overall standard of living.

Japan), and still others make no provision for such ballots at any level of government (Israel). Another difference can be found in voter registration; in most advanced democracies it is the responsibility of the state to ensure that all eligible voters are automatically registered to vote, yet in a few (the United States and France), it is contingent on the individual voter to register. Voting rights and obligations may also differ. In Norway, Sweden, the

Netherlands, and Denmark, any foreigner who has taken up permanent residence may vote in local elections. In Australia, Argentina, Uruguay, and Belgium, voting is mandatory; those who do not vote can be fined.

Nor is competition uniform across the advanced democracies. Its variations include the ways in which political parties and campaigns are funded: some countries impose specific limits on the amount of money that can be contributed by private actors to any political party or candidate, laws that require the disclosure of the source of private political contributions. To take one example, in the United States, there are no limits on how much can be spent by a legislative candidate running for office, and campaigns often cost millions of dollars; in New Zealand, the spending limit is 20,000 New Zealand dollars (about $8,500 U.S.). The separation of powers also varies greatly, with unicameral and bicameral systems, strong and weak constitutional courts, presidents and prime ministers.

In short, the advanced democracies are politically diverse. All advanced democracies guarantee participation, competition, and liberty, but at the same time they differ in where the boundaries of these freedoms are defined or how these freedoms are exercised. Freedom is a basic guarantee, but the form and content of freedom varies from case to case.

In addition to a commitment to freedom, advanced democracies also share in common a similar approach to equality that emphasizes capitalism, that is to say, private property and free markets. This approach appears to have generated a great deal of economic wealth—overall basic standards of living are higher in the advanced democracies than elsewhere in the world, and average life expectancy is high, at over seventy years—yet this wealth exists alongside inequality.

Yet here, too, we see variation. Looking again at the arc on the matrix of freedom and equality, we can see that advanced democracies range widely in the degree of economic equality they afford. Recall from Chapter 4 that the Gini index, a measurement of inequality around the world, found a surprising degree of difference among countries even when their levels of economic development were roughly the same. For example, Germany and the United States have comparable levels of economic development as measured by GDP, but very different levels of inequality as measured by the Gini index. The United States is much more unequal than in Germany or other advanced democracies such as Sweden.

This difference in equality is in part a function of the role of the state. Across advanced democracies, states differ greatly in their economic functions, including their role in the distribution of wealth. In liberal and mercantilist countries such as the United States and Japan, the state provides relatively low levels of social expenditure. Individuals or families have a greater responsibility for funding basic needs, and the total tax burden on the public in these countries is typically lower as a result. This is not to say, however, that inequality is necessarily the end result; in Japan and South Korea, a small welfare state coexists alongside a higher level of economic equality than in the United States. In social-democratic systems, such as those found in much of Europe, taxation is much higher and these resources are used for income redistribution through a strong system of social expenditures. However, these variations in the state's approach to inequality do not change the fact that in each of these countries private property and free markets are fundamental institutions.

In short, the advanced democracies hold in common a basic set of institutions to reconcile freedom and equality. These institutions include liberal democracy, with its emphasis on participation, competition, and liberty, and capitalism, with its emphasis on free markets and private property. Yet each of the advanced democracies has constructed these institutions in different ways, resulting in quite significant variations among them.

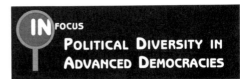

IN FOCUS
POLITICAL DIVERSITY IN ADVANCED DEMOCRACIES

Participation

- Standards of voter eligibility differ.
- Referenda and initiatives are used in varying degrees.
- Some, but not all, states automatically register all eligible voters.
- Voting is compulsory in some nations, but voluntary in most.

Competition

- Different methods and levels of funding for political parties and campaigns.
- Separation of powers varies greatly, and is based primarily on the relative strength of different branches of government.

Liberties

- Distinctions in the regulation, allowance, or prohibition of activities such as abortion, prostitution, and hate speech.
- Different degrees of individual privacy from state and corporate intrusion.

ADVANCED DEMOCRACIES IN THE NEW MILLENNIUM

The institutions that the advanced democracies share are part of what makes these countries **modern**—that is, secular, rational, materialistic, technological, bureaucratic, and placing a greater emphasis on individual freedom than on collective equality. But like any other set of countries,

GLOBAL COMPARISONS
INCOME REDISTRIBUTION IN ADVANCED DEMOCRACIES

Country	Political-Economic System	Taxes as a percentage of GDP, 1996	Gini Index, 1990s
Sweden	Social democratic	52	25.0
Denmark	Social democratic	52	24.7
France	Social democratic	46	32.7
Germany	Social democratic	38	30.0
United Kingdom	Liberal	39	36.1
Canada	Liberal	37	31.5
United States	Liberal	29	40.8
Japan	Mercantilist	28	24.9

Sources: Organization for Economic Cooperation and Development, World Bank

the advanced democracies are not static; their institutions are subject to change under the influence of domestic and international forces. And indeed, some argue that the advanced democracies are currently undergoing a profound set of social, political, and economic changes, marking what many call the rise of a new, **postmodern** era, characterized by a new set of values centered on "quality of life" considerations and less concern with material gain. If true, this would mean that existing modern institutions are giving way to new ones as these countries make a transition from modernization to postmodernization. Such a change, if it is indeed happening, is likely to be profound. Because institutions are typically resistant to change, when such change does occur it is likely to be dramatic, and revolutionary rather than evolutionary.

Are the advanced democracies moving from away from modernity to something radically different and new? How would we know this? And what might this change portend for the relationship between freedom and equality in the advanced democracies? These are big questions that lie in the realm of speculation and rely on fragmentary evidence, so we must be careful. But to get at some answers, we need to look at how political, societal, and economic institutions may be changing in the advanced democracies, so that we may draw our own conclusions about whether modernity, as we understand it, is really giving way to something new.

In delving into these matters, we will look both at the broad spectrum of advanced democracies and at two specific cases: Sweden and Japan. In many ways these two countries are as different as any pair within the set of advanced democracies, which can create some problems in making comparisons. Yet at the same time they reveal some interesting similarities. By using two distinct cases we can better determine whether the changes discussed above are truly emerging across a variety of countries within the advanced democracies.

Japan is a late democratizer and industrializer. Its economic changes were directed in large part by the state, and its democratic system was imposed from the outside—by the U.S. occupation after World War II. Since the war, Japan has become a major power in the international system, a fact that many attribute to its mercantilist political-economic system. This system was forged in large part by the Liberal Democratic Party, which has dominated the Japanese government and state almost continuously since 1955. During the 1970s and 1980s many other countries looked on with a mixture of envy and fear at the rapid pace of Japanese development, viewing "Japan, Inc." as a nearly unstoppable economic force (although the recession that Japan has experienced over the past decade or so has called its momentum into question).

Sweden is in many ways quite the opposite of Japan in terms of history and policies. Sweden has a much longer tradition of democracy: its history of early representative institutions (such as a legislature) goes back as far as those of England. Another contrast with Japan can be found in Sweden's political economy. Unlike Japan's mercantilism, in which the state directs economic growth while providing a relatively low level of social expenditures, Sweden is perhaps best known for its social-democratic orientation. During the Great Depression the Social Democratic Party came into government in Sweden, and it held power, either alone or in coalition, from 1945 to 1976, as well as through much of the 1980s and 1990s. The Social Democrats enacted a wide range of policies to expand social expenditures in such areas as pensions, health care, and education, creating one of the most generous welfare states in the world. The high rates of taxation that have helped pay for these social expenditures have also limited the freedom of individuals to amass personal wealth as they have produced a more equal redistribution among the public as whole.

Yet in spite of their different histories and political-economic systems, Sweden and Japan share some of the highest levels of economic equality in the world. Both countries also experienced a long tenure by a single political party, meaning that their governments could construct and institutionalize new regimes that have fundamentally transformed these countries. Finally, both countries have been held up as models of progress. In short, Japan and Sweden have pursued very different paths of economic development, under the political guidance of a single dominant party, creating countries that stand apart among the advanced democracies.

In spite of their exemplary natures, both Sweden and Japan confront the same challenges facing all the advanced democracies. Old institutions and policies are encountering new problems and opportunities brought on by changes in the political, economic, and social environments. The relationship between freedom and equality, something many observers thought had been permanently reconciled in each of these countries, is threatening to break down. The following sections will illustrate some of these challenges and the possible changes underway, both generally and in the specific cases of Sweden and Japan.

STATES AND SOVEREIGNTY: CHALLENGES AND OPPORTUNITIES

In Chapter 2 we discussed a number of different ways in which states can be analyzed and compared. In particular we spoke about state sovereignty and the way in which state power can be viewed in terms of autonomy and capacity. Although advanced democracies differ in their levels of autonomy and capacity, they are all distinguished by the ability to formulate and carry out the basic tasks expected of them by society. In other words, advanced democracies are notable for their sovereignty, or their ability to act independent of outside actors, which ever since the rise of the modern state has been a hallmark of power.

Yet in recent decades these concepts have come under challenge. In particular, within the advanced democracies we have seen a movement toward greater integration between countries, and greater devolution within countries. **Integration** is a process by which states pool their sovereignty, surrendering some individual powers in order to gain political, economic, or societal benefits in return. Integration blurs the line between countries by forging tight connections, common policies, and shared rules that bind them together. In contrast, **devolution** is a process by which political power is devolved, or "sent down," to lower levels of government. This process is intended to increase local participation, efficiency, and flexibility, as tasks once handled at the national level are managed by local authorities. These two processes differ in the direction in which power is flowing—either "above" the state in the case of integration, or "below" the state in the case of devolution. But in both cases state capacity, autonomy, and sovereignty are affected, influencing the relationship between freedom and equality. Although both integration and devolution can be found to varying degrees around the world, it is among the advanced democracies that such processes are the most advanced and profound, and it is there that they are shaping the very future of the state.

Integration and the European Union: The Future of the Advanced Democracies?

The most important example of integration is without a doubt the European Union (EU), a project without precedent and whose long-term implications are profound and uncertain. Following World War II, a number of European leaders argued that the repeated conflicts in the region were caused by a lack of interconnection between the countries themselves— which in turn fostered insecurity, inequality, and nationalism. These lead-

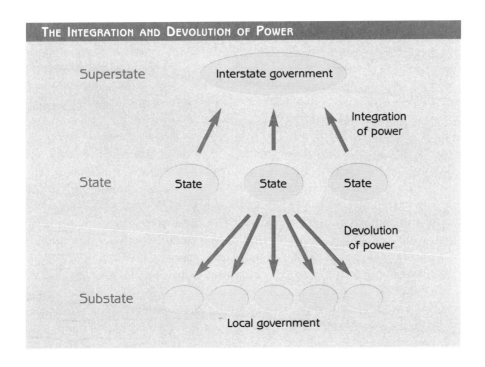

THE INTEGRATION AND DEVOLUTION OF POWER

Superstate   Interstate government

                                    Integration
                                    of power

State   State   State   State

                                    Devolution
                                    of power

Substate

        Local government

TIMELINE: EUROPEAN INTEGRATION	
1951	European Coal and Steel Community founded by Belgium, France, Germany, Italy, Luxembourg, and the Netherlands
1957	European Economic Community created
1967	European Community (EC) created
1973	Denmark, Ireland, and the United Kingdom join EC
1979	Direct elections to the European Parliament
1981	Greece joins EC
1986	Spain and Portugal join EC
1993	European Union (EU) created
1995	Sweden, Finland, and Austria join EU
1999	Monetary union created between most EU member states
2002	Euro currency enters circulation; most EU national currencies eliminated

ers believed that if their countries could be bound together through economic, social, and political institutions, they would reject war against each other as an irrational act. Moreover, they argued, a common political agenda would give European states greater international authority in a postwar environment that had become dominated by the Soviet Union and the United States. With these motivations, a core of western European countries began the process of integration in the early 1950s. As you can imagine, this was a radical step away from sovereignty, and not an easy one for any state or society to swallow. As a result, integration moved forward slowly.[1]

As the timeline above shows, the EU developed incrementally over time, from a small organization that dealt primarily with the production of steel and coal to one with many more members and vastly greater responsibilities. Out of these changes a basic set of institutions has developed, with sovereign power in many areas over the member states themselves. The European Commission, made up of representatives appointed by the member-state governments, develops legislation; the Council of Ministers, made up of ministers from the countries' respective national governments, approves or rejects this legislation (with each minister voting in accordance with his or her country's concerns). A third body, the European Parliament, is directly elected by the member states' citizens. In other words, EU citizens vote in elections both for their national legislatures and for the European Parliament. The European Parliament is able to modify or reject most legislation that comes from the Commission, as well as approve the addition of new members to the EU. Finally, the European Court of Justice plays an important role in resolving disputes over legislation once it has been adopted; it also decides matters of EU law. These state-like institutions have gained power over time, so much so that now many people no longer speak of the EU as an **intergovernmental system**, with countries cooperating on issues, but as a **supranational system**, with its own

European Union Members and Candidates for Membership, 2003

Source: British Parliament

Note: Numbers in parentheses indicate population size, in millions.

sovereign powers over the member states themselves. As a result, the reconciliation of freedom and equality has become as much an international task as a domestic one.

Each of the individual states of the EU has had to weigh the benefits of integration against the loss of sovereignty. For example, Sweden is a latecomer to the EU, having joined only in 1995. Its long resistance toward membership stemmed in part from its tradition of political neutrality (Sweden did not take sides during World War II) and from the fear that membership would require changes in domestic institutions and policies in order to conform to EU standards. Of greatest concern were Sweden's large social expenditures, created to ensure greater collective equality. However, the end of the Cold War changed Swedish thinking about neutrality, and in the 1990s the government moved to apply for membership, although public skepticism remained. Even though a public referendum on EU membership passed in Sweden in 1994, the vote was only 52 percent in favor.

The growing breadth and depth of the EU have been further underscored by two recent projects. The first is monetary union. On January 1, 1999, the majority of EU member states linked their currencies to the euro, a single currency eventually meant to replace those of the member states as a means to promote further economic integration and growth. On January 1, 2002, all EU member states that joined this monetary union withdrew their own currencies from circulation and replaced them with the euro. In Chapter 4 we noted that one important facet of a state's power is its ability to print money and set interest rates; in the European monetary union, this power has been surrendered to the European Central Bank. This monetary union represents the largest single transfer of power to date within the EU; it has also been one of the most contentious.

As for Sweden, since joining the EU it has continued to pursue a somewhat ambivalent relationship. Along with Denmark and the United Kingdom, for example, Sweden has declined to join the monetary union. Many Swedes continue to fear that a single currency would force the state to enact tax and budget reforms to align more with the other EU member states, which would undermine the Swedish welfare system. Although the Swedish government has stated that it expects to hold a referendum on monetary union in the next few years, opinion polls indicate that a significant number of Swedes oppose adopting the euro, and a large number would support leaving the EU altogether. Sweden's ambivalence toward monetary union and the EU might be stronger than that of other member states, but in general it mirrors a widespread ambivalence about how integration will affect state power and the ability to reconcile freedom and equality at the domestic level.

A second important development is the ongoing expansion of the EU. Since 1951 the EU has grown from six member states to fifteen, and currently more than ten other countries have applied for membership. With such expansion the EU could have a population of over 400 million (compared to the 280 million people in the United States) and a GDP as large as that of the United States (around $10 trillion). This kind of enlargement would require a radical reorganization of the EU; structures that work for six or even fifteen countries would not be able to handle so many different members and interests. For some, expansion presents an opportunity to forge new institutions to manage the challenges of such a large political system. Moreover, the accession of postcommunist members would help complete their transition into advanced democracies. Others, however, view enlargement as a threat to further integration, for it would create an EU too cumbersome to further deepen connections between its member countries. Interestingly, this very problem is viewed by others in a positive light; they hope that the problems of enlargement will put a brake on integration and the loss of state sovereignty.

In other words, the very successes of the EU have generated concerns and opposition. Some of this opposition stems from the loss of sovereignty and the reduced ability of the public to exercise control over those in power. Critics of the integration process decry what has been called the **democratic deficit**: as the EU has taken on greater power, more and more state capacity has shifted to supranational institutions that are highly autonomous and not under direct democratic control. In fact, the only directly elected EU body, the European Parliament, is one of its weakest institutions in terms of political authority. As the EU takes on more responsibility, there will likely be more debates over how to make the body a more democratic institution. Should, for example, the EU have its own prime minister or directly elected president?

This leads us to a final consideration, that of whether the EU will become a sovereign state in its own right. Although currently the EU does exercise sovereignty in many areas of law, it lacks some of the key elements of a state, among them the monopoly of force. Will in time the EU, too, have its own armed forces and police? Or will it become something truly different, a political entity that is different from the modern state? These questions are relevant not just for Europe, but across many of the advanced democracies that are engaged in integration projects. The North American Free Trade Agreement between the United States, Canada, and Mexico, for example, has far less power than the EU—but only fifty years ago the EU itself was little more than a free-trade agreement. Will the Americas eventually forge a supranational body of their own?[2]

Devolution and Democracy

While many advanced democracies are confronting the pull of integration from above, they are also facing the tug of devolution from below. As mentioned earlier, devolution is a process by which powers and resources are transferred away from central state institutions and vested at a lower level. What is interesting about this process is that it is a reversal of the historical development of the state, which is noteworthy for its centralization of power over time. Over the decades, ever greater power has moved from the local level to the national level on issues such as social welfare. Yet across the advanced democracies, powers seem increasingly to be flowing in the opposite direction.

Why this apparent reversal? Among political leaders in many advanced democracies is a concern that the public mistrusts the state, viewing it as too large, too distant, and too inflexible. Devolution is viewed as a way to counteract this distrust by bringing government closer to the public, thereby increasing local control and participation. By increasing the public voice, and the public's capacity to shape politics, it is hoped, democracy can be reinvigorated.[3]

How does devolution take shape in reality? One way is through the transfer of responsibility and funds to local authorities, giving them greater say in how policies are crafted and executed. When local institutions have more control, they can craft policy to meet their own particular conditions. One example of such devolution occurred in the United States in the 1990s, when welfare reform created bulk transfers of funds to the states, which could then use this money to design and implement their own particular social-welfare policies. Another is through the creation of wholly new political institutions to provide a new level of public participation. An example of such innovation was seen in Canada in 1999, when an entirely new province, Nunavut, was created out of a portion of the Northwest Territories. The creation of this new province was intended to give the native Inuit people self-government and control the natural resources in the region where they live. Similarly, in 1999 the United Kingdom created new, directly elected assemblies for the

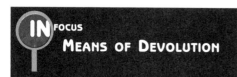

IN FOCUS

MEANS OF DEVOLUTION

- Transfer of policy-making responsibility to lower levels of government.

- Transfer of funds and powers to tax to lower levels of government, affording them more control over how resources are distributed.

- Creation of new political institutions at lower levels of government.

regions of Scotland and Wales and reinstated an assembly for Northern Ireland that had been dissolved in the 1970s as a result of nationalist conflict. Each of these bodies has been given varying degrees of power. Interestingly, across the EU devolution has gone hand in hand with integration, as local governments become increasingly connected to the EU. Regions and cities are able to directly influence EU policy-making, bypassing their national governments in the process, and local authorities are often empowered to directly implement EU policy. This increased power at the local level has in part been promoted as a way to respond to the democratic deficit, but some observers fear such semifederal arrangements will undermine central authority. Sweden and Japan, for example, are both highly centralized states where local officials have little authority; in both countries, devolution has been less popular among those in power. In those countries where ethnic divisions exist, there are also concerns that devolution could be a slippery slope, leading eventually to the disintegration of the countries themselves. Indeed, for some Scottish and Welsh nationalists, independence as sovereign states within the EU is their goal. But others argue that greater local participation will increase public trust in the state, not weaken it.

As with integration, it is not certain whether devolution is a trend among the advanced democracies that will continue to spread and deepen in the future, nor is it clear what the long-term implications of such a process would be. Devolution may be a means to rebuild democratic participation by making people more directly responsible for policy-making. However, it may also undermine the capacity and autonomy of the central state, especially if coupled with integration.

How will devolution shape freedom and equality? Whereas integration implies that these values become reconciled increasingly at the international level, devolution implies that this process becomes increasingly local. These would seem to be contradictory processes, then. By pulling in two different directions, integration and devolution might lead to future conflicts over individual freedom, collective equality, and the proper location and role of political power—below and above the state.

SOCIAL CHANGE AND CONFLICT

Just as advanced democratic states are undergoing a number of challenges and changes in the new millennium, societies are in transition as well. And as with states, societies seem to be pulled from two directions. A new set of shared norms and values appears to be emerging across the advanced democracies, while at the same time a greater emphasis on local concerns is pulling these same societies inward. These processes are strongly connected to the struggle over integration and devolution. Whether these social forces are complementary or contradictory, and whether such developments are a sign of greater cooperation or conflict, is still a matter of debate.

Postmodern Values and Organization

In recent years a number of political scientists have begun to track the emergence of what they see as the development of postmodern values in the advanced democracies.[4] In premodern societies, people were focused to a greater extent on traditional forms of authority and on basic survival; this focus led to authoritarian systems with clear standards of obedience and collectivism. Starting in the eighteenth century those countries that would become the advanced democracies began to embrace the notions of rationality and science, individualism, and autonomy. The modern state, society, and economy promised a world of progress, development, and limitless possibilities, and it did enable unprecedented economic growth, material abundance, and improved standards of living for hundreds of millions of people.

Yet by the 1960s modern values came under attack, just as they themselves had challenged premodern ones more than two centuries earlier. These challenges took several forms. Economic development came into question because of environmental damage that it causes. Modern values stressed the environment as an instrument for the achievement of material goals, but critics argued that the environment should be valued for its own sake—a public good to be shared by all. Science, too, was similarly viewed with greater skepticism. Technological innovation did not lead to unmitigated benefits, but rather carried with it risks and uncertainty. Fears over nuclear power and chemical contamination underscored the belief among many that the very notion of "progress" was a questionable goal. In politics, too, postmodern values challenged nationalism and patriotism, questioning authority, hierarchy, and deference to the state. In general, these criticisms indicated the possible emergence of a new set of social norms and values.

Postmodern values differ from modern ones in a number of ways. As indicated above, postmodern values are much less focused on the idea of progress as embodied by material goods, technological change, or scientific innovation. Instead, postmodern values center on what have been called "quality of life" or postmaterialist" issues, which give primary attention to concerns other than material gain. These include concerns over the environment, health, and leisure as well as a greater focus on personal equality and diversity. At the same time, postmodern values are skeptical of state power while supportive of democracy, especially in the form of direct participation and action. These values in many ways reflect both integrationist and devolutionary tendencies, with their concern for greater tolerance among people (integration) and their greater hostility toward centralized power (devolution).

To what extent are these postmodern values reshaping the societies of the advanced democracies? Public-opinion surveys conducted over the past ten years in the advanced democracies do point to the rise of postmodern values, though their spread is less even than one might expect. For example, the box below reveals that in the United States and the European Union, there is little support for traditional gender roles, although support for such roles is much higher in Japan. Similarly, the surveys detailed in the box on page 198 show that in Japan and the United States a slight majority of the population says that it favors environmental protection, even if it means material sacrifices in return.

POSTMODERN VALUES AND GENDER: PUBLIC OPINION SURVEYS IN EUROPE, THE UNITED STATES, AND JAPAN

European Union survey, 1998
"A husband's job is to earn money and a wife's role is to stay at home."

Agree:	25%
Disagree:	73%

United States survey, 1997
"Women should return to their traditional roles in society."

Agree:	24%
Disagree:	73%

Japan survey, 1998
"The man's job is to earn income while the woman's job is to look after the house and family."

Agree:	35%
Difficult to say:	27%
Disagree:	37%

Source: European Union; *Asahi Shimbun*

POSTMODERN VALUES AND THE ENVIRONMENT: PUBLIC OPINION SURVEYS IN THE UNITED STATES AND JAPAN

United States, 1997
"People should be willing to pay higher prices in order to protect the environment."
Agree: 55%
Disagree: 43%

Japan, 1999
Willingness to accept a less comfortable life in order to protect the environment:
Willing: 51%
Unwilling: 39%

Sources: Pew Research Center for the People and the Press; *Asahi Shimbun*

We must be careful not to overstate these findings, however. Although data appear to confirm the spread of postmaterial values across the advanced democracies, researchers also note that other factors continue to shape the belief systems of individual countries. For example, although Europeans from predominantly Protestant countries such as Sweden do not place a high priority on religion, religion remains strong in the predominantly Catholic countries of Europe, the United States, and Canada, even though all these countries enjoy roughly similar levels of development. Similarly, although there is rising acceptance of homosexuality and gender equality in North America and Europe, this has not been the case in Japan or South Korea. These differences indicate that cultural factors in each country remain important in shaping the value systems of societies, even as they undergo a general process of development and consequent change. This persistence of cultural factors raises some questions. Are postmodern values the inevitable outcome of a development and democracy, or are they particular facets of Western culture? Will postmodern values inevitably spread outward from the advanced democracies, or will they be limited by non-Western cultural and religious barriers?[5]

One important implication of postmodern values in the advanced democracies may be in the very debate over freedom and equality, as new issues develop that transform the way in which we think about this dilemma. Environmentalism is one such issue; as noted earlier, rising environmental consciousness is a hallmark of postmodern values; people are concerned not simply with material security or free will, but with the preservation of the natural environment. This concern is not simply guided by self-preservation—a concern reflected in advocacy of laws or regulations to prevent catastrophe—but is also shaped by the belief that nature itself supercedes human demands and wants. In this logic, individual freedom and collective equality are human concerns that do not take into consideration the world around them. Environmentalism thus takes on many characteristics of a new ideology, though one that does not fit on our matrix of freedom and equality. It may therefore represent a challenge to the way in which political scientists have thought about politics during the modern era.

Resurgent Ideologies: Anarchism and Fascism

Value change in the advanced democracies may also breathe life into older ideologies that have long been marginalized—specifically, anarchism and fascism. Some observers see a potential renewal of anarchism in the ongoing devolutionary and integrationist tendencies in advanced democratic states. Devolutionary tendencies further the spread of small, grassroots organizations focused on local and regional issues. At the same time, integrationist tendencies allow for these myriad groups to link up nationally or internationally. The development of new technologies such as the Internet has contributed to this process; the Internet, lacking hierarchy, borders, a central authority, or even a physical location in some ways seems to capture the anarchic ideal. Over the past few years this fusion of the local and the global, of old ideas with new technology, has resulted in an array of activity against institutions that symbolize the advanced democracies. Protests against the World Trade Organization, the International Monetary Fund, and the World Bank, although often ostensibly centered on those institutions' policies toward less-developed countries, are at the same time critiques of the basic values and institutions of the advanced democracies themselves. Similar, sometimes lethal protests have also emerged against the European Union. These new forms of political activity in many ways reflect and draw from the ideology of anarchism. Viewing states as oppressive structures, anarchism believes that individual freedom and collective equality can be best achieved by eliminating centralized authority and replacing it with a system of cooperation. As states and societies continue to be transformed within the advanced democracies, these changes may pave the way for a reconsideration of anarchist ideas and their call for radical change.[6]

At the same time, however, value change in the advanced democracies may also be fostering a counter-reaction. Whereas some see anarchism as an ideology whose time may finally have come, others are reviving ideas that advocate centralized power and the inherent inequality of people: fascism and other forms of extremism.[7] Over the past decade various groups, ranging from white supremacists to religious cults that embrace violence, have proliferated in all of the advanced democracies. Although the sentiments they express are not new, what is of concern to observers is how widely these groups have spread. According to the Southern Poverty Law Center, in the United States in 2000 there were more than 600 groups in operation that openly advocated hatred toward ethnic groups and other nationalities. Particularly striking about these developments in the United States is the fact that they fly in the face of the assumption that with postmodern values come growing tolerance and a weakening of nationalism and racism. The bombing of the federal office building in Oklahoma City in 1995 shocked Americans in large part because it as the work not of some foreign terrorist from a "backward" country but of an American engaged in terrorism against his own compatriots. Terrorist attacks from outside of the advanced democracies may only add fuel to this movement by rekindling xenophobia.

Similarly, in Europe a number of political parties have gained support for their hostility toward immigration. In Austria, the nationalist Freedom Party joined a coalition government in 1999, much to the dismay of other EU member states. France's National Front criticizes the EU for "destroying nations and opening Europe to Third World immigrants and foreign products." This party controls some local governments and during the 1990s regularly polled around 15 percent of the national vote, and its leader, Jean-Marie Le Pen, came in second place in France's 2002 presidential election. Violence against immigrants has also risen dramatically in recent years; in Germany in 1999 alone more than 10,000 criminal offenses with xenophobic or racist motives were reported.

Extremism has had a profound effect on Japan, too. Most notable is the Aum Shinrikyo cult, which during the 1980s and 1990s attracted thousands of well-educated Japanese through its promise of spiritual enlightenment through its charismatic leader, Shoko Asahara. But Aum Shinrikyo was not only a religious movement; it also espoused anti-Semitism and conspiracy theories, justifying violence as a means to hasten what it saw as the coming Armageddon. In 1995, the year that the cult released poisonous nerve gas in the Tokyo subway system, killing twelve people, it was also busy attempting to construct or purchase chemical, biological, and nuclear weapons. The size, devotion, and apparent power of this group has led many Japanese to question what led so many of their fellow citizens to join such a movement.

In short, many political scientists believe that there are important societal changes under way in the advanced democracies that reflect and reinforce the changes taking place within the state. Whereas some emphasize the emergence of postmodern values, others point to the strengthening of fascist and other extremist views. These seemingly polarized reactions may not be as contradictory as they appear. Dramatic changes within the advanced democracies are disorienting for many who feel that older values, norms, and ways of life are being cast aside. Many feel that they have no say in these changes and no longer can find meaning in their lives. For some, anarchism may offer a vision of a world where everyone can be free and equal. For others, fascism and other forms of extremism offer attractive notions of domination and control. Both of these views share a fusion of radicalism and reaction, a vision of a future utopia and a return to a mythic past. As the advanced democracies confront issues such as integration and devolution, migration and multiculturalism, and environmental and technological change, the old ways of thinking about the world may fail us. In the face of these challenges, fascism and anarchism may offer attractive ways of thinking about how political power can be used, and to what end. Of course, these views may be nothing more than isolated and futile responses to a deepening liberal democratic and economic order. Or, perhaps they are an indication of new ideological battles to come.

ECONOMIC CHANGE

Our discussion so far has asked to what extent postmodernization is changing the power and legitimacy of states and societies. Our last area of interest is that of economic development, and it is in this area that postmodernization is most obvious. Dramatic changes have taken place in the economic structures of the advanced industrialized democracies over the past generation, to such an extent that it may no longer be logical to refer to them as "industrial" at all. At the same time, long-standing assumptions about the role of the state in such areas as the redistribution of income have come under attack, challenging the welfare state. These changes may overturn existing ideas about the proper balance of freedom and equality in the advanced democracies.

Postindustrialism

So far we have considered postmodernization and how it may affect states and societies. In both of these arenas, the evidence and implications of change are largely unclear and open to debate. In the economic realm the advanced democracies have experienced a dramatic shift during the last half-century, a shift from economies based primarily on industry and manufacturing to postindustrial economies. In **postindustrialism**, the majority of people are employed in and the bulk of profits made in the **service sector**—work that involves not the creation of tangible goods, such as cars or computers, but such industries as finance, insurance, real estate, education, retail sales, transportation, communication, high technology, utilities, health care, and business and legal services. Just as modern economies made the transition from agriculture to industry, they are now moving away from their industrial orientation. As the table below indicates, this shift has been occurring across the advanced democracies over the past several decades. In these countries, anywhere from 60 to 75 percent of the population is now employed in the service sector. This shift

EMPLOYMENT BY ECONOMIC SECTOR, 1960–99

	Percentage of Total National Employment in		
	Services	Industry	Agriculture
United States			
1960	58%	33%	9%
1999	75%	22%	3%
Canada			
1960	55%	32%	13%
1999	74%	22%	3%
Japan			
1960	42%	29%	30%
1999	64%	31%	5%
France			
1960	39%	37%	23%
1999	72%	25%	4%

Source: U.S. Bureau of Labor Statistics

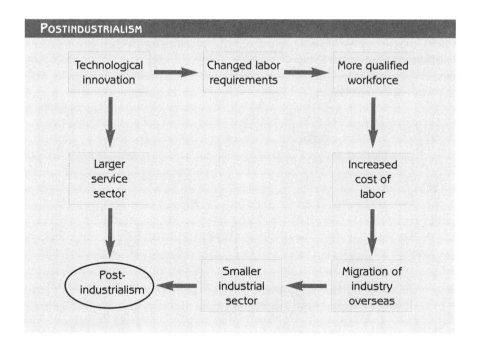

POSTINDUSTRIALISM

Technological innovation → Changed labor requirements → More qualified workforce

Larger service sector

Increased cost of labor

Post-industrialism ← Smaller industrial sector ← Migration of industry overseas

has occurred for a number of reasons. Much industrial production has migrated outside of the advanced democracies in search of lower labor and other costs. Furthermore, technological innovation in the advanced democracies is changing the requirements of labor. Employees are also expected to have higher levels of education than they were forty years ago; whereas in 1960 only 8 percent of Americans had completed college, that figure now stands at nearly 25 percent.

Postindustrialism in some ways reflects and may reinforce the political and social trends discussed earlier. The emergence of an information-based economy, for example, may contribute to a greater devolution of power within the economy, as firms become less hierarchical and more decentralized, less physical and more "virtual," less national and more international, with much greater individual autonomy and flexibility. This shift, in turn, may well reinforce postmodern values that question hierarchical structures and authority. However, for those without specialized training and education, postindustrialism may mean less freedom and equality; the growing importance of knowledge could marginalize these workers, creating an educational underclass whose prospects for upward mobility are limited. The resulting frustration among such workers could in turn inspire reactionary or radical politics.

But as always, we should be careful not to overestimate postindustrialism's impact. Although it is clear that the advanced democracies are moving toward economies centered more on information and less on industry, this does not automatically mean that the old economic system will necessarily disappear. The rise of the Internet does not mean that "bricks and mortar" businesses are doomed; the recent demise of many dot-com businesses only underscores this argument. Nor does it mean that hierarchical forms of organization have outlived their usefulness. Finally, the elimination of industrial jobs does not automatically mean that those without education will no longer find work—only that the nature of unskilled labor will change, bringing different advantages and problems. As these transformations proceed, states will be called on to manage the marketplace in new ways, reconciling freedom and equality in the face of social and economic change.

The End of the Welfare State?

This leads us to the final aspect of economic transformation in the advanced democracies: the future of the welfare state. As we discussed in Chapter 4, for the past half-century a defining element of the advanced democracies has been the development of social expenditures as a way to reduce inequality and provide public goods through such programs as national pension plans, public health care, education, and unemployment benefits—programs collectively known as the "welfare state." There can be no doubt that the welfare state has provided a wide array of benefits among the advanced democracies: extreme poverty has been reduced, infant mortality has declined and life expectancy has increased, literacy and education have improved dramatically. Social expenditures have played an important role in socializing risk—that is, making the uncertainties that come with work, health, and age a community, rather than an individual, concern.

But the welfare state has brought costs and controversies. First, although social expenditures have been lauded as an essential part of a humane society, they are increasingly expensive. During the early part of the twentieth century, social expenditures typically amounted to around 10–15 percent of the advanced democracies' GDPs. By the late 1990s, however, in most of these countries social expenditures in such areas as unemployment, pensions, and health care consumed more than one-third of GDP. This increased spending has required higher taxes: in western Europe, where in 1965 taxes consumed around one-quarter of GDP, they

DEMOGRAPHICS AND THE FUTURE OF THE WELFARE STATE

Concerns about the future viability of social expenditures are compounded by the demographic transformation of the advanced democracies. One benefit of economic development in these countries has been the dramatic increase in life expectancy. In 1900, residents of these countries had an average life expectancy of around 40–50 years, whereas by 2000 they could expect to live 70–80 years. Life expectancy in the advanced democracies is expected to increase to over 80 years by 2050. At the same time, people in the advanced democracies are having fewer children. As people live longer and fewer children are born, national populations will age, with an ever larger number of citizens seeking to draw on such things as retirement and health-care benefits. At the same time, there will be fewer and fewer young workers to tax in order to support the elderly. In short, welfare states will be unable to afford the level of benefits they currently provide.

This "graying" of the advanced democracies looms large, and there are no easy solutions. Governments will confront some unpleasant options, such as increasing the retirement age. But few democratically elected governments are eager to tackle such reforms, especially since they risk raising the ire of senior citizens.

Another option for countries may be to increase the number of younger workers by encouraging migration, thus offsetting an aging population and filling shortages in labor. The United Nations estimates that in order to prevent population decline in Japan, for example, the country will need to accept nearly 400,000 immigrants a year between 2005 and 2050. As a result, by 2050 nearly 20 percent of the Japanese population would be made up of migrants and their descendents—a huge demographic shift in a country noted for its ethnic homogeneity. Such migration may solve economic problems, but it will undoubtedly raise new questions about citizenship and nationality in many of the advanced democracies.

migration into Japan

now average more than half of GDP. Even in more liberal or mercantilist countries such as the United States and Japan, public expenditures have risen dramatically over the past half-century, requiring new taxes or government borrowing. This trend is likely to be magnified by demographic changes within the advanced democracies, particularly as their populations age. Some fear that if such expenditures continue to rise, businesses and labor will be inclined to leave high-tax countries for places where taxes are lower. Sweden's high taxes, for example, have prompted some large businesses and young professionals to move to other advanced democracies;

in 1999, the Swedish telecommunications firm Ericsson, known world-wide for its cellular phones, relocated its headquarters to London.

There is a widespread recognition that the welfare state will have to be reformed in the future, but how, and how much, is hotly contested.[9] Some favor the increased privatization of welfare—allowing, for example, the investment of public retirement funds into stocks and bonds. Such investments might produce a higher rate of return, but they also pose the danger that an economic downturn would wipe out not only personal investments but public retirement funds as well. Other plans have included limiting benefits for unemployment, or shifting the costs of education and health care onto those who use them. None of these solutions is easy; although they may increase one's freedom to make choices regarding one's own personal welfare, the trade-off may be greater risk and inequality as the basic social safety net contracts.

In Sum: The Advanced Democracies in Transformation

The advanced democracies are in many ways unique, both in their institutions and in the challenges they face. Although there is variation among them, these countries are characterized by liberal democracy and high levels of economic development. They represent in many ways what we consider to be modern social, economic, and political life. Yet none of these institutions is set in stone. State sovereignty is confronted by the twin dynamics of devolution and integration, transferring power above and below. Social norms are similarly in flux, as postmodern values challenge the status quo and anarchist and fascist ideologies reappear. Modern industrial structures have given way to a new, information-based economy that empowers some and dislocates others, and that calls into question how countries provide public goods to their people. All of these factors challenge the existing balance of freedom and equality.

In the coming chapters we will turn to these same issues as they exist outside the advanced democracies. Communist and postcommunist, less-developed and newly industrializing countries all confront issues of state sovereignty, social values and ideology, industrialization, and the welfare of the public. What unique challenges each group faces in these areas will be the focus of the next two chapters. Will these countries eventually join the ranks of the advanced democracies in a convergence of political, economic, and social institutions around the globe? This question will remain with us through the next two chapters and culminate in our final discussion of the prospects for globalization.

NOTES

1 For details on the historical development of the EU see *The Community of Europe : A History of European Integration since 1945* (New York: Addison-Wesley, 1995).

2 For more details see Walter Mattli, *The Logic of Regional Integration: Europe and Beyond* (Cambridge: Cambridge University Press, 1999).

3 For a broader discussion of devolution see Larry Diamond with Svetlana Tsalik, "Size and Democracy: The Case for Decentralization," in Larry Diamond, ed., *Developing Democracy: Toward Consolidation* (Baltimore: Johns Hopkins Press, 1999).

4 Robert Cooper, *The Postmodern State and the World Order* (London: Demos, 1996).

5 For a further discussion see Ronald Inglehart and Marita Carballo, "Does Latin America Exist? (And Is There a Confucian Culture?): A Global Analysis of Cross-Cultural Differences," *PS: Political Science and Politics* 30, no. 1 (March 1997): 34–46.

6 Jeff Ferrel, *Tearing Down the Streets: Adventures in Urban Anarchy* (New York, Palgrave, 2001).

7 See Peter H. Merkl and Leonard Weinberg, eds., *The Revival of Right-Wing Extremism* (Portland: Frank Cass, 2002).

8 The classic study on this topic is Daniel Bell, *The Coming of Post-Industrial Society* (New York: Basic Books, 1999).

9 See Evelyne Huber and John D. Stephens, *Development and Crisis of the Welfare State* (Chicago: University of Chicago Press, 2001).

8 COMMUNISM AND POSTCOMMUNISM

The advanced industrialized democracies we studied in Chapter 7 have become the wealthiest and most powerful countries in the world. In spite of this success, however, these countries continue to struggle with a number of issues, among them economic inequality—both within their societies as well as between themselves and the rest of the world. Their dilemma is no small matter: Must freedom always come at the expense of equality? Particularly with the rise of economic and political liberalism and the retreat of the welfare state, it would seem that the answer is yes. But throughout history humans have struggled to find a way in which equality might be secured, providing benefits for all.

This concern goes to the heart of communism in both theory and practice, for it seeks to create a system that limits individual freedoms in order to divide wealth in an equitable manner. This vision of a world without economic distinctions drove the formation of communist regimes around the world, eventually bringing hundreds of millions of people under its banner.

Yet in spite of the lofty ideals of communist thought, and in spite of its dramatic emergence as a political regime in the early part of the twentieth century, within less than a century the majority of the world's communist regimes began to unravel. Why? What brought the quest for collective equality to a dead end? Was there a mistranslation of theory into practice, or were the theories themselves inherently suspect, unable to be realized in any practical manner?

In this chapter we will look at how communism attempted to reconcile freedom and equality and why communist systems in practice have largely failed at that endeavor. We will begin by looking at the original theories of modern communism, particularly the ideas of Karl Marx. From there we will investigate how communism was changed from theory into practice, as communist regimes were built around the world, most notably in the Soviet Union, eastern Europe, and China. How did these systems seek to create equality and bring Marx's ideas to life? Our answer will discuss the nature of government, regime, and state under communism. Of equal importance for our purposes is the nature of communist political economies. Because markets and property were both viewed as sources of inequality, communist regimes sought to replace them with a state-directed economic order. Society, too, was refashioned to conform to communist theory, although as in the areas of politics and economics, the changes were often incomplete and the effects unintended.

After examining the dynamics of communism in practice, we will study its demise. What were its shortcomings, and why could these limitations not be corrected? Why did attempts at reform in the Soviet Union and eastern Europe turn into a rout? And what lessons can we draw from this when we look at the only major communist country to survive, China? Our look at the downfall of communism will take us to our last issue: What comes after it? How are political, economic, and societal institutions rebuilt after communism? What are the obstacles in developing democracy and market economies where both have been long absent or never existed at

COMMUNIST REGIMES IN THE 1980s

Europe	Asia	Africa and the Middle East	Latin America
Albania	Afghanistan	Angola	Cuba*
Bulgaria	Cambodia	Benin	
Czechoslovakia	China*	Ethiopia	
East Germany	Laos*	Mozambique	
Hungary	Mongolia	South Yemen	
Poland	North Korea*		
Romania	Vietnam*		
Soviet Union			
Yugoslavia			

*Still communist as of 2003.

all? And where does this leave these countries in terms of reconciling freedom and equality, when both may now be uncertain? In addressing each
of these questions, we will uncover the enormous scope and vision of communist thought, the tremendous challenges of putting it into practice, the
serious flaws and limitations that this implementation entailed, and the
daunting work of building new political, social, and economic institutions
from the rubble of communism's demise.

COMMUNISM, EQUALITY, AND THE NATURE OF HUMAN RELATIONS

Communism is a set of ideas that view political, social, and economic
institutions in a fundamentally different manner than most political
thought, essentially challenging much of what we have studied so far.
Because communism views the world and human relations in such a dramatically different way, we must first understand the logic behind these
ideas before we can understand how it functioned in practice.

In modern politics, communism as a political theory and ideology can
be traced primarily to the German philosopher Karl Marx (1818–83).[1]
Marx began with a rather straightforward observation: human beings are
able to create objects of value by investing their own time and labor into
their creation. That "surplus value of labor" stays with the object, making
it useful to anyone, not just the maker. It is this ability to create objects
with their own innate value that sets people apart from other animals, but
it also inevitably leads to economic injustice, Marx concluded. He argued
that as human beings develop their knowledge and technological skills, an
opportunity is created for those with political power to essentially extract
the surplus value from others, enriching themselves while impoverishing
others. In other words, once human beings learned how to produce things
of value, others found that they could gain these things at little cost to
themselves simply by using coercion to acquire them.

For Marx, then, the world was properly understood in economic terms;
all human action flowed from the relations between the haves and the
have-nots. Specifically, Marx spoke of human history and human relations
as being based on what he termed the "base" and the "superstructure."
The base is the system of economic production, including the level of technology (what he called the "means of production") and the kind of class
relations that exist as a result (the "relations of production"). Resting on
the base is the superstructure, which represents all human institutions—
politics and the state, national identity and culture, religion and gender,

etc. Marx viewed this superstructure as a system of institutions created essentially to justify and perpetuate the existing order. People consequently suffer from "false consciousness," meaning that they believe they understand the true nature of the world around them, but in reality they are deluded by the superstructure imposed by capitalism.

This notion of false consciousness can be illustrated with some examples. States were seen by Marx as purely coercive mechanisms, monopolizing force not in order to generate security, as Max Weber discussed, but

TERMS IN MARXIST THEORY

Surplus value of labor: the value invested in any man-made good that can be used by another individual. Exploitation results when one person or group extracts the surplus value from another.

Base: the economic system of a society, made up of technology (the means of production) and class relations between people (the relations of production).

Superstructure: All non-economic relations in a society (i.e., religion, culture, national identity, etc.). These ideas and values derive from the base and serve to legitimize the current system of exploitation.

False consciousness: Failure to understand the nature of one's exploitation; essentially "buying in" to the superstructure.

Dialectical materialism: Process of historical change that is not evolutionary but revolutionary. The existing base and superstructure (thesis) would come into conflict with new technological innovations, generating growing tensions between the exploiters and the exploited (antithesis). This would culminate in revolution, overthrowing the old base and superstructure.

Dictatorship of the proletariat: Temporary period after capitalism has been overthrown during which vestiges of the old base and superstructure are eradicated.

Proletariat: The working class.

Bourgeoisie: The property-owning class.

Communism: According to Marxists, the final stage of history once capitalism is overthrown and the dictatorship of proletariat destroys its remaining vestiges. In communism, state and politics would disappear, and society and the economy would be based on equality and cooperation.

Vanguard of the proletariat: Lenin's argument that an elite communist party would have to carry out revolution, because due to false consciousness, historical conditions would not automatically lead to capitalism's demise.

definitions

States to defend the haves against the have-notes and to allow the elites of various countries to wage war against each other in the ongoing pursuit of wealth. National and ethnic identity, citizenship, and patriotism, too, are simply mechanisms to divert people's attention from the real sources of their problems, by instilling false pride in the nation and the state and by fostering animosity toward other groups. This animosity in turn blinds people to the sources of their true oppression; their fears are focused on strangers when the true danger is the economic elites in their midst. Men fight wars and die, believing they are doing so for "king and country" when in reality they are fighting only for the economic benefit of those few who control the state. Democracy, too, was rejected by Marx and most other communists as a system created to delude the exploited into thinking they have a say in their political destiny, when in fact those with wealth actually control politics.

REVOLUTION AND THE "TRIUMPH" OF COMMUNISM

Having dissected what he saw as the nature of politics, economics, and society, Marx used this framework to understand historical development and to anticipate the future of capitalism. In many ways Marx saw himself as a social scientist—someone who wanted not to forge revolution but to explain and predict human development. As such, Marx concluded that human history developed in specific phases, each driven by the particular nature of exploitation at that point in time. In each historical case, he argued, the specific form of exploitation was built around the existing level of technology. For example, in early agrarian societies feudalism was the dominant political and economic order; the rudimentary technology available tied individuals to the land so that their labor could be exploited by the aristocracy. But although such relations may appear stable, technology itself is always dynamic. Marx recognized this and asserted that the inevitable changes in technology would increase tensions between rulers and ruled, as new forms of technological development empowered new groups who clashed with the base and the superstructure. Again, in the case of feudalism, emerging technology empowered an early capitalist, property-owning middle class or bourgeoisie, whose members sought political power for themselves and the remaking of the economic and social order in a way that better fit capitalist ambitions.

Eventually, this tension would lead to revolution; those in power would be overthrown and a new ruling class would come to power. In each case, change would be sudden and violent and would pave the way for a new economic base and superstructure. This entire process is termed "dialectical materialism." The dialectic portrays history as a struggle between the existing order (the thesis), the challenge to that order (the antithesis), and the resulting historical change (the synthesis). Revolutions inevitably come about as a result of this tension between economic classes.

On the basis of these ideas, Marx concluded that capitalist democracy, which had displaced feudalism, would itself eventually be overthrown by its own internal flaws. As capitalism developed, competition between firms would intensify. The working class, or "proletariat," would find itself on the losing end of this process, as firms introduced more and more technology to reduce the number of workers and as unprofitable businesses began to go bankrupt in the face of intense competition. The bourgeoisie would grow smaller and smaller as the wealth of society became concentrated in fewer and fewer hands, and large monopolies would come to dominate the economy. The wages of the working class would decline in the face of increased competition (an oversupply of labor as technology reduces the number of workers needed) and the ranks of the unemployed would swell.

Alienated and driven to desperation by these conditions, eventually the proletariat would "gain consciousness" by realizing the true source of their poverty and rise up in rebellion. They would carry out a revolution, seizing control of the state and the economy. Marx saw this process not sim-

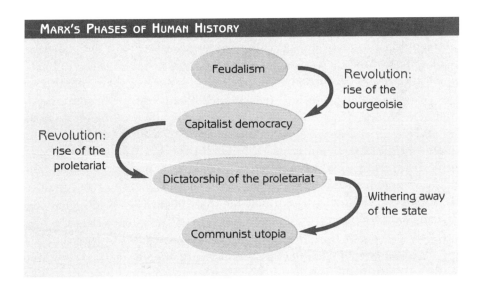

MARX'S PHASES OF HUMAN HISTORY

Feudalism

Revolution: rise of the bourgeoisie

Capitalist democracy

Revolution: rise of the proletariat

Dictatorship of the proletariat

Withering away of the state

Communist utopia

ply as a national phenomenon, but as an international one. When the conditions were right, he hypothesized, revolution would spread among all the capitalist countries, sweeping away this unjust order in a relatively short period of time.

Once world revolution had taken place, Marx foresaw, there would be a temporary "dictatorship of the proletariat," during which the last vestiges of capitalism, particularly the old remnants of the superstructure, would be swept away. All economic activity and property would be shared by the people, creating pure freedom and equality. After the institutions of capitalism had been decisively eliminated, the institutions of the state itself would begin to "wither away." If this sounds like an odd result, recall that according to Marx the state exists only to reinforce inequality; thus, once inequality had been solved the state would no longer have a purpose. There would be no more need for laws or police, since all people would share equally in the fruits of labor. No longer would there be a need for armies or flags, since people would be united in equality rather than blinded by the false consciousness of nationalism. People would live in a stateless world, and history, which in Marx's view had been fundamentally drive by exploitation and class struggle, would essentially come to an end. Only then could one actually speak of "communism"—which is why communist parties usually speak of their own countries as being "socialist" since they are still controlled by the state.

PUTTING COMMUNISM INTO PRACTICE

Communism thus provides an entire worldview, explaining the course of human history and the inevitable ascent into utopia as the product of economic interaction. As one might imagine, such a sweeping theory has proven extremely convincing for many people, including those who sought to put Marx's ideas into practice. Two of the most notable followers of Marx's ideas were Vladimir Ulyanov, more commonly known as Lenin, and Mao Zedong, who came to lead communist revolutions in Russia (1917) and China (1949), respectively. Yet although both Mao and Lenin were inspired by Marx, they departed from his ideas by seeking to carry out revolution in two countries that were weakly industrialized and far from being capitalist. (Marx had argued that revolution would occur only where and when capitalism was most advanced, and thus most prone to collapse.) But Lenin and Mao had believed that revolution could be carried out in less-advanced countries if leaders constructed a "vanguard of the proletariat"—Lenin's term for a small revolutionary movement that could seize power on behalf of the people.[2]

This departure from Marx's views meant that in reality communism spread where the level of economic development was relatively low—exactly the opposite of what Marx predicted. Whereas communism made no headway in the developed countries, it continued to spread in much of the less-developed world, often with the backing of the Soviet Union and

IMPORTANT FIGURES IN COMMUNISM

Karl Marx (1818–83) First philosopher to systematically construct a theory explaining why capitalism would fail and be replaced by communism; father of modern communist thought.

Lenin (Vladimir Ulyanov) (1870–1924) Applied Marxist thought to Russia, leading successful revolution in 1917; modified Marxist ideas by arguing that revolution would occur not in most developed societies, but rather in struggling countries such as Russia.

Stalin (Josef Dzhugashvili) (1879–1953) Succeeded Lenin as leader of the Soviet Union; embarked on rapid industrialization of the country, modifying Marxism to argue that socialism could be built in a single country; extended communism to eastern Europe after World War II; denounced by Nikita Khrushchev in 1956 for his use of a personality cult and terror.

Mao Zedong (1883–1976) Led Chinese Communist Party and fought against Chinese rivals and Japanese occupiers during World War II; modified communism to focus on peasantry instead of working class, given primarily agrarian nature of China; unleashed Cultural Revolution in 1966 to weaken party and increase his own power.

Fidel Castro (1926–   ) Led Cuban revolution in 1959 and defended the communist system against anticommunist forces and U.S. opposition; continues to defend Cuban socialism in spite of the collapse of the Soviet Union and other Communist regimes in eastern Europe.

Deng Xiaoping (1905–1997) Fought with Mao Zedong against Chinese nationalists and Japanese invaders during World War II; named general secretary of the Chinese Communist Party in 1956; stripped of all posts during the Cultural Revolution, but emerged as country's leader after death of Mao; pursued economic liberalization in 1980s and supported repression of Tiananmen Square protests.

Mikhail Gorbachev (1931–   ) Made general secretary of the Communist Party of the Soviet Union in 1985; initiated twin policies of perestroika (economic restructuring) and glasnost (political liberalization), which eventually led to increasing discord within the country and a failed coup attempt by hard-line communists who opposed further reform; the resulting dissolution of the Soviet Union left Gorbachev without a country to lead.

China. By the 1980s communist regimes accounted for approximately one-third of the world's population.

Over the first half of the twentieth century, communism expanded by leaps and bounds, striking fear among the capitalist states. Although it took hold largely in less-developed countries or where it had been imposed by military might (such as in eastern Europe after World War II), people in noncommunist countries feared that they would be next. Yet at the same time, the leaders of these communist countries faced a common dilemma: how exactly did one go about building communism? Marx had left no blueprint for that task. Indeed, many devout communists expected in 1917 that world revolution was just around the corner; they did not expect to have to confront the day-to-day aspects of political power. In 1917 the revolutionaries who created the Soviet Union literally waited by the telegraph, expecting word of new revolutions in Germany, France, and the United States. But the world revolution did not come, leaving communist leaders with the daunting task of building a new state, society, and economy that would pave the way for true global equality in a distant communist future.

Politics and the State under Communism

In part because Marx provided no specific outline for how communism would be built, the systems that were created varied widely, shaped by domestic economic and political conditions, historical context, cultural factors, and the ideas and authority of those in power. But beyond these differences they share a basic set of institutions, first developed in the Soviet Union after 1917, to control and transform human activity and generate collective equality as a result. Because of the desire to so fundamentally reshape human relations, communist states have accrued a high level of autonomy and capacity; their authoritarian regimes have at times become totalitarian in their desire to transform virtually all basic human institutions, from work to prayer to gender to art.

The task of this transformation was entrusted to the communist elite who came to direct and staff the state.[3] At its apex, political power rests within the communist party, a relatively small "vanguard" organization (typically comprising less than 10 percent of the population) whose leading role in the country is typically written directly into the constitution—meaning that there is no constitutional way to remove the party from power. The party and the communist regime are a central part of the communist state. Since the communist party embodies what it sees as the "correct" view of human history and future relations, alternative organizations and

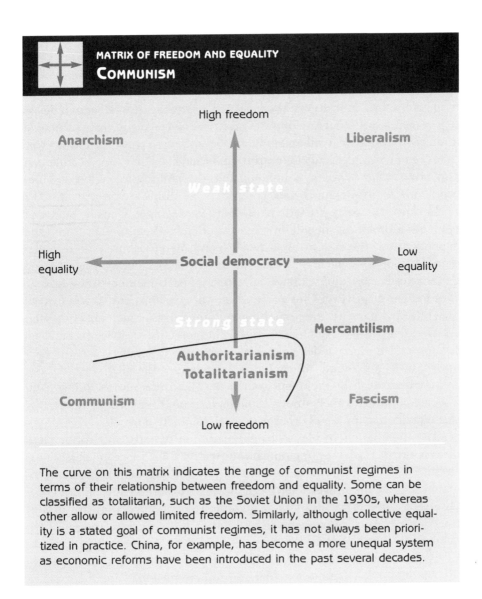

MATRIX OF FREEDOM AND EQUALITY
COMMUNISM

High freedom

Anarchism

Liberalism

Weak state

High
equality

Social democracy

Low
equality

Strong state

Mercantilism

Authoritarianism
Totalitarianism

Communism

Fascism

Low freedom

The curve on this matrix indicates the range of communist regimes in terms of their relationship between freedom and equality. Some can be classified as totalitarian, such as the Soviet Union in the 1930s, whereas other allow or allowed limited freedom. Similarly, although collective equality is a stated goal of communist regimes, it has not always been prioritized in practice. China, for example, has become a more unequal system as economic reforms have been introduced in the past several decades.

ideologies are seen as hostile to communism, products of the capitalist superstructure to be repressed and destroyed.

But as we discussed in Chapter 5, no system of authoritarian rule can survive through the threat of force alone. Communist parties maintain control over society not only through repression, but also by carefully allocating power throughout the country's various political, social, and economic institutions—a thorough form of cooptation. This cooptation can be seen clearly in the **nomenklatura**, politically sensitive or influential jobs in the state, society, or the economy that are staffed by people chosen or approved by the communist party. The *nomenklatura* encompasses a wide range of important positions: the head of a university, the editor of a newspaper, a military officer, a film director. Not surprisingly, party approval often requires party membership, making joining the party the easiest way to prove one's loyalty and rise up the career ladder. Party membership can also bring other benefits: better housing, the ability to travel abroad, or access to scarce consumer goods.

In short, the party uses the *nomenklatura* system as a means to co-opt talented or ambitious people in society and make them benefit from (and dependent on) the system. As a result, party membership is often driven more by opportunism than by idealism; many join so that they can pursue certain careers or simply gain the benefits that party membership will buy.[4] This system of privileges for party elites works against the Marxist quest for collective equality, since many party elites live better (sometimes far better) than the average citizen. But by and large these divisions between the top and bottom under communism are much smaller than the economic divisions found in capitalist economies. Equality, even if not achieved to the full extent envisioned by Marx, was and is still greater under communism than under capitalism, though one could retort that this equality means simply that everyone is equally poor.

The dominant role played by the communist party and the *nomenklatura* creates a power relationship different from those in democratic and many other authoritarian systems. Power, rather than being centered within the state and government, rests within the party. For example, when observers refer to the "leader" of a communist country, they are usually referring not to a government official but to the general secretary of the communist party. Indeed, top party leaders often do not hold any important position within the state. Because of the dominance of the communist party over the state, the actual government positions are of secondary importance. Thus, the term **"party-state"** is often used in place of "government" when referring to communist countries, indicating that power flows from the party directly to the state, bypassing governmental structures. One result of such a system is that leadership turnover takes place not through elections, but rather through power struggles among the party elite.

As for the actual structure of the government and the state, these by and large resemble political systems we see elsewhere in the world, typically with a prime minister or president, a parliament, a judiciary, and local government—all encompassing positions that are part of the *nomenklatura* and thus staffed by party members. Although such trappings of democracy, such as parliamentary elections, typically exist, electoral candidates are almost exclusively communist party members; there is no real competition. Moreover, parliaments and other organs of power are little more than "rubber-stamp" institutions, approving of decisions sent down the party hierarchy.

As for the party itself, in many ways it intentionally mirrors the state, with a general secretary serving as chief executive, and a **Politburo** (short for "Political Bureau") and **Central Committee** acting as a kind of cabinet and legislature, respectively, shaping national policy and confirming the decisions of the party leadership. Below the Central Committee various other bodies extend all the way down to individual places of work or residence, where party members are organized into basic party organizations or "cells." These cells are ostensibly intended to represent the inter-

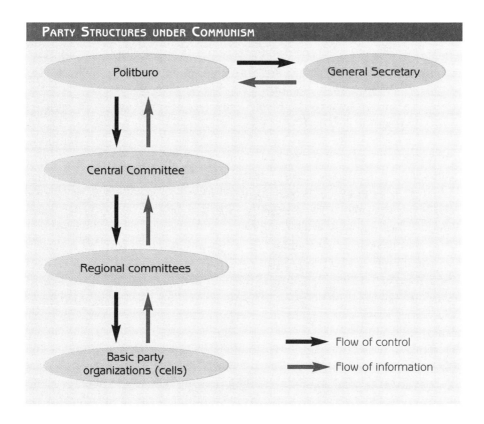

ests of the people, but they are primarily mechanisms by which the party can closely monitor the population. Traditionally the party holds a congress every few years at which its leadership is elected by delegates sent from the party cells—though these elections tend to be little more than confirmations of those already in power. Those who come to power within the party typically do so through informal alliances within the party or even through violent elimination of rivals.

While the party and its *nomenklatura* control key organizations, communist ideology shapes policy and seeks to legitimize authoritarian control. Based fundamentally on the theories of Marx as adapted by Lenin, communist ideology focuses on the elimination of inequality and the promotion of economic development. Because of the expansive nature of communist ideology and its promise of a future utopia, many have argued that it is in fact a secular religion, requiring unquestioning faith in a set of beliefs and sacrifice for a future reward, and boasting its own collection of saints, martyrs, and devils. In this view, adherents venerate charismatic leaders who served as prophets of communism, such as Lenin, Mao, Josef Stalin, and Fidel Castro. Many charismatic communist leaders have reinforced their position through elaborate personality cults (discussed in Chapter 5).

The quest for and exercise of this monopoly on power, as expressed through the *nomenklatura* and the deep penetration of the state and society by the party, down to the most basic level of home and work, proved to be dangerous and lethal. In the first decades of communist rule in the Soviet Union, China, and eastern Europe, terror was used to eliminate opposition and to maintain control. Tens of millions perished in such campaigns, especially in the Soviet Union under Stalin in the 1930s and in China under Mao in the 1960s and 1970s. Under the rule of Stalin, many people were purged from within the Soviet Communist Party itself and executed for imaginary crimes. These were not cases of mistaken punishment: Stalin used terror and victimized symbolic "criminals" as a way to cow the Communist Party and the population as a whole.[5] Similarly, in China Mao unleashed the Cultural Revolution in the late 1960s to encouraging the public (students, in particular) to attack any institution or individual that was seen as either a remnant of precommunist China or someone who had lost his or her revolutionary zeal. Mao's targets included the party-state, which he believed had grown conservative over time, and was restricting his power. During the next decade, not only did countless Chinese die (the total number killed remains unknown and may be in the millions), but books were burned, art destroyed, and cultural relics demolished—all for the crime of being "reactionary."[6]

COMMUNIST POLITICAL ECONOMY

If the communist party's singular quest for power led in the cases of Stalin and Mao to its gross abuse, the centralization of economic power similarly created problems that Marxist theory did not anticipate. Communist political economic systems share a set of institutions fundamentally different from liberal, mercantilist, or social democratic alternatives. Unlike these other forms of political economy, where the state exercises various degrees of influence over markets and property, under communist systems both markets and property are essentially absorbed by the state.[7] Certainly private ownership of personal possessions unrelated to economic production is allowed under communism, and in some countries limited forms of private property and market forces continued or continue to exist. However, most of the means of production—factories, land, homes—are nationalized by the state on behalf of the people as a whole. With the means of production held by the state, many of the typical aspects of capitalism that we take for granted—individual profit, unemployment, competition between firms, bankruptcy—are eliminated. Individuals lose their right to control property, including their own labor; the party-state makes the decisions about how these resources should be used. A communist economy functions in essence as a single large firm, with the public as employees of that firm. In turn, communist leaders can redirect national wealth toward the goal of collective equality, through such mechanisms as social expenditures. As communist systems take control over private property, in return they establish a universal system of public education, health care, retirement, and other benefits.

Alongside the elimination of private property, communist systems also eliminate the market mechanism, believing that it is incapable of equitably distributing wealth. To people who live under capitalism, this elimination of the market would seem to be impossible. Markets have their own logic and spontaneity in valuing and distributing resources—how can one replace them? Communist countries by and large choose to replace the market with the state bureaucracy, which explicitly allocates resources by planning what should be produced and in what amounts, setting the final prices of these goods, and deciding where they should be sold. This system has come to be known as **central planning**.

As one might imagine, planning an entire economy is an extremely difficult task. A market economy responds to the relationship of supply and demand in a spontaneous and decentralized manner. If there is a market for something, a producer will often come along to fill that need in the hope of making a profit. In a centrally planned economy, however, bureaucrats must centralize these decisions. How much steel should be produced this year? How many women's size eight shoes? How many apartments? Determining needs for each and every good produced in a country requires huge amounts of information. Equally difficult is determining the role of the factories themselves. Which factories should be in charge of producing what, from where should they should get their resources, and how should these final goods be distributed?

As communist planners have found, matching up all these inputs and outputs is overwhelming. There are simply too many things to plan—in the Soviet Union, for instance, some 40,000–50,000 items—and too many unforeseen outcomes, such as a factory's failing to deliver its full output, or a change in demand. Since most entities in an economy are interdependent, small problems can have a huge effect on the entire plan. A miscalculation resulting in the underproduction of steel, for example, would have disastrous effects on all those goods dependent on steel, some of which would themselves be components in other finished goods—such as nails or bolts. Any mistakes or changes in the central plan, and production begins to go out of balance.

IN FOCUS
COMMUNIST POLITICAL ECONOMY

- Markets and property are wholly absorbed by the state.

- Central planning replaces the market mechanism.

- Individual property rights, individual profit, unemployment, competition between firms, and bankruptcy are all virtually eliminated.

- Most of the nation's means of production are nationalized.

- The economy functions in essence as a single large firm, with the public as its sole employees.

- The state provides extensive public goods and social services, including universal systems of public education, health care, and retirement.

Another problem encountered in centrally planned economies is the lack of worker incentives. Factories and farms are unconcerned about the quality of their goods, since central planners simply indicate a numerical quota they have to fulfill. Workers do not have to fear losing their jobs, nor factories going out of business as a result of shoddy work, since under communism employment is guaranteed and firms, being owned by the state, cannot go bankrupt. For example, one scholar noted that shortages in certain kinds of small pipe in the Soviet Union could be traced to the fact that the factories producing these pipes were evaluated on how many tons of pipe they produced. As a result, they concentrated on producing large-scale and heavy-diameter pipe so they could most easily meet their quota. This not only wasted metal but also created shortages in the supply of smaller-diameter pipes.

In a market system, such substandard producers would be driven out of business by a competitor. In a communist system, however, there is no competition. As a result, poor work is not punished, and exceptional work is not rewarded, since this would lead to economic inequality., The lack of rewards stifles innovation and motivation. This explains in part why all communist countries eventually have fallen behind economically. In the absence of competition and incentives, innovation and efficiency disappear, leaving these systems to stagnate.

SOCIETAL INSTITUTIONS UNDER COMMUNISM

In addition to re-engineering politics and economics in order to eliminate the inequality and exploitation associated with capitalist systems, communist parties also seek to reorder human relations, hoping to sweep away the old superstructure held responsible for generating false consciousness. Individual freedoms are also repressed, since they are viewed as an expression of false consciousness and therefore a threat to communist goals.

One example of this hostility can be seen in communism's view of religion. Marx is known for his oft-cited statement that "religion is the opiate of the masses," meaning that it is part of the superstructure that serves to perpetuate inequality and legitimize suffering in return for rewards in some afterlife. As a result, in most communist countries religion is strongly suppressed. In the Soviet Union most places of worship were closed, converted to other uses, or torn down. In China during the Cultural Revolution most temples and other religious shrines were destroyed. Even where religion is tolerated to a greater extent, it is still harassed or directly controlled by the communist party. As a result, in most countries traditional religious institutions are very weak.

Traditional gender relations are also seen by Marxists as a function of capitalism; specifically, gender relations are seen to be class relations in microcosm. Men exploit women through the family structure just as the proletariat exploits the bourgeoisie, and sexual morality serves as a means to perpetuate this gender inequality. Communism envisions complete economic, social, and political equality between men and women. Even the repressive institution of marriage, like the state, will fade away, replaced by what Marx called "an openly legalized community of free love."[8] This was quite a radical view of gender relations for its time—Marx was writing in the late nineteenth century, when women did not even have the right to vote anywhere in the world.

In spite of Marxist ideals, gender relations have only partially changed under communist rule. In most communist countries women are given much greater opportunities than they experienced previously. To promote industrialization, communist parties have encouraged women to enter the workforce and to increase their education. Most countries have also enacted liberal divorce and abortion laws and provided social benefits such as state-run child care. These changes increased opportunities for women, such that by the 1970s in communist countries such as Czechoslovakia and East Germany, 75 percent of women worked outside the home.[9]

In spite of these changes, however, women's traditional roles as house-keepers and mothers have not changed. The "new socialist woman" has not been complemented by a "new socialist man"; traditional patterns of sexism persist and women have found themselves burdened by the double duty of work inside and outside the home. In addition, while many women work in important occupations, few have risen to positions of any signifi-cant political or economic power. The top ranks of the party membership, the state, and the economy remain dominated by men. In most countries the Politburo is dominated entirely by men, and not a single woman has ever served as party general secretary in a communist country. Finally, many communist countries remain very sexually conservative, a far cry from the society of "free love" that Marx envisioned.

SOCIETAL INSTITUTIONS UNDER COMMUNISM

Ideal	Reality
Religion, the "opiate of the masses," will disappear.	Religion was suppressed but not eliminated.
Men and women will be economically, socially, and politically equal.	Opportunities for women increased, but women were still expected to fulfill traditional duties in the home.
Repressive institutions such as marriage will be replaced by "an openly legalized system of free love."	Many communist countries remained sexually very conservative.
Nationalism, exposed as part of the elite's "divide and conquer" strategy, will be eliminated.	Though discouraged from doing so, people clung to old national and ethnic identities.

A final aspect of society that communism seeks to change is national identity. As we discussed earlier, as part of the superstructure nationalism is seen as a mechanism by which the ruling elites pit the working classes of different countries against one another in a tactic of divide and rule. With the advent of world communist revolution, such divisions were expected to disappear, to be replaced by equality and harmony among all peoples. Nations, perhaps even different ethnicities, would eventually vanish.

As a result, communist parties tend to reject any overt expressions of nationalism, though such identities often lurk beneath the surface. For example, encompassed within the vast Soviet Union were many ethnic groups, although the Communist Party tended to be dominated by Russians, who made up the single largest ethnic group in the country. Many citizens of non-Russian ethnic groups resented this Russian domination, a resentment further aggravated by Russian migration into traditionally non-Russian parts of the Soviet Union and by the predominance of Russian language and culture in the country as a whole. Many eastern Europeans also viewed communist rule as little more than Russian imperialism; their national identity was therefore sharpened, not erased. This simmering nationalism played an important role in the fall of communism in eastern Europe and the Soviet Union.

THE COLLAPSE OF COMMUNISM

In retrospect it may seem obvious that communism was bound to fail, and yet even in the mid-1980s few expected that it would happen anytime soon. Two factors played an important role in bringing about its sudden decline.

The first was the re-emergence of Cold War struggles between the Soviet Union and the United States. After the tense decades of the 1950s and 1960s, which were marked by international competition, arms races, and harrowing events such as the Cuban missile crisis, the United States and the Soviet Union settled into a period of détente in which peaceful coexistence became the main goal. But détente lasted less than a decade. The Soviet Union's invasion of Afghanistan in 1979 in order to prop up a failing communist regime there, and the election of Ronald Reagan as U.S. president in 1980, soured relations between the two countries. Reagan, who viewed the Soviet Union as an "evil empire," embarked on a new policy of military buildup. But growing economic stagnation made it difficult for the Soviet Union to meet this expensive challenge.

At the same time as the United States and the Soviet Union entered a new and costly stage of the Cold War, a new generation of political leaders rose to power in the Soviet Union, among them Mikhail Gorbachev, who was chosen as general secretary of the communist party in 1985. Unlike his predecessors, Gorbachev recognized the stagnation of the Soviet system and understood that a new arms race would bankrupt his country. He thus proposed reforming both international and domestic relations, revitalizing both the Soviet Union and communist thought.

At the domestic level, Gorbachev initiated the twin policies of glasnost (openness) and perestroika (restructuring), intended to liberalize and reform communism. **Glasnost** encouraged public debate, with the hope that a frank discussion of the shortcomings of the system would help foster change and increase the legitimacy of the regime. **Perestroika**, or actual institutional reforms in the economy and political system, would flow from these critiques. These reforms were expected to include some limited forms of democratic participation, or market-based incentives in the economy. Moderate reform, not wholesale transformation, was Gorbachev's goal.[10]

In the international arena, Gorbachev similarly proposed widespread, if moderate, changes. In order to reduce the Soviet Union's military burdens and improve relations with Western countries, he began to loosen his country's control over other communist states, particularly those in eastern Europe, which had been under the thumb of the Soviet Union since the end of World War II. Gorbachev hoped that some limited liberalization in the region would ease tensions with Europe and the United States, enabling expanded trade and other economic ties.

But as Alexis de Tocqueville famously wrote with regard to the French monarchy, the most dangerous moment for a bad government is usually when it begins to reform itself. All of these policies wound up backfiring against Gorbachev and the Soviet Union. Glasnost encouraged public

GORBACHEV'S TWIN POLICIES FOR REFORMING COMMUNISM

Glasnost (openness)	Perestroika (restructuring)
Discussion of system's shortcomings	Institutional reforms in politics and economy
Intended to foster change	Intended to flow from glasnost
Intended to increase regime's legitimacy	Reforms were meant to be moderate

debate, but rather than simply criticize corruption or the quality of con-sumer goods (which is what Gorbachev expected), the public began to challenge the very nature of the political system. Ethnic groups within the Soviet Union and citizens of eastern European states used glasnost to agi-tate for greater freedom from Russian domination.

Perestroika had similarly unexpected effects. By seeking political and economic reform Gorbachev threatened those within the party who had long benefited from the status quo. Political leaders, administrators, fac-tory bosses, and many other members of the *nomenklatura* resisted reform, leading to infighting and instability. This problem was compounded by Gorbachev's actual reforms, which were largely half-hearted measures. Confusion deepened within the party, the state, and society as to where communism was heading.

As this confusion deepened, among the Soviet Union's satellite states change was proceeding faster than anyone expected. In 1989, opposition movements across eastern Europe used Gorbachev's new hands-off policy to attack their countries' communist regimes, demanding open elections and an end to one-party rule. Eastern European communist party leaders, realizing that the Soviet Union would no longer intervene militarily to sup-port them, had little choice but to acquiesce. As a result, by 1990 com-munists had been swept from their monopolies on power across the region. In most cases this revolutionary change was largely peaceful.

The Soviet Union would not be far behind. By 1991 the country was in deep turmoil: limited reforms had increased the public's appetite for greater change; the end of communism in eastern Europe further emboldened oppo-sition within the Soviet Union; and ethnic conflict and nationalism were on the rise as various groups sought political power. Communist hard-liners even-tually tried to stop the reform process through a coup d'état, seizing power and detaining Gorbachev. However, these leaders lacked the support of impor-tant actors such as the military and other segments of the state, and public demonstrations helped bring the poorly planned coup to an end.[11]

In the aftermath of the 1991 coup and in response to their own ethnic constituents, the individual republics that made up the Soviet Union broke up, forming fifteen new independent countries, of which Russia is one. Shortly thereafter these republics (with the exception of the Baltic states of Latvia, Lithuania, and Estonia) formed a close confederation known as the Commonwealth of Independent States (CIS). However, unlike such broad international institutions as the European Union, the CIS exercises little power. Each country had to contend on its own with building a new polit-ical system, economy, and society out of the ruins of communism.

TIMELINE: COMMUNIST HISTORY

1848	Karl Marx and Freidrich Engels write *The Communist Manifesto*, a central document in communist thought
1917	Lenin leads Russian Revolution, creating the Soviet Union as the world's first communist country
1930s	Stalin begins to arrest and execute Soviet Communist Party members and others to consolidate power and terrorize the population
1945	Soviet Army occupies eastern Europe, imposing communist regimes; tensions between the United States and the Soviet Union lead to Cold War
1949	Chinese Communist Party, led by Mao Zedong, gains control over mainland China after a long struggle against local opposition and Japanese occupiers
1953	Stalin dies
1956	Nikita Khrushchev denounces Stalin's use of terror and allows limited open debate; debate turns to unrest in parts of eastern Europe; protests in Hungary lead to open revolution against communism; Hungarian revolution put down by Soviet army
1966–76	Mao unleashes Cultural Revolution in China; student "Red Guard" attacks symbols of precommunism and party leaders accused of having grown too conservative; Cultural Revolution used to eliminate Mao's political rivals
1976	Mao Zedong dies; China and the U.S. begin to improve relations; rise to power of Deng Xiaopeng, who enacts widespread economic reforms
1979	Soviet Union invades Afghanistan, worsening relations between U.S. and Soviet Union; reintensification of the Cold War
1985	Gorbachev becomes general secretary of the Soviet Communist Party and begins to carry out economic and political liberalization
1989	Student protests for political reform in China's Tiananmen Square crushed by the military
1989–90	East Europeans seize on reforms in the Soviet Union to press for dramatic political change; largely peaceful political protests lead to free elections and the elimination of communist rule in eastern Europe
1991	Increasing turmoil in Soviet Union leads communist conservatives to oust Gorbachev and seize power; coup fails due to weak military support and public demonstrations; Soviet Union breaks into fifteen separate states

But communism did not collapse everywhere. Although in eastern Europe and the Soviet Union, 1989 marked liberalization and the first moves toward democracy, in China similar protests that year in Tiananmen Square, led by students and encouraged by Gorbachev's example, were met with deadly military force. Communist leaders in China did not heed public demands for reform and political liberalization, and showed themselves both willing and able to use the army to violently quell peaceful protests. Why this difference? One reason may be that in China the Communist Party had already begun to carry out a set of wide-ranging economic reforms in the late 1970s. These reforms were not accompanied by simultaneous political reform, however. In fact, in China the Communist Party used economic reform as a way to stave off public discontent and increase the party's own legitimacy. Having been focused on economics and not politics, and already involved in an extended period of reform, the Chinese Communist Party in 1989 did not confront the kind of rapid decompression and disarray that the Soviet Union or eastern Europe did. Furthermore, by initiating reforms primarily in the area of economics, the Chinese limited political mobilization and so were able to effectively crack down against public protest. Change is still under way in China, but the Communist Party intends to control and limit its course. Whether this will be possible in the long run is anyone's guess.

POLITICAL INSTITUTIONS IN TRANSITION

So far, we have discussed how communist theory saw the origins and solutions to inequality, the difficulties in translating theory into reality, and how eventually these institutions unraveled across most of the communist world. Yet although the downfall of communism was dramatic, what followed was no less awesome. Postcommunist countries faced, and continue to face, the challenge of building new political, social, and economic institutions to strike a new balance between freedom and equality. No country had ever made such a dramatic change in all three areas at once, and this task has met with varying degrees of success.

Reorganizing the State

An underlying task in the transition from communism is to reorganize the state in terms of its autonomy and capacity. Under communism the party-state was able to dominate virtually all aspects of human relations without any effective check. State autonomy and capacity were extremely high. But with the collapse of communism, the party was ejected from its leading role in political life, and new leaders had to change the very role and scope of the state. No longer could it dominate all aspects of human relations. But reducing state power was not easy, in part because new leaders saw high capacity and autonomy as vital to carrying out painful reforms. This is a paradox of political transitions: dramatic political change occurs alongside a substantial weakening of the state precisely when state power is most needed. Many postcommunist countries thus sought to narrow their states' capacity and autonomy without making them ineffective—a difficult task.

Another important aspect of postcommunist reform is the establishment of the rule of law. In Chapter 6 and elsewhere we have seen that laws and regulations are essential institutions in political life; they are the basic "rules of the game" that the majority of people obey because it is in their best interest. Under communist systems the rule of law was weak. The communist party could make, break, or change laws as it saw fit, and as a result people came to view laws rather cynically. Laws were not considered legitimate, neither by the public nor by those in power. This attitude encouraged evasion and corruption, problems that expanded dramatically once the repressive power of the state was retracted or weakened.

As a result, postcommunist countries have been challenged by the task of building the rule of law. Those in power must adhere to regulations and legal structures, not acting in a capricious manner or taking advantage of their authority. In society, too, the rule of law must be instilled in such a way that people willingly obey the system even when it is not in their personal interest to do so. Unless and until rules can be institutionalized, postcommunist states find it difficult to be effective and to have their laws obeyed by citizens and leaders.

Constructing a Democratic Regime

Alongside reconstructing state power and the rule of law, postcommunist countries have faced the prospect of building a democratic regime where authoritarianism has long been the norm. This project requires numerous tasks: revising or rewriting the constitution to establish civil rights and freedoms, creating a separation of powers between branches of government, revamping judicial bodies and high courts, generating electoral laws and regulating political parties, and doing all of this in such a way as to generate support on the part of the majority of actors in society. If a large portion of the public does not accept these structures as legitimate, political instability and violence will result.

Creating all of these institutions requires many decisions as to their final shape and form. For example, should these countries follow the European model of prime ministers, or opt for a presidential system like that of the United States? Prime ministers may allow for greater political party control and flexibility in a time of great change, but presidents may wield much more power and be a symbol of leadership during trying times. In fact, most communist countries have opted for the prime ministerial model, but some, such as Russia, adopted a semi-presidential system like that found in France. Another issue is that of electoral rules. Supporters of proportional representation (PR) favor that system as a way to include many different political ideologies and actors in the government, thus increasing legitimacy; opponents favor a greater use of first-past-the-post (FPTP) districts to create two large parties that they believe will be more effective in passing legislation. Many postcommunist countries opted for pure PR, but several, such as Russia and Hungary, opted for the German model of mixed PR and FPTP.

Civil rights are a final area of concern. Under communism constitutions typically established an elaborate set of civil liberties, though in reality these were largely ignored by those in power. With the collapse of communism, leaders were faced with deciding how civil liberties should be constitutionally protected. This meant not only strengthening the rule of law so that those once-hollow rights could be enforced, but also deciding what kinds of rights should be enshrined in the constitution. For example, in the case of freedom of speech and assembly, should the constitution ban communist parties, as the post-1945 German constitution had the Nazis? Do communists deserve the right to participate in the newly emerging democracy? Should ethnic minorities be granted special rights in education or government jobs? To what extent should communist-era rights, such as the rights to health care and education, be retained? Finally, who should be the final arbiter of disputes over these rights? The role of constitutional courts became a major issue in countries where traditionally the judiciary had been anything but independent.

Evaluating Political Transitions

More than a decade has passed since the fall of communism in eastern Europe and the Soviet Union. How have their political transitions fared? In short, the picture is mixed. Freedom House, a liberal nongovernmental organization that studies democracy around the world, ranks countries on a 1 to 7 freedom scale, with countries given a 1 being the most free and those given a 7 being the least free. This ranking is based on such considerations as electoral competition, freedoms of speech and assembly, rule of law levels of corruption, and protections of human and economic rights.

As shown in the table below, a number of postcommunist countries have made dramatic strides toward democracy and the rule of law, to such an extent that Freedom House now considers them to be consolidated democracies—meaning that their democratic regimes have been highly ranked on the Freedom House scale for a decade or so, and are therefore stable and fully institutionalized. The majority of these consolidated democracies can be found in central Europe (such as Hungary, Poland,

GLOBAL COMPARISONS

FREEDOM IN SELECTED POSTCOMMUNIST SYSTEMS AND CANADA, 2000

	Political Rights	Civil Liberties
	(1 = most free, 7 = not free)	
Canada	1	1
Poland*	1	1
Hungary*	1	2
Estonia†	1	2
Czech Republic*	1	2
Latvia†	1	2
Bulgaria*	2	3
Moldova†	2	4
Russia†	4	5
Tajikistan†	6	6
Belarus†	6	6
China	7	6

Source: Freedom House
*a formerly communist country of eastern Europe
†a former republic of the Soviet Union

and the Czech Republic) and the Baltics, areas that share a precommunist history of greater economic development, democratic institutions, and the rule of law, and that enjoyed more contact with western Europe and a shorter period of communist rule. All of these factors may help explain why democratic transition in these regions has been more successful.

But this group only makes up around 40 percent of all the postcommunist countries in eastern Europe and the former Soviet Union. In the majority of countries, democracy is either weakly institutionalized or completely absent. These countries tend to be poorer, with little historical experience of democracy and a long period of Soviet control, such as most of the former republics of the Soviet Union. In many of these countries a new set of authoritarian leaders has consolidated power, many of them former members of the communist *nomenklatura*. Democratic rights and freedoms are still restricted, and those in power have frequently enriched themselves through corrupt practices. In many of these cases it is difficult to speak of the rule of law. Equally disturbing, many of these countries have become less democratic and less lawful over time—including Russia, whose Freedom House score has dropped steadily in the last ten years.

Outside of eastern Europe and the former Soviet Union the picture is even less clear, for not only has democracy been slow to spread, several communist regimes continue to hold on to power. China, Laos, Vietnam, North Korea, and Cuba remain steadfastly authoritarian; only China has initiated significant economic reforms. Elsewhere in Asia and Africa communist regimes have fallen, in many cases resulting in state collapse and civil war, as in Afghanistan. Upon the Soviet Union's withdrawal from that country in 1989, civil war raged until 1996, when the Taliban gained power over most of the country. Thus not everywhere has the end of communism been peaceful and democratic.

ECONOMIC INSTITUTIONS IN TRANSITION

In addition to transforming the state and the regime, transitions from communism have also confronted the task of re-establishing some separation between the state and the economy. This involves two processes: **marketization**, or the re-creation of market forces of supply and demand, and **privatization**, the transfer of state-held property into private hands. In both cases, decisions about how to carry out these changes and to what end were influenced by different political-economic alternatives: Should social democracy, liberalism, or mercantilism be the country's new path? Let's consider the ways in which privatization and marketization can be approached before we investigate the different paths postcommunist countries have taken in each area.

Privatization

The transition from communism to capitalism requires a redefinition of property. In order to generate economic growth and limit the power of the state, economic resources must be re-entrusted with the public, placing them back into private hands. But the task of privatization is neither easy nor clear. In fact, prior to 1989 no country had ever gone from a communist economy to a capitalist one, so no model existed. Among the many questions and concerns facing the postcommunist countries was how to place a price on the various elements of the economy—factories, shops, land, apartments. In order to privatize these assets states first must figure out their values, something difficult in a system where no market has existed.

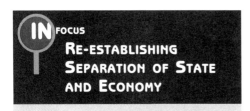

IN FOCUS

RE-ESTABLISHING SEPARATION OF STATE AND ECONOMY

- *Privatization*, the transfer of state-held property into private hands.

- *Marketization*, the re-creation of the market forces of supply and demand.

Second, who should get these assets? One option would be to simply give the assets away—transferring ownership of a factory to its workers, for example, or a house to its occupants. On the surface this strategy might seem to preserve a certain degree of equality among society (something social democrats might applaud). But inevitably some workers would wind up owning a factory that turns out to profitable, while others are saddled with a money-losing enterprise. Is this just? Another option would be to sell assets to the highest bidder (consistent with a liberal approach). But again, this strategy poses a problem. In a society where wages and profits have been restricted under communism, who would have the money to buy something as large as a factory? Often only the old *nomenklatura* would be expected to have amassed any significant wealth, which would mean that the old party bosses would now become the new capitalist bosses. A third alternative would be to allow foreign buyers, which would bring not only foreign investment but also Western managerial skills and technology. Yet this alternative could have political repercussions, as such sales could generate public anger that the results of their hard labor were being sold to foreigners (a critique similar to mercantilist thought). In all of these options old questions of inequality resurface.

Privatization was eventually carried out in a number of different ways, depending on the country and the kind of economic assets concerned. In many cases small businesses were sold directly to their employees. Some countries did sell many large businesses to the highest bidder; foreign investors such as General Electric purchased many large businesses in Hungary and Estonia. Other countries, such as the Czech Republic, relied on what is known as "voucher privatization," under which citizens were given vouchers that they could use to purchase shares in firms. Imagine, if you will, a huge auction in which everyone has a number of vouchers, which they can then use to bid for shares in a business. Although this method has the advantage of being more rapid and superficially more equitable, it posed the disadvantage that a firm was not sold outright to a new investor, who could bring new capital and expertise. Direct sales and voucher privatization were both fraught with the danger that those in power might use the process to enrich themselves or their political allies.

No matter what the privatization process, in the end there are many firms in postcommunist countries that are overstaffed, outdated, and unable to turn a profit in a market economy. Most problematic are very large industrial firms, such as coal mines and steel plants built in the early years of industrialization; these antiquated behemoths are uncompetitive in the international market. Such firms cannot be sold or even given away, but must be closed, leading to unemployment in a society where previously employment had been guaranteed. In some cases, such firms employ thousands of people and represent the main source of work in a city or region. To close down such firms is not an easy task for any politician, especially in a newly democratic system in which people are likely to vote with their pocketbooks and turn such leaders out of office. As a result, in some countries privatization has preceded slowly for fear of widespread unemployment and resulting social unrest.

Marketization

In addition to re-creating private property, states must re-create a market in which property, labor, goods, and services can all function in a competitive environment to determine their value. On the surface marketization appears easier than privatization—a simple matter of eliminating central planning and allowing the market to naturally resurface. But marketization too is a complicated process. One issue of debate concerns how rapidly marketization should take place. Some have argued that, given the profound nature of the economic transformation in postcommunist states, changes should be gradual to minimize any social disruptions that might undermine these fledgling economies and democracies. In particular, supporters of this "gradualism" feared that sudden marketization would lead to a wild jump in prices as sellers became able to charge whatever they wanted for their goods. Inflation and even hyperinflation could result, undermining confidence in the transition process and generating widespread poverty.

Others rejected these arguments, advocating rapid market reforms that would free prices and bring an end to central planning and state subsidies for businesses virtually overnight—a policy known as **shock therapy**. Such change would be painful and might initially involve a high degree of inflation, but the pain would be shorter than that accompanying gradualism. Shock therapy, particularly favored by some liberal Western advisers, was pioneered in Poland and later was attempted in Russia.

Evaluating Economic Transitions

How successful have all of these reforms been? The answer depends on what country you are looking at.[12] The table on page 237 shows some of the results of ten years of transition, which are decidedly mixed. In some cases marketization and privatization have led to relatively high rates of growth. Poland's shock therapy in 1990 had an initial dramatic and painful effect on the economy, as prices rose and inflation soared. Standards of living and the gross domestic product (GDP) declined. However, by the mid-1990s the economy began to recover, and now Poland's GDP is higher than it was in 1989. But in spite of this success Poland still struggles with privatization, and its unemployment rate is now over 16 percent. In the Czech Republic and Hungary, marketization was much more gradual, but privatization was carried out more rapidly than in Poland. The Czech Republic relied heavily on voucher privatization, while Hungary sold off many firms to foreign investors. In spite of these differences, these three countries are often cited as the most successful examples of postcommunist economic transition. All three countries also embraced aspects of economic liberalism and social democracy.

Russia and most of the other republics that once made up the former Soviet Union have not fared as well. Russia also attempted shock therapy, but with disastrous results. Freeing up markets led not to economic growth,

GLOBAL COMPARISONS

ECONOMIC INDICATORS IN THE COMMUNIST AND POSTCOMMUNIST WORLD AND THE UNITED STATES

	Per capita GDP, 2000 (PPP, in U.S. $)	Percentage of GDP Privately Owned, 1999	Average Annual GDP Growth Rate, 1990–98	Percentage of Labor Force Unemployed, 1999–2000
United States	36,200	99	3.0	4
Poland*	8,500	65	4.6	12
Hungary*	11,200	85	0.5	9.4
Estonia†	10,000	70	−2.2	11.7
Czech Republic*	12,900	75	0.9	8.7
Latvia†	7,200	65	−6.3	7.8
Bulgaria*	6,200	65	−3.1	17.7
Moldova†	2,500	50	−12.6	not available
Russia†	7,700	70	−7.0	10.5
Tajikistan†	1,140	30	−9.8	39 (est.)
Belarus†	7,500	20	−4.3	10–30 (est.)
China	3,600	60	11.2	10 (urban est.)

Sources: World Bank, European Union, Central Intelligence Agency
*a formerly communist country of eastern Europe
†a former republic of the Soviet Union

but to uncontrollable inflation and a rapid decline in the standard of living as people found their savings wiped out and their salaries unable to keep up with rising prices. Russia's problems were compounded by the way in which privatization was carried out: the old *nomenklatura*, rather than new private entrepreneurs, were able to buy up many of best industrial assets and natural resources. According to various sources, as of 1999 one-third or more of the Russian population was living in poverty.[13] In most other countries that were once part of the former Soviet Union, economic growth has been similarly stunted by incomplete economic reforms, insider privatization, and continued government intervention and ownership of the economy. Among the members of the CIS, average GDP is now only around 60 percent of where it stood in 1989.[14] In these countries one sees a political-economic system that has strong elements of mercantilism in its desire for state influence over the economy and its belief that markets must serve national goals. This postcommunist version of mercantilism also carries within it an anti-Western sentiment that rejects liberalism as a foreign ideology that helped bring down the Soviet Union and wreaked economic ruin on its former communist republics.

One theme that runs through all these cases is the correlation between economic growth and the rule of law. Where the rule of law is weak, economic transition is much less successful. Entrepreneurs (both domestic and international) lack a predictable environment in which to invest, while political leaders and state officials use their positions to siphon off resources for themselves, often hiding the money overseas. In these conditions the result is referred to as **crony capitalism**, in which a small group of elites gets extremely rich, often through highly questionable means, while most others see their standards of living decline as businesses are closed and inflation destroys their savings. Some observers expect greater growth across the region in the future as reforms slowly take hold. Yet even if growth does resume it will take years or even decades before some countries achieve even the standard of living they had in 1989.

Outside of eastern Europe and the former Soviet Union, economic transition is equally varied. Much attention has been focused on China, which historically had a much more weakly institutionalized system of central planning and control over property (which may in part explain China's early experimentation with reform). Since the 1970s China's reforms have included a dramatic expansion of private business and agriculture, all with the support of the Chinese Communist Party. The slogan of this economic reform—"To get rich is glorious"—sounds anything but Marxist, but it is rooted in the practical realization that earlier drives for rapid economic growth led to disaster. Some observers argue that these reforms have succeeded where many other communist countries have failed, introducing economic transition while restricting political change so as to better manage the course of reform.

Yet the Chinese model has its drawbacks. Alongside economic growth and the development of a free market and private property, problems such as inflation, rampant corruption, unemployment, and growing inequality have also surfaced, many of them exacerbated by the still-powerful presence of the state in the Chinese economy. The lack of a strong rule of law

COMMUNISM COMPARED: HUNGARY AND ROMANIA BEFORE AND AFTER 1989

Although many institutional features were common across communist countries, there was quite a bit of country-to-country variation in practice, shaped by history, culture, and the political leaders themselves. This affected not only communist rule, but also how formerly communist countries have managed since communism's collapse. A comparison of Hungary and Romania, two neighboring countries in eastern Europe, illustrates this point.

Historically Hungary has had a long connection to political, economic, and social institutions in western Europe. Although Hungary came under Soviet occupation in 1945, many Hungarians resisted Soviet domination, which they saw not as a source of economic progress but as imperial rule by an economically and culturally backward country. This tension came to a head in 1956, when attempts at liberalization in the Soviet Union fostered open dissent in Hungary and eventually an outright revolution against the Soviet-supported government. Although communist power was quickly restored by Soviet troops, party leaders in Hungary sought to pacify the public by allowing a limited degree of political and economic freedom. Private businesses, somewhat open debate, and even foreign travel were allowed to a limited extent. As a result, by 1989 many Hungarians had rather broad exposure to a wide range of political, social, and economic ideas, making postcommunist reforms much easier.

In contrast, before 1945 Romania had been a largely agrarian society cut off from broader European developments and institutions. The imposition of communist rule by the Soviets included the development of a highly personalistic and oppressive regime under Nicolae Ceausescu, who constructed an elaborate cult of personality around himself and elevated his various family members into positions of power. A huge security apparatus tapped phones and spied on the public, instilling terror and preventing even mild dissent. But 1989, growing public awareness of political change in other communist countries spilled out into public demonstrations; Ceausescu ordered military troops to fire on the demonstrators, and the resulting revolution led to Ceausescu's overthrow and execution. Since then Romania has found it much more difficult to construct the unfamiliar institutions of democracy and a market economy. As a result of these different histories, over the past ten years Hungary's and Romania's fortunes have been radically different. While Hungary has witnessed steady economic growth and stability, Romania's fate has been one of economic stagnation and political incapacity.

only compounds these problems. The hardships suffered by those who are not benefiting from China's economic changes have also led to sporadic public unrest. Finally, is it unclear where exactly these reforms are heading. The party sporadically carries out "strike hard" campaigns against corruption, arresting and executing thousands for economic crimes, but these crackdowns seem to have little effect. Will growing market forces and private property eventually come into conflict with the party's monopoly on power? And what will be the result—more democracy or more conflict?

SOCIETAL INSTITUTIONS IN TRANSITION

Like political systems and economies, societies too are being fundamentally transformed in postcommunist countries. Where once communist control asserted one interpretation of human relations, people now face a future much more uncertain and unclear. Postcommunist societies have the potential for greater individual action, but with this potential comes greater risk. The elimination of an all-encompassing ideology from people's lives has created a social vacuum that must be filled. In all of these countries the transition from communism has been a wrenching process, as people adjust to new realities and seek new individual and collective identities.

National Identity and Religion

This transformation of society has manifested itself in a number of different ways. Religion, once suppressed by communist parties, has resurfaced in many countries. In eastern Europe and parts of the former Soviet Union, Western evangelical movements have made many new converts, while in other parts of the former Soviet Union such as Central Asia, Islam has re-emerged as a powerful force, with many thousands of mosques and religious schools built in part with funds from other Muslim countries such as Saudi Arabia. In many countries this return to religion has helped rebuild social norms and values, although in other cases it has also led to the emergence of new forms of extremism, including Islamic fundamentalism. In China, too, where communism has not relaxed its control, new and old religious movements are gaining strength. Most notable is the spiritual group Falun Gong, which has attracted somewhere between 70 million and 100 million followers and is the target of a harsh crackdown by government authorities. Denouncing Falun Gong as a "cult," the Chinese leadership clearly fears any organization that may command greater loyalty than the state.[15] In the face of economic hardship, corruption, and often still-oppressive regimes, this religious resurgence should not be surprising: religion can play an important role in providing people with a sense of community and purpose.

Like religion, ethnic and national identities have re-emerged as potent forms of group identification. In many postcommunist countries both leaders and publics have sought to re-instill national pride and resurrect the values, symbols, and ideas that bind people together. The scope of this task varies among the postcommunist countries. In much of eastern Europe a clear sense of ethnic and national identity has existed for many generations, and in spite of communist rule many of these social structures not only remained intact but were reinforced by authoritarianism. In contrast, across the diverse ethnic groups of the former Soviet Union national identity has historically been much weaker. Many of these peoples have few ethnic or national institutions to draw on, and their identities are not simply being resurrected but are being created from scratch, with new words, anthems, symbols, and myths.

All such identities can be a double-edged sword, of course. Although they can help mobilize the public and provide stability in a time of great transition, religious, ethnic, and national identities can also generate division and conflict, particularly when several identities coexist in one country, and where political leaders exploit such divisions as a way to garner power.

Gender

The changes underway in social identities cannot help but affect gender relations as well. Recall our earlier discussion of how communist theory advanced the radical notion of gender equality. Although equality was not truly realized in practice, women were incorporated into the workforce and provided with social benefits that generated new opportunities. With the end of communism, however, many of these policies and institutions have been weakened or challenged. Critics have attacked many communist-era practices such as easy access to abortions, while economic reforms have cut back much of the elaborate social safety net that once benefited women. The re-emergence of traditional or fundamentalist religious practices has also challenged women's role in society.

Evaluating Societal Transitions

New societies in postcommunist countries have developed in very different ways. In some cases, the emergence of new religious and national identities has contributed to violence and civil war, most notably in parts of the former Soviet Union and the former Yugoslavia. Ethnic and religious differences have erupted in horrific conflict, often fomented by political leaders seeking to exploit these differences. In parts of the former Soviet Union these divisions have contributed to a decade of violent conflict, as in Tajikistan, Chechnya (part of Russia), Uzbekistan, Moldova, Azerbaijan, and Armenia, among others. In eastern Europe, the dissolution of Yugoslavia claimed more than 200,000 lives. In China, in addition to new religious challenges such as the rise of Falun Gong, the Communist Party must also contend with secessionist movements among Tibetans and Uighurs, conflicts that have resulted in violence and fierce state repression. Finally, the almost endless wars in Afghanistan since the 1970s are yet another tragedy whose consequences have rippled throughout the domestic and international communities.

These conflicts paint a gloomy picture. Less recognized, however, is that by and large the transition from communism has been rather peaceful, quite the opposite of what most observers expected in the early 1990s. Tense ethnic relations within and between many countries have been effectively resolved, with citizenship and religious freedom extended to different groups. In fact, in some countries national identity may again be on the decline. Studies done since the 1990s in eastern Europe show that in recent years people have shifted away from identifying themselves primarily in terms of their nation or their town, toward viewing themselves primarily either in terms of their larger region or more generally as Europeans. Although one must be careful not to read too much from a single finding, these data do echo the twin processes of devolution and integration seen in the advanced democracies. Whether these changes reflect these same forces at work is unclear and requires further research.

Gender relations in postcommunist countries also show signs of progress and setback, as the rhetoric of equality espoused under communism has given way. For example, as parliaments have become more powerful, few women are winning seats. In communist Hungary in 1980, 30 percent of parliamentarians were women; by 2001, however, this number had fallen to less than 10 percent. At the same time, studies show that women in many postcommunist countries have increased their roles in local politics and are particularly active in civil society—in some countries accounting for more than half of the leadership positions in nongovernmental organizations.[16] Reductions in state social expenditures, too, have had a dramatic impact on women, particularly in the area of maternal support. Unemployment has also hit women disproportionately hard: Women

NATIONAL IDENTITY AFTER COMMUNISM

Citizens of former Communist countries were asked the following question in 1991 and 1998: "With which of the following do you most closely identify yourself?"

	Bulgaria		Poland		Romania	
	1991	**1998**	**1991**	**1998**	**1991**	**1998**
Town	30%	6%	27%	5%	39%	8%
Region	0	63%	0	32%	0	27%
Country	65%	6%	68%	9%	68%	15%
Europe	3%	17%	3%	47%	3%	42%

Source: New Democracies Barometer

are more likely than men to lose their jobs, and many industries once dominated by female employees have been closed down. Of the estimated ten million unemployed in postcommunist eastern Europe and the former Soviet Union, 60 percent are women. However, research also indicates that women are active in starting new businesses, and that self-employed women now represent an important part of the private sector in many postcommunist countries.

IN SUM: THE LEGACY OF COMMUNISM

According to Marxist thought, capitalism inevitably led to great industrialization but also to great injustice, a contradiction that would result in its downfall. Communism would build upon capitalism's ruins to generate a society of total equality. But constructing communism proved to be a daunting task. People within communist systems found little incentive for hard work and innovation and had few freedoms to express themselves individually.

For the Soviet Union and eastern Europe, attempts to solve these problems led to outright collapse. One might use the analogy of renovating a dilapidated house only to find that the whole structure is unsound, and that renovations are only making the situation worse. At that point, one has to either demolish the whole structure or be demolished by it. In 1989 people in a number of eastern European countries chose to demolish the institutions of communism. Communist structures in the Soviet Union eventually collapsed on the Communist Party and Soviet society. China seems to be in a process of endless (and perhaps precarious) remodeling, while other communist countries, such as Cuba and North Korea, have yet to carry out any major reforms.

It is not clear what the coming decades will bring to the postcommunist world. All of these societies are attempting to grapple again with the dilemma of freedom and equality. New political, economic, and social institutions are needed, but in many cases they must be forged out of the rubble of the old order, a situation that is creating unique difficulties and contradictions. Over the past decade both individual freedom and collective inequality have grown in many countries. Increased civil liberties have arisen alongside poverty, and the rebirth of society alongside conflict and hostility.

The results of this diverse process have been dramatically different across the communist and postcommunist world. In some countries we see the institutionalization of democracy and capitalism; in others, authoritarianism and state-controlled economies remain in place. Moreover, it is apparent that over time these countries will grow increasingly dissimilar. Democratic consolidation and economic growth in eastern Europe appear to have placed many of these countries on the slow path to becoming advanced democracies. Within much of the former Soviet Union, however, economic stagnation or decline, political instability, and authoritarianism are more common; those countries are starting to resemble the less-developed world. China remains an enormous question mark. But whatever their paths, all these countries will continue to struggle to balance freedom and equality, a concern as pressing now as it was on the eve of the Russian Revolution in 1917.

NOTES

1 For a good overview of communist theory see Alfred Meyer, *Communism* (New York: Random House, 1984).

2 See V. I. Lenin, *What Is to Be Done? Burning Questions of Our Movement*, trans. Joe Fineberg and George Hanna (New York: International Publishers, 1969).

3 For a comparative discussion of different communist systems see Stephen White, John Gardner, George Schöpflin, and Tony Saich, *Communist and Post-Communist Political Systems* (New York: St. Martin's, 1990).

4 See Michael Voslensky, *Nomenklatura: Anatomy of the Soviet Ruling Class* (Garden City, N.Y.: Doubleday, 1984).

5 See Robert Conquest, *The Great Terror: A Reassessment* (New York: Oxford University Press, 1990).

6 See Lowell Dittmer, *China's Continuous Revolution: The Post-Liberation Epoch, 1949–1981* (Berkeley: University of California Press, 1987).

7 Robert W. Campbell, *The Socialist Economies in Transition: A Primer on Semi-Reformed Systems* (Bloomington: Indiana University Press, 1991).

8 Karl Marx and Friedrich Engels, *Manifesto of the Communist Party,* available online at www.marxists.org/archive/marx/works/1848/communist-manifesto/.

9 Joni Lovenduski and Jean Woodall, *Politics and Society in Eastern Europe* (Bloomington: Indiana University Press, 1987), 158.

10 Marcy McAuley, *Soviet Politics 1917–1991* (Oxford: Oxford University Press, 1992).

11 On the collapse of communism in eastern Europe see Timothy Garton Ash, *The Magic Lantern: The Revolution of 1989 Witnessed in Warsaw, Budapest, Berlin and Prague* (New York: Random House, 1990); on the Soviet Union see David Remnick, *Lenin's Tomb: The Last Days of the Soviet Empire* (New York: Random House, 1993).

12 For an analysis see World Bank, *Transition—The First Ten Years: Analysis and Lessons for Eastern Europe and the Former Soviet Union* (Washington: World Bank, 2002).

13 See United Nations, *2000 Human Development Report for the Russian Federation* (Moscow: United Nations Development Programme, 2000).

14 World Bank, *Transition—The First Ten Years,* xiii.

15 See the Web site of Falun Gong at www.falundafa.org/; for the Chinese government's view of Falun Gong see english.peopledaily.com.cn/special/fagong/home.html.

16 See *MONEE 1999 Regional Monitoring Report 6: Women in Transition* (Florence: UNICEF, 1999), 95–102, available at eurochild.gla.ac.uk/Documents/monee/pdf/MONEE6/monee6.htm.

9 LESS-DEVELOPED AND NEWLY INDUSTRIALIZING COUNTRIES

So far we have investigated two major parts of the world—the advanced democracies, often described as the First World, and communist and post-communist countries, or what had been known as the Second World. But these two categories leave out the majority of countries around the world, especially those in Latin America, Asia, and Africa. These regions are populated with countries that historically have had neither liberal-democratic nor communist regimes. Moreover, the vast majority of these countries have levels or economic industrialization far below those in the advanced democracies or the communist and postcommunist world. The traditional labeling of these countries as belonging to the "Third World" unhelpfully grouped together a diverse range of people and political systems according to what they were not, rather than what they were.

How then should we understand this important and vast part of the world? Whereas the advanced democracies are noted for their early capitalist development and the possible emergence of a postmodern system, and the communist states for their later rapid modernization and industrialization directed by the state, those countries that are the subject of this chapter are characterized by their mixture of premodern and modern institutions, a hybrid of economic, societal, and political institutions both foreign and indigenous.

In this chapter we will attempt to develop some ideas and categories to investigate and understand this part of the world. We will begin by distinguishing between newly industrializing and less-developed countries, and examining how the relationship between freedom and equality is structured in each. From there we will look at some of the fundamental experiences and institutions that these countries share, particularly those associated with imperialism and colonialism. Although imperialism had different effects in different parts of the world, similar legacies resulted from this form of rule. Next we will consider what challenges and obstacles these countries have faced after gaining independence. How does a country reconcile freedom and equality when the conditions may favor neither? And how is it that some countries have managed to enjoy economic and political development while others have stagnated or declined? These topics will lead us in to a final discussion of the prospects for political, economic, and societal development in this part of the world. What policies might help generate greater democracy, political stability, and economic prosperity in these countries? The difficulties they face are great, and the tasks daunting. But out of such dilemmas can emerge new ideas and innovations with the potential for positive change.

FREEDOM AND EQUALITY IN THE NEWLY INDUSTRIALIZING AND LESS-DEVELOPED COUNTRIES

The countries of what was traditionally referred to as the "Third World" are in fact often divided into two groups that indicate differences in their levels of development. Over the past fifty years some countries, particularly in Asia and parts of Latin America, have experienced dramatic rates of economic growth and democratization, to the point where they now resemble the advanced democracies in many ways. These are typically known as **newly industrializing countries**. Although this name emphasizes their rapid economic growth, in recent years the newly industrializing countries have also shown a marked tendency toward democratization and political and social stability. South Korea is one such country. A relatively poor agricultural country in the early 1960s, divided and damaged by the Korean War, South Korea would over the next fifty years become one of the world's largest economies and slowly develop a set of demo-

LESS-DEVELOPED AND NEWLY INDUSTRIALIZING COUNTRIES, 2003

Central and South America	Asia	North Africa and Middle East	Sub-Saharan Africa (continued)
Antigua & Barbuda	Afghanistan*	Algeria	Equatorial Guinea
Argentina	Bahrain	Egypt	Gagon
Belize	Bangladesh	Eritrea	Gambia
Bolivia	Bhutan	Ethiopia*	Ghana
Brazil	Brunei	Iran	Guinea
Chile	Burma	Iraq	Guinea-Bissau
Colombia	(Myanmar)	Jordan	Ivory Coast
Costa Rica	Cambodia*	Lebanon	Kenya
Dominica	Cyprus	Libya	Lesotho
Dominican	Fiji	Morocco	Liberia
Republic	India	Oman	Madagascar
Ecuador	Indonesia	Qatar	Malawi
El Salvador	Kiribati	Saudi	Mali
Grenada	Korea (South)	Arabia	Mauritania
Guatemala	Kuwait	Syria	Mauritius
Guyana	Malaysia	United Arab	Mozambique*
Haiti	Maldives	Emirates	Namibia
Honduras	Marshall	Yemen	Niger
Jamaica	Islands		Nigeria
Mexico	Micronesia	**Sub-Saharan Africa**	Rwanda
Nicaragua	Nauru		Sao Tome and
Panama	Nepal	Angola	Principe
Paraguay	Palau	Benin*	Senegal
Peru	Pakistan	Botswana	Seychelles
St. Kitts & Nevis	Papua New	Burkina Faso	Sierra Leone
St. Lucia	Guinea	Burundi	Somalia*
St. Vincent & the	Philippines	Cameroon	South Africa
Grenadines	Samoa	Cape Verde	Sudan
Suriname	Singapore	Central	Swaziland
Trinidad & Tobago	Solomon	African	Tanzania
Uruguay	Islands	Republic	Togo
Venezuela	Sri Lanka	Chad	Tunisia
	Taiwan	Comoros	Uganda
	Thailand	Congo (Republic of)	Zambia
	Tonga	Congo (Democratic	Zimbabwe
Europe	Turkey	Republic of)	
	Tuvalu	Djibouti	
Turkey	Vanuatu		

*Former communist regimes

cratic institutions alongside its growing wealth. In countries such as South Korea one finds stable and democratizing political institutions, an expanding web of nongovernmental institutions, and a growing economy. Such countries, however, tend to be in the minority. In many other cases, economic and political structures have remained weak or grown weaker over the past decades; these countries are marked by economic stagnation or even decline, with some sliding into poverty, violence, and civil conflict. These cases are often referred to as the **less-developed countries** (LDCs), a term that implies a lack of significant economic development or political institutionalization. An example here might be the country of Ghana. Despite expectations in the 1960s that this newly independent country was on the road to rapid political and economic development, Ghana sank into economic stagnation, political instability, and authoritarian rule. Perhaps most curious, in the early 1960s Ghana had a higher per capita gross domestic product (GDP) than did South Korea. This reversal of fortune will be explored later on in this chapter.

Although newly industrializing and less-developed countries seem in many ways to be increasingly dissimilar, what they still have in common is the relative weakness of both freedom and equality. Newly industrializing countries may have progressed toward greater democracy and economic development, but these processes remain incomplete and shaky, and could still be undermined. Indeed, in some cases democratic and economic change has raised new problems in reconciling freedom and equality, particularly where gaps have grown between rich and poor and where politics have become polarized as a result. The situation is particularly bad in the less-developed countries, where both freedom and equality are often circumscribed, with economic and political power tightly held in the hands of a very few.

Let's turn once again to the matrix of freedom and equality (shown on page 250). The wide range of countries in those categories are represented on it with a long dashed line. A number of newly industrializing countries lie along the upper end of the line, with increasingly liberal economic systems and democratizing regimes, though with growing inequality as one possible result. Toward the lower end of the line we find many less-developed countries. In some, where greater equality has been the regime's emphasis, individual freedom is limited. Still others provide little by way of either freedom or equality, not because of any particular ideology but because of the sheer inability of the state to guarantee economic or political stability. Under these conditions poverty and authoritarianism are the norm.

Why are freedom and equality so weak in these countries? Social scientists do not agree on the reasons, but many point to the important role played by imperialism and colonialism. Virtually all of the countries that we describe as newly industrializing or less developed were formerly part

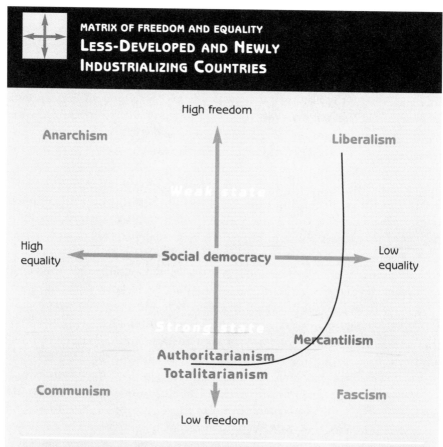

MATRIX OF FREEDOM AND EQUALITY
LESS-DEVELOPED AND NEWLY INDUSTRIALIZING COUNTRIES

High freedom

Anarchism   Liberalism

Weak state

High equality ⟵ —— Social democracy —— ⟶ Low equality

Strong state

Mercantilism

Authoritarianism
Totalitarianism

Communism   Fascism

Low freedom

The curved line on this matrix shows the range of regimes in newly industrializing and less-developed countries. A number of newly industrializing and less-developed countries fall along the upper portion of the line, having increasingly embraced liberal democracy and liberal political-economic systems. But in many more countries freedom is much lower. In some countries it is coupled with a greater emphasis on equality, but in others, neither freedom nor equality is upheld by the state.

of much larger empires, possessions of more powerful states. This imperial rule, which in some cases lasted for decades or even centuries, dramatically and often rapidly transformed economic, political, and societal institutions in these countries. Although resistance eventually brought down imperial rule, the changes wrought by this system could not be unmade. In order to better understand these legacies, it is worth our time to look at this form of political control in some detail.

IMPERIALISM AND COLONIALISM

In the first three chapters of this book we saw that over the past millennium Europe, the Middle East, and Asia embarked on a series of dramatic social, economic, and political changes that formed the outlines of what are now recognized as the hallmarks of modern society: ethnic and national identity, technological innovation, political centralization. This growing power was soon projected outward to conquer and incorporate new lands and peoples that could contribute to this rapid development. The result was the emergence of **empires**, which are defined as single political authorities that have under their sovereignty a large number of external regions or territories and different peoples. Although this definition might lead one to conclude that any large, diverse country is an empire, central to the definition is the idea that lands and peoples that are not seen as an integral part of the country itself are nonetheless under its direct control. The term **imperialism** describes the system whereby a state extends its power in order to directly control territory, resources, and people beyond its borders. The term "imperialism" is often used interchangeably with the word "**colonialism**," a word that indicates to a greater degree the physical occupation of a foreign territory through military force, businesses, or settlers. Colonialism, then, is often a central goal of imperialism—a means to consolidate one's empire.

Although imperialist practices date back many thousands of years, modern imperialism can be dated from the 1500s, when technological development in Europe, the Middle East, and Asia—advanced seafaring and military technology in particular—had advanced to such an extent that these countries were able to project their military might far overseas. In Asia, the powerful Chinese empire turned away from this path. Having consolidated power hundreds of years before the states of Europe did, the Chinese state had grown conservative and inflexible, interested more in

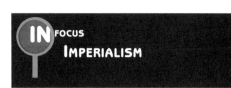

IN FOCUS

IMPERIALISM

- A system in which a state extends its power beyond its borders to control other territories and peoples.
- Propagated by European powers from the sixteenth to the twenty-first centuries.
- Driven by economic, strategic, and religious motives.
- Often led to *colonialism*, the physical occupation of foreign territories.

maintaining the status quo than in striking out to acquire new lands. Indeed, at the same time that Europeans were setting out for the Americas, the Chinese were actually retreating from overseas voyages; by 1500 it had become illegal for Chinese subjects to build oceangoing vessels. Similarly, in the Middle East the powerful Ottoman Empire expanded its power over much of the Arab world and into Asia, North Africa, and parts of Europe, nearly conquering Vienna in 1683. But the Ottoman Empire also turned inward and lost interest in technological innovation and in expanding power beyond the Islamic world. In contrast, the Europeans saw imperialism as a means to expand their resources, markets, subjects, and territory in order to gain the upper hand in their frequent battles with one another.

Thus, starting in the sixteenth century Europe began a process of imperialism that would not end for nearly five centuries. Driven by economic and strategic motives, as well as by a belief that Christianity and Western culture needed to be brought to the rest of the world, European empires stretched their power around the globe. First, Spain and Portugal gained control over South and Central America. By the seventeenth century, British, French, and other settlers began to arrive in North America, displacing the local population. In the eighteenth century, Europeans began to assert control over parts of North Africa and the Middle East, shocking Ottoman elites who had long viewed Europeans as technologically and culturally backward. This shock was shared by the Chinese in the nineteenth and early twentieth centuries as European imperialism rapidly expanded into Asia. Nearly all of Africa, too, was eventually divided up by the European states. This European imperialist expansion was joined briefly by Japan, which in the early twentieth century established its own empire across parts of Asia. In each of these cases imperial powers possessed well-organized political systems, military structures, technological advances, and economic resources; these advantages were combined with a belief that imperial control was not only possible, but necessary and just.[1]

TIMELINE: MODERN IMPERIALISM	
1494	Following European discovery, Spain and Portugal partition the Americas between their two empires
1519–36	Indigenous groups (Aztecs, Incas) are defeated by imperial powers in South America
1602–52	Dutch begin to establish control over parts of Indonesian archipelago and southern Africa. English settlement begins in North America
1810–25	Wars of independence in Latin America; Spanish and Portuguese rule is brought to an end
1839–58	United Kingdom expands control into Asia, notably Hong Kong and India
1884	The Berlin Conference: Africa is rapidly divided among European powers, notably France, Portugal, and Belgium
1939–45	World War II catalyzes the eventual decolonization of Asia and Africa
1947	Independence of India; first major decolonization of twentieth century
1956–68	Independence of most British, French, and Belgian colonies in Africa after local rebellions against imperial rule
1975	Independence of most former Portuguese colonies in Africa and Asia
1999	Hong Kong (United Kingdom) and Macau (Portugal) returned to China

INSTITUTIONS OF IMPERIALISM

The effects that imperialism had on those societies that came under foreign rule differs across time and place, but some common elements resulted from the imposition of modern political, social, and economic systems onto largely premodern societies. As we shall see, the imposition of modern institutions onto premodern peoples had a traumatic effect that continues into the present.[2]

Exporting the State

One of the first major effects of imperialism was the transfer of the state to the rest of the world. Recall from Chapter 2 how the modern state that we take for granted today emerged as a result of a long historical process in Europe; prior to that time, political units tended to have much weaker control over land and their subjects, and territorial sovereignty was rather tenuous. States, however, eventually succeeded in consolidating power over other forms of political organization, eliminating their rivals, clearly delineating their borders, and establishing sovereignty.

When European empires began to expand around the world, new territories were incorporated into these state structures, territories carved up by rival states in the quest for economic resources and strategic advantages. The borders drawn by imperial states were often reflections of their own power rather than existing geographic, religious, or linguistic realities. In turn, many of these arbitrary and externally imposed boundaries would later become the demarcations for independent countries once imperial rule was overthrown.

Having conquered these territories, imperial powers went about establishing state power and authority. In many empires this meant establishing bureaucratic structures similar to those found in the home country, in an attempt to "civilize"—to modernize—these premodern peoples. These structures commonly included a national language (typically that of the imperial power rather than a local language), police, taxation and legal systems, and basic public goods such as roads, schools, and hospitals. How this process was carried out and enforced differed. Some empires relied on local leaders to enforce their will, whereas others bypassed indigenous elites in favor of their own centralized forms of authority. In both cases few if any democratic practices were introduced, even if they were the norm in the home country. Individuals under colonial rule were considered subjects, not citizens, and thus had few political rights.

This imposition of the state had mixed effects, the benefits of which are open to debate. Many subject peoples experienced increased education and the benefits of a basic infrastructure that improved communication and transportation. Life expectancies rose and infant mortality rates declined, although when those trends were combined with traditional family practices they produced a population explosion that in many poor countries continues today. Traditional institutions such as local religions and customs were eroded and replaced by a greater awareness (and mimicry) of modern practices and institutions. But this transition was incomplete and uneven. Imperial territories remained economically and politically underdeveloped, placing many subject peoples in a kind of limbo—no longer part of a premodern system but not fully incorporated into the modern one. The frustration that grew out of this conflict over identity helped fan the flames of anti-imperialism, the desire for freedom from foreign control.

Ethnicity, Nationalism, and Gender

The imposition of organizational forms from outside included notions of ethnicity and nationality, which were relatively unknown or weak prior to the arrival of the Europeans. In much of the world that came under imperial control, people identified themselves by tribe or religion, by economic position, or by vocation rather than by some ethnic or national identity. But just as empires brought their own political institutions with them, the concepts of ethnicity and nation were also introduced by the new ruling powers. Imperial elites, themselves shaped and defined by national and ethnic identities, took great interest in identifying and classifying different ethnic groups in the regions they came to occupy, and structuring their political and economic control around these classifications.

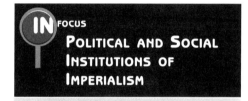

IN FOCUS

POLITICAL AND SOCIAL INSTITUTIONS OF IMPERIALISM

- The state, as a form of political organization, was imposed on much of the world outside of Europe.

- Ethnic and national identities were created where none had existed prior to colonization.

- Gender roles from the imperial country were often imposed on colonies.

Suddenly, people who had never thought of themselves being part of an ethnic group found that their basic rights were tied to how they had been ethnically defined by the empire. In some cases this ethnic classification was tied to early-modern notions of race, which held that certain ethnic groups were naturally superior to others. European and the Japanese empires were influenced by the assumption that the colonizing race was superior to the colonized, and thus destined to rule them. Different peoples within the empire, too, were subject to hierarchical classification. Certain ethnic groups were promoted to positions of power and economic advantage while other groups were marginalized (recall the discussion of Rwanda in Chapter 3). Colonialism often further exacerbated these hierarchies, as nonindigenous peoples migrated into colonies. Sometimes these migrants were settlers from the home country; in other cases they were peoples from other parts of the empire (for example, Indians migrating into Africa). These foreign presences further sharpened ethnic divisions, especially when such groups were accorded specific economic or political privileges. In short, inequality and ethnicity became tightly interconnected.

In addition to ethnicity, imperial powers also introduced the idea of national identity. During the late nineteenth and early twentieth centuries, in particular, national identity grew to be a powerful force in the industrializing world, helping give shape to the imperialist cause. But the peoples brought under imperial control had little familiarity with national identity, little notion of any right to a sovereign state. This combination of nationalism and imperialism proved dangerous. Empires viewed the peoples living in their overseas possessions as inferior subjects and gave them only a limited ability to improve their standing within the empire. Yet the imperial powers' own concept of nationalism provided these subject peoples with the very means to challenge foreign rule. If nationalism meant the right for a people—any people—to live under their own sovereign state, did this not mean that subject peoples had a right to rule themselves? Empires would thus provide the very ideological ammunition that their subjects would eventually use to overturn imperialism.

Colonialism also affected gender roles within the colonies. It is hard to make generalizations in this area, since in each region existing gender roles differed greatly and each imperial power viewed gender in a somewhat different way. Some scholars argue that on balance imperialism brought a number of benefits to women, increasing their freedom and equality by improving their access to health care and education. Others reject this argument, asserting that quite the reverse occurred in many cases. In many premodern societies gender roles may have been much less fixed than those found in the modern world, allowing women particular areas of individual freedom and relative equality with men. For example, in precolonial Nigeria, the women of the Ibo people wielded substantial political power. Under British imperialism, however, gender roles in Nigeria became much more rigid and hierarchical. Imperial powers brought with them their own assumptions regarding the subordinate status of women, views they imposed through such policies as education and the legal system. The economic systems imposed by the colonizers marginalized women in many ways. On balance, although imperialism may have provided new avenues for women, this progress may have come at the costs of other freedoms or areas of equality that women once held in their premodern societies.[3]

Dependent Development

Just as imperialism transformed political and social institutions in colonial areas, creating an amalgam of premodern and modern forms, economic change similarly occurred in a dramatic and uneven way.[4] The first important change in most imperial possessions was the replacement of a traditional agricultural economy by one driven by the needs of the industrializing capitalist home country. Systems based largely on subsistence agriculture and barter were transformed into cash economies, in which money was introduced as a means to pay for goods and labor.

Alongside this introduction of a cash-based economy came the transformation of economic production. Using a mercantilist political-economic system, empires sought to extract revenue from their colonies while at the same time using these territories and their people as a captive market for finished goods from the home country. Free trade thus did not exist for the colonies, which were obliged to sell and buy goods within the confines of the empire. In addition, colonial production was organized to provide those goods that were not easily available in the home country. Rather than finished goods, local economies were rebuilt around primary products such as cotton, cocoa, coffee, tea, wood, rubber, and other valuable commodities that could be extracted from the natural environment. Large businesses were established to oversee these so-called extractive economies, which were often dominated by a single monopoly. For example, in Indonesia, the United East India Company, a Dutch firm, gained control over lucrative spice exports while monopolizing the local market for finished goods from Europe, thereby destroying indigenous trade networks that had existed in the region for centuries. Export-oriented imperialism also led to the creation of large plantations that could produce vast quantities of rubber, coffee, or tobacco.

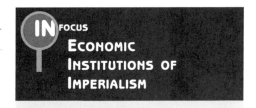

IN FOCUS

ECONOMIC INSTITUTIONS OF IMPERIALISM

- Traditional agricultural economies were transformed to suit the needs of the imperialist power.

- Free trade was often suppressed as colonies were forced to supply goods only to the imperial country, creating extractive economies in the colonies.

- Economic organization under imperialism impeded domestic development in the colonies.

This form of economic organization was quite different from that of the home countries and in many respects ill-suited to domestic development. Infrastructure was often developed only to facilitate effective extraction and export, rather than to improve communication or movement for the subject peoples; jobs were created in the extractive sector but local industrialization and entrepreneurialism were limited; the development of agriculture for export instead of for subsistence damaged the ability of these peoples to feed themselves, and the creation of large-scale agricultural production drove many small farmers off the land. Many colonies saw a resulting boom in urbanization, typically centered around the colonial capital or other cities central to imperial politics and trade. By the late 1500s, for example, the Spanish had established more than 200 cities in Latin America, which to this day remain the central urban areas in the region.

Let us take a moment to summarize what we have considered so far. By virtue of their organizational strengths, modern states expanded their power around the globe, establishing new political, economic, and social institutions. In some cases, these institutions were reflections of the home country; in others, they were designed specifically to consolidate imperial rule. The result was an uneasy mixture of indigenous and foreign structures, premodern and modern. New political institutions and new societal identities were imposed while participation and citizenship were restricted; economic development was encouraged but in a form that would serve the markets of the home country. Imperialism thus generated new identities and conflict by classifying people and distinguishing between them—between rulers and ruled, and between subject peoples themselves. At the same time, the contradictions inherent in this inequality and limitation on freedom became increasingly clear to subject peoples as they began to assimilate modern ideas and values. By the early twentieth century, the growing awareness of this system and its inherent contradictions helped foster public resistance to imperialism and would pave the way for eventual independence.

THE CHALLENGES OF POSTIMPERIALISM

Despite the power of empires to extend their control over much of the world, their time eventually came to an end. In Latin America, where European imperialism first emerged, Napoleon's invasion of Spain and Portugal in 1807–8 led to turmoil in the colonies and a series of wars for independence, which freed most of the region by 1826. In Africa and Asia, where imperialism reached its zenith only in the nineteenth century, decolonization came after World War II. Numerous independence movements emerged within the Asian and African colonies, catalyzed by the weakened positions of the imperial powers and promoted by a Western-educated indigenous leadership able to articulate nationalist goals and organize resistance. Many imperial powers resisted bitterly: Portugal, for example, did not fully withdraw from Africa until 1975. For the most part, however, colonies in Africa and Asia gained independence in the 1950s and 1960s.

The elimination of imperialism, however, did not mean a sudden end to the problems of the newly industrializing and less-developed countries. Over the past half-century these countries have continued to struggle with political, social, and economic challenges to development and stability, freedom and equality. In many cases these problems are a legacy of imperial rule, although in others they stem from particular domestic and international factors that have developed in the years since independence.

Building State Capacity and Autonomy

One central problem that many newly industrializing and less-developed countries have faced in the years after imperialism has been the difficulty in creating effective political institutions. In Chapter 2 we distinguished between weak states and strong states and noted that many scholars look at state power by distinguishing between state capacity and state autonomy. Recall that capacity refers to the ability of a state to achieve basic policy tasks, and autonomy refers to the ability of a state to act independently of the public. Both are necessary in order to carry out policy, and both have been difficult for the newly industrializing and less-developed countries to achieve.

In terms of capacity, states are frequently unable to perform many of the basic tasks expected by the public, such as creating infrastructure, providing education and health care, or delivering other public goods. This lack of capacity can often be traced to the absence of a professional bureaucracy to run the government. The foreigners who ran the imperial bureaucracies in the colonies typically left upon independence, precluding a gradual transition to a local bureaucracy. These initial problems of capacity have since been further exacerbated by the politicization of the state; in many cases the bureaucracy has become an important source of jobs, resources, and benefits that are doled out by political leaders as a way to solidify control. Civil servants thus become part of a system of clientelism

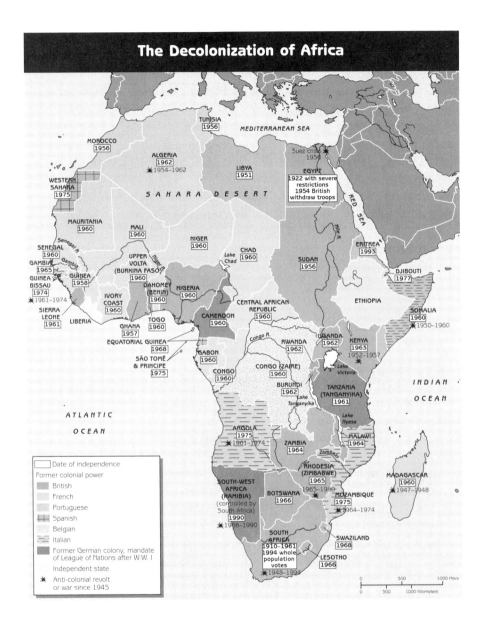

The Decolonization of Africa

and rent-seeking, in which they assist in providing goods and benefits to certain members of the public in return for political support. At a more extreme level, this cooptation takes the form of patrimonialism, in which the state is packed with officials whose only qualification is their support for those in power, and whose main goal is to siphon resources from the state for their own enrichment.[5]

Autonomy has been equally problematic in the postimperialist world. On the surface, many newly industrializing and less-developed countries appear to be highly autonomous, able to function without consulting the population at all. The prevalence of authoritarianism in much of the newly industrializing and less-developed world only seems to reinforce this

GLOBAL COMPARISONS
CORRUPTION INDEX, 2000

Country	Score (10 = least corrupt)
Finland	10.0
Canada	9.2
United Kingdom	8.7
United States	7.8
Botswana	6.0
Taiwan	5.5
South Africa	5.0
Mauritius	4.5
South Korea	4.0
Brazil	3.9
India	2.8
Philippines	2.8
Bolivia	2.7
Côte d'Ivoire	2.7
Venezuela	2.7
Ecuador	2.6
Uganda	2.3
Mozambique	2.2
Kenya	2.1
Angola	1.7
Indonesia	1.7
Nigeria	1.2

Source: Transparency International

impression. Indeed, many of these states are highly autonomous—they can repress or terrorize the population as they see fit—but this autonomy is quite limited, built largely (and dangerously) around force alone. In many cases the state is not a highly independent actor, but is instead penetrated by actors and organizations who see the state as a resource to be exploited rather than a tool for achieving policy. Frequently the result of such penetration is high levels of corruption—what has been termed "kleptocracy," or government by theft. For example, during military rule in Nigeria in the 1990s officials stole more than $1 billion from the state treasury. To be fair, not all newly industrializing and less-developed countries are corrupt; Chile, Singapore, and Botswana all rank among the least corrupt countries in the world. However, many more are concentrated toward the highly corrupt end of the spectrum. On a scale of one to ten, with ten being the least corrupt and one the most corrupt, more than 65 percent of the countries scoring four or below are newly industrializing and less-developed countries (the remaining 35 percent are communist or postcommunist). The table on page 261 lists a selection of countries and their scores on this corruption index.

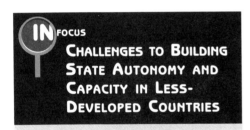

IN FOCUS

CHALLENGES TO BUILDING STATE AUTONOMY AND CAPACITY IN LESS-DEVELOPED COUNTRIES

- Absence of professional bureaucracy (following departure of foreign imperial bureaucrats).
- Clientelism, rent-seeking, and corruption in the struggle for state jobs and revenue.
- Sovereignty often compromised by external actors (other states, international organizations).

In addition to constraints on autonomy from domestic sources, the states of the newly industrializing and less-developed world are often also limited in their autonomy by international factors. Less-developed and newly industrializing countries are subject to pressure from other, more powerful states or international actors such as the United Nations, the World Bank, multinational corporations, or even organizations such as Amnesty International or the Red Cross. Frequently wielding much greater economic and political power than the states themselves, these actors can significantly influence the policies of these countries, shaping their military and diplomatic alliances, trade relations, local economies, and domestic laws.

These constraints on state autonomy and capacity have clear implications for freedom and equality. A state with weak capacity and autonomy is unlikely to be able to establish the rule of law. Laws will not be respected by the public if the state itself is unwilling or unable to enforce and abide by them. Freedom is threatened by conflict and unpredictability, which in turn hinder economic development. A volatile environment and the absence of basic public goods such as roads or education will dissuade long-term investment. Wealth flows primarily into the hands of those who control the state, generating a high degree of inequality. There is no clear regime, and no rules or norms for how politics is to be played.

Unfortunately, where instability is so high there is often only one institution with a great deal of autonomy and capacity: the military. Where states are weak, military forces often step in and take control of the government themselves, either to stave off disorder or simply to take a turn at draining the state. Military rule has been common in the newly industrializing and less-developed countries. Even where it has ended, as in many countries of Latin America, the military often remains a powerful actor behind the scenes.

This discussion of autonomy and capacity may offer one explanation for why some countries have managed to develop and democratize in the aftermath of imperialism while others have fallen behind. Many political scientists have in past noted that newly industrializing countries are marked by relatively high degrees of state autonomy and capacity. Their capabilities are made possible in part by the existence of a well-trained bureaucracy as well as by the relatively weak ability of society to make demands that would compromise state power. In countries such as Chile, Taiwan, and South Korea, for example, the state was able to resist (and often violently destroy) public resistance to the regime, giving the government a much greater scope for dramatic action. One disconcerting implication of this argument, however, is that economic success may necessitate an iron hand, and that democracy can come about only once basic economic goals have been met.

Still, this discussion begs the question of why some countries were able to build their autonomy and capacity while others were not. In part this disparity may be the luck of the draw, influenced by historical circumstances, the form and legacies of imperialism, international economic relations, or a country's strategic relationship with advanced democracies. But another important factor that should not be discounted is the crucial role played by postcolonial leaders themselves. In some cases, the leaders of newly independent countries used their political legitimacy to strengthen and institutionalize state capacity and autonomy, viewing these as central to future stability and growth. In other cases such goals were rejected. In Ghana's case, at the time of independence the country boasted a relatively developed infrastructure and professional bureaucracy. But those who came to power favored cooptation rather than autonomy, fostering clientelism, rent-seeking, and corruption that contributed greatly to the country's decline.[6]

Forging Social Identities

In the aftermath of colonialism, many less-developed and newly industrializing countries have struggled with the challenge of forging a single nation out of highly diverse societies. Initially, where centralized political authority did not exist prior to imperialism, societies were not homogenized. Their diversity became problematic when imperial powers began categorizing societal groups and establishing political boundaries and economic and social hierarchies. Migration within empires further complicated these relations. Upon independence, several problems rose to the surface.

First, group divisions often have economic implications, just as they did under colonial rule. Some ethnic groups favored under colonialism continue to monopolize wealth in the postindependence society. For example, in Malaysia and Indonesia, ethnic Chinese continue to hold a disproportionate share of national wealth, generating resentment among non-Chinese groups. Similarly, in Kenya, Uganda, and Fiji, the Indian population, originally brought in by the British as indentured labor, came to control a large portion of the business sector. The resulting outbursts of violence appear to be on the surface ethnic in nature, but in fact their origins are economic. In 1972 the Ugandan government under the notorious dictator Idi Amin expelled all Indians from the country, seizing their lands and businesses. Indigenous populations are among the poorest across Latin America, a situation that has sparked rebellions such as the Chiapas uprising in southern Mexico in 1995. Many civil conflicts in the less-developed and newly industrializing countries are driven in large part by economic concerns overlaid onto ethnic or religious differences.

Second, ethnic and religious divisions can similarly divide politics. In countries where populations are heterogeneous, the battle for political power often falls along ethnic or religious lines, with each side seeking to gain control over the state in order to serve its own group's particular ends. Each ethnic or religious group competes for its share of public goods or other benefits from the state. This struggle may foster authoritarian rule, for a group that gains control over the state may be unwilling to relinquish or share it, and no one group can be confident that it could successfully

dominate politics simply through the democratic process. As a result, where ethnic or
religious divisions are strong we often see
the state dominated by one group while others are effectively frozen out of the political
process.[7] In some countries a majority or
plurality may dominate politics, as people of
European origin do in Mexico, while the
minority indigenous population has little
political power. The Angolan state is dominated by the Ovimbundu people, who hail
from the north of the country and make up
37 percent of the population; their opposition has come from the Kimbundu people

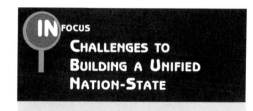

IN FOCUS

CHALLENGES TO BUILDING A UNIFIED NATION-STATE

- Arbitrary political boundaries imposed by imperial powers.

- Ethnic and religious divisions among different groups in heterogeneous societies (often exacerbated by economic inequality).

in the south, who make up 25 percent of the population. The result has
been a civil war that has devastated the country since 1975 and may only
now be drawing to a close. In still other cases, a minority may dominate
a much larger minority; in Iraq, where the majority population is of the
Shia sect of Islam, the ruling Ba'ath Party is dominated by members of
the minority Sunni sect.

The economic and political difficulties that arise from such social divisions make the creation of a single national identity difficult. Amid such
ethnic and religious diversity, many populations are much less inclined to
see the postcolonial state as a true representation of their group's wishes,
and states themselves have little beyond the initial struggle for independence on which to build a shared political identity for their people. At an
extreme level, these ethnic and religious conflicts may take on the goal of
secessionism, as disaffected groups seek to create their own autonomous
or wholly independent territories.

Gender is another important social issue in less-developed and newly
industrializing countries. Gender roles imposed or reinforced by colonial rule
persisted in many societies following independence, reinforced by rapid
urbanization and the commercialization of agriculture, which tended to favor
male labor and property rights. Because males are privileged in this way,
society tends to view males as a more valuable addition to a family than
females, an attitude that can limit women's access to important resources
such as education and, consequently, greater economic advancement. At an
extreme level, this favoritism can be deadly, taking the form of female infanticide. Estimates indicate that in India approximately 10,000 baby girls are

killed each year, and an unknown number of female fetuses are aborted once their sex has been determined by ultrasound examination. Female infanticide is also practiced in China, Taiwan, and South Korea.[8]

As a result, we might conclude that sexist institutions in these countries are a result of imperialism. But the situation is more complicated than that. Imperialism also brought with it many liberal notions of female autonomy, which these countries have since sought to reconcile with more traditional cultural values. For example the rise of Islamic fundamentalism in many countries has been strongly supported by some women who view feminism as another example of foreign values being imposed on them by the advanced democracies. For other women, however, such fundamentalism threatens to deny them their basic freedoms—education, careers, individual autonomy.

As with state and economic institutions, these distinctions may also help explain differences between the newly industrializing countries and the less-developed ones. Some scholars have suggested that development is connected to the degree to which a society is divided along ethnic lines. Under conditions where economic and political power are the exclusive preserves of specific ethnic groups, the resulting uneven development and lack of mobility and opportunity across ethnic lines can lead to conflict and instability, setting back development. In the island country of Fiji economic power has remained in the hands of Europeans, Chinese, and Indians who settled there when Fiji was a British colony. After independence in 1970, resentment grew among indigenous Fijians, who saw themselves as an ethnic underclass that could only watch while the traditional economic wealth of other ethnic groups continued to expand. Such animosity helped spark a military coup in 1987 against the Indian-dominated government, and another, failed coup was launched as recently as 2000. As a result of this turmoil, many skilled workers have left Fiji, thereby weakening the state and its economy; in the years immediately following the 1987 coup, the World Bank estimated that Fiji lost half of its doctors to emigration.[9] Similarly, it has been argued that unequal relationships between women and men contribute to lower levels of economic development. Inequality, whether between groups or between genders, appears to hamper growth.

Generating Economic Growth

And it is economic growth that attracts the most focus among those who study the less-developed and newly industrializing countries. Indeed, when we think of development, typically it is economic progress that comes to mind. In addition to the difficulties already mentioned, numerous challenges face the less-developed and newly industrializing countries. Because of imperialism, rather than undergoing economic modernization on their own terms, these countries experienced rapid changes directed by the colonial powers—their economic development was geared to suit European needs and tailored to provide specific goods to specific external markets. Their experience is a far cry from those of Europe or North America, where economic development spurred by internal needs took place over the course of several centuries.

As a result, upon independence many of these countries found themselves in a continued state of economic dependency on the former colonial powers. Language ties, infrastructure, and production all favored the continuation of these relationships. But such dependent relationships did not bode well for long-term development, since they stressed the production of agricultural and other basic commodities in return for finished products. The production of basic commodities does not require high-skilled labor, nor does it promise large profits in return; if anything, this form of economic production is much more unstable, subject to uncontrollable factors such as the weather or unexpected changes in the global market. For example, in the mid-1980s Western consumers became concerned about the amount of saturated fats in their diets, particularly palm and coconut oils, the dangers of which were played up by American producers of soybean oil, a chief competitor. In Southeast Asia, large-scale production of tropical oils dates back to imperial rule. The change in Western attitudes translated into reduced demand for and fewer exports of these oils to the United States—Malaysia alone saw its oil exports decline by nearly half. For many less-developed countries, this unequal relationship was simply a new, indirect form of imperialism, or what has been called **neocolonialism**.

Breaking this cycle of dependent development was thus the greatest concern for the less-developed countries following independence. Because the industrial democracies dominated domestic and global markets through their sheer size and technical sophistication, it appeared that no poorer country could ever compete against them in the global economy. Less-developed countries looked to the examples of the Soviet Union and China, where rapid industrialization was taking place by essentially withdrawing from the global economy, and they concluded that they too could find a different path to development, built on their own unique conditions.

This mindset resulted in two distinct economic policies that were applied throughout the less-developed world.[10] The first, known as **import**

substitution, is based on the idea that because the poorer countries cannot compete with the advanced industrialized democracies, it is necessary for the state to create more positive conditions for the development of local industry. The logic behind import substitution is straightforward. Less-developed countries restrict imports, making them more expensive. This in turn helps spur demand for local alternatives, and new businesses to fill this demand could be built with state funds. Once these firms had tapped and fulfilled local demands, they would have developed the productive capacity to compete domestically and internationally, and trade barriers could be lifted. Import substitution would thus create businesses able to compete not only in the local market, but in the export market as well.

In practice, import substitution followed several specific steps. Tariff or nontariff barriers were established to raise the price of foreign goods. In some cases, these barriers were accompanied by reduced restrictions on patents and intellectual-property rights, allowing local business to copy foreign-made goods such as pharmaceutical products. The state often played a direct role in the creation of these industries. Many states took responsibility for industrialization, developing partially or fully state-owned businesses in such areas as steel or chemical production. As you might suspect, import substitution is not a liberal strategy, but one influenced much more by mercantilism (and, to a lesser extent, communism). Countries that adapted this economic strategy believed that their states had to play a strong role in directing their economies and their nations toward independence from the dominant power of the advanced democracies. Following World War II, import substitution was commonly used across Latin America and was also taken up in Africa and parts of Asia.

How successful was it? Most observers have since concluded that import substitution did not produce the benefits expected and may have set back economic development in these countries. Some have described import substitution as creating a kind of "hothouse economy," an analogy that deserves some attention. In a hothouse one is able to grow all kinds of produce even when the outside weather would not support it: one can have tomatoes in winter, or grow tropical plants in New England. Similarly, import substitution allowed the creation of domestic producers, which were often subsidized or owned by the state. Although these firms did initially lead to economic growth, they existed in a kind of economic hothouse, where the cold blasts of outside competition were kept at bay through artificial trade barriers. Insulated from the global economy, these firms could dominate the local market, but lacking competition they were much less innovative or efficient than their international competitors, and they tended to draw money from the state rather than generate profits. The idea that these economies would eventually be opened up to the outside world became hard to envision; the harsh climate of the international market would have quickly killed off these less-competitive firms.

Import substitution thus resulted in economies with large industries reliant on the state for economic support and unable to compete in the international market. By making losses rather than profits, these firms became a drain on state treasuries, compounding the problem of international debt in these countries, for states had to borrow internationally in order to build and subsidize their industries. These economies were eventually opened up to the outside world after they were prodded to do so by liberal lending organizations such as the International Monetary Fund. Whether simply opening up to the outside world will produce benefits, however, is uncertain. If one can no longer afford to keep up one's hothouse, it may make sense to tear it down, but it is unlikely that the plants inside will survive.

INDUSTRIALIZATION, IMPORT SUBSTITUTION, AND THE BRAZILIAN COMPUTER MARKET

In the 1970s, the Brazilian government decided that computers were an important enough product that they should be developed domestically. The Brazilian government passed a "national law for informatics," which sought to create a national computer industry independent of IBM and the other major international manufacturers. The Brazilian state limited the imports of foreign computers through high tariffs, provided subsidies to local producers, and created a state-owned computer producer. Within a short time, Brazilian producers were dominating the local market for personal computers. However, it would be difficult to describe this action as a success. According to observers, this policy led to higher prices as well as lower-quality computers. Some of the computers supposedly made in Brazil turned out to be imports that were dismantled and reassembled under a local brand name. By the 1990s, these problems of low quality and high prices led the Brazilian government to end its protection of the local computer industry. Many Brazilian computer firms subsequently formed joint ventures with major international businesses such as IBM and Fujitsu. In the end, the attempt to create a wholly local industry failed, and critics argued that Brazil lost a whole decade during which it could have benefited from a more open market for computer technology.

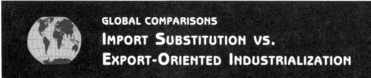

GLOBAL COMPARISONS
IMPORT SUBSTITUTION VS. EXPORT-ORIENTED INDUSTRIALIZATION

Country	Economic System	GDP per capita (PPP, U.S. $)		Per Capita Annual Growth Rate, 1975–2000 (percent)
		1960	2000	
Ghana	Import substitution	1,049	1,964	0.1
Brazil	Import substitution	1,404	7,625	0.8
Argentina	Import substitution	3,381	12,337	0.4
South Korea	Export-oriented	690	17,380	6.2
Thailand	Export-oriented	985	6,402	5.5
Malaysia	Export-oriented	1,783	9,068	4.1

Source: United Nations

Not all less-developed countries pursued import substitution. Over the past several decades the world has witnessed the rise of "Asian tigers"—Hong Kong, South Korea, Taiwan, Singapore, with Thailand, Malaysia, and Indonesia often touted as the next wave—that achieved astounding levels of growth within a generation. Many observers have attributed their success to cultural factors, arguing about the superiority of a Confucian work ethic, but others have asserted that the credit is due to their states, which pursued very different economic policies than those found in Africa or Latin America.

Among the Asian tigers import substitution was eventually discarded in favor of what has been termed **export-oriented industrialization**, which seeks to directly integrate into the global economy by concentrating on economic production that can find a niche in international markets. Like import substitution, export-oriented industrialization is not a liberal economic policy, but rather mercantilist in its assignment of a strong role for the state in promoting domestic growth. Export-oriented states, like their import-substituting counterparts, also used tariff barriers to protect their industries in their initial stages.

In Asia, countries pursuing an export-oriented strategy sought out technologies and developed industries that were focused specifically on export, capitalizing on what is known as the "product life cycle," a concept that describes the way in which goods and technologies are diffused in international markets. Initially, the innovator of a good produces it for the domestic market and exports it to the rest of the world. As this product spreads, other countries find ways to make the same good more cheaply or more efficiently, eventually exporting their own version back to the country that originated the product. By this time, the originator country has moved on to a new innovation. Export-oriented growth seeks to capitalize on the produce life cycle by seeking out these advantages, embracing technological advances in order to create new exports. Thus in South Korea, initial exports focused on basic technologies such as textiles and shoes, but eventually moved into more complex areas such as automobiles and computers. Although countries that pursued export-oriented industrialization have also faced problems with high levels of government subsidies and have in recent years been hurt by economic recessions, overall this strategy of development has led to much higher levels of economic development. Some export-oriented countries, such as South Korea and Thailand, in 1960 had per capita GDPs far below those of many Latin American and even some African countries, but by the mid-1990s they had come to far surpass many of their import-substituting rivals.

Clearly, less-developed and newly industrializing countries diverged widely in their economic policies. Why did some countries choose import substitution while others opted for export-oriented industrialization? One important factor was geopolitical. In Latin America, import substitution was influenced by the region's economic domination by the United States. During the Great Depression, Latin America's market for raw materials and agricultural exports to the United States dried up, devastating many of its economies; later, during World War II, although markets for some exports improved, finished goods became scarce as the United States directed its industrial production toward the war effort. As a result of these dislocations Latin American scholars and leaders concluded that import substitution would be a means to insulate their countries from this unpredictable and, in their eyes, neocolonial relationship.

In Asia, however, development strategies were directly influenced by the Cold War and the role of the United States in this struggle. Backed by extensive American financial and technical support, many Asian states specifically developed export-oriented industries; they were encouraged to tap into the American market as a way to industrialize their economies while protecting their own. The United States tolerated these more mercantilist policies as the price to pay for drawing these countries closer to

COMPARING CONCEPTS
THREE PATHS TO ECONOMIC GROWTH

Import substitution	Based on mercantilism
	State plays a strong role in the economy
	Tariffs or nontariff barriers are used to restrict imports
	State actively promotes domestic production, sometimes creating state-owned businesses in developing industries
	Criticized for creating "hothouse economies," with large industries reliant on the state for support and unable to compete in the international market
Export-oriented industrialization	Based on mercantilism
	State plays a strong role in the economy
	Tariff barriers are used to protect domestic industries
	Economic production is focused on industries that have a niche in international market
	Seeks to integrate directly into the global economy
	Has generally led to a higher level of economic development than import substitution
Structural adjustment	Based on liberalism
	State involvement is reduced as the economy is opened up
	Foreign investment is encouraged
	Often follows import substitution
	Criticized as a tool of neocolonialism and for its failure in most cases to bring substantial economic development

the U.S. and preventing the spread of communism in the region. In short, the specific regional and geopolitical contexts of Latin America and Asia—and their countries' relationships with the United States in particular—influenced the paths of development they took.[11]

In recent years both import substitution and export-oriented industrialization have been challenged by critics. Although import substitution has long been criticized by liberals as inefficient and prone to corruption, the downturn of many Asian economies in the 1990s also cast doubt on the long-term viability of export-oriented industrialization as well. Liberals charged that this system, too, with its close ties between business and the state, has engendered corruption and inefficiency and contributed to the Asian economic downturn. Whether they are import substituting or export oriented in their approach, in the wake of these economic difficulties many less-developed and newly industrializing countries have turned to the International Monetary Fund and the World Bank for help, and in return for financial support have been compelled to adopt more liberal economic policies. These policies of liberalization (often known as **structural adjustment programs**) have often required privatizing state-run firms, ending subsidies, reducing tariff barriers, shrinking the size of the state, and welcoming foreign investment. Opening up the economy and shrinking the state, liberals believe, will generate faster and more consistent growth.

Some observers, however, are skeptical of such policies and point to evidence that underscores their concerns. A recent study by the United Nations found that although many less-developed countries have adopted highly liberal economic systems in the past decade, they have not reaped great benefits in terms of economic growth—the majority of such countries achieved average growth rates of less than 1 percent between 1990 and 1998.[12] Thus some have concluded that the advancement of liberalism into the newly industrializing and less-developed countries is little more than another permutation of neocolonial policies, or least another example of policies generated in the advanced democracies and misapplied in countries where the situation is vastly different.

PROSPECTS FOR DEMOCRACY AND DEVELOPMENT

It is unclear where the less-developed and newly industrializing countries are heading in the new millennium. Optimists (liberals in particular) see the coming decades as a period of great opportunity for this part of the world, where more open societies and markets will generate prosperity and democracy. Other observers see many more obstacles than opportunities; some go so far as to predict a "coming anarchy" that will overtake many of the weakest countries. Neocolonialism, poverty, and violence will be their future, these critics assert, making freedom and equality impossible. Nor will this danger be confined to the less-developed countries they say; it will spread around the world through such avenues as mass migration and terrorism. The events of September 11, 2001, and the subsequent U.S. war in Afghanistan would seem to be evidence of this growing danger.

But speculating about what the future holds is of limited value. Perhaps more useful is the observation that greater order or more chaos, or more or less freedom and equality are all possible; the outcomes depend on the choices made inside and outside these developing and less-developed parts of the world. If we assume that anarchy is not a desirable outcome, and that some mix of freedom and equality is a worthy goal, how can these goals be realized? Again, there are no certainties, but scholars point to several possible paths.

Building State Capacity

State capacity, as noted earlier in this chapter, is one vital area that shapes both freedom and equality. In the past, international organizations and the governments of less-developed and newly industrializing countries themselves often did not pay much attention to idea of an efficient and efficacious state; instead systems that were wasteful, corrupt, and mismanaged were allowed to emerge. These systems in turn created a risky environment for entrepreneurialism, fostered kleptocratic policies and political instability, and led to large (if weak) states that crowded out the private sector and organizations that promoted the public good.

Yet at the same time, simply rolling back state power, as liberalism would suggest, will not in and of itself generate stability. New economic opportunities generated in such circumstances may only increase corruption, as those with political connections seek to corner the market while the poor, lacking economic resources and political power, are further marginalized. Effective development that reaches the majority of society requires the rule of law as a basic foundation, and the rule of law requires a state that can generate and enforce those institutions. But identifying the need for state capacity and autonomy does not tell us how to achieve it. How does one make good government, weed out corruption, make certain that laws are enforced and enforced fairly, and create a state bureaucracy that has the expertise and independence to enact and enforce policy?

A number of possible solutions have been proposed, each dependent on the context. Where state capacity is hobbled by clientelism and rent-seeking, administrative reforms tend to concentrate on developing an ethos of professionalism and **meritocracy**, or rule by merit (rather than by personal or political connections). Reforms here include developing entrance exams as conditions for employment as well as a tenure system that insulates government administrators from being fired for political reasons. Botswana, for example, has been able to improve state capacity and autonomy and also shows higher rates of economic growth and lower levels of corruption than most of its less-developed counterparts.[13]

Where state capacity is limited by inefficiency, reforms can include the decentralization of state bureaucracies along the lines of the devolutionary policies being enacted in the advanced democracies. State capacity can also be improved by increased democratization within a government administration, perhaps by increasing oversight of and participation by the citizenry in policy formulation and implementation. Although these policies may seem like a dangerous weakening of autonomy, such reforms involve turning more power over to the people as a whole, as opposed to simply renting out parts of the state to the few who are well-connected.[14]

Each one of these reforms poses its own difficulties and possible problems, but in general many observers now agree that helping to achieve structural change within the state is an important first step toward economic and political development. Newly industrializing countries, too, are not exempt from such reforms; the Asian financial crisis persuaded many that these countries need greater state capacity to prevent such crises through such tools as effective regulation and bureaucratic independence from political pressure. Politics and economics cannot be played effectively if the rules are not clear and clearly enforced.

Supporting Civil Society

Administration may be the foundation for economic and political development, but of equal importance is the role of the public. Of particular importance is the development of **civil society**, or those organizations outside of the state that help people define and advance their own interests. Civil society binds people together in a society, creating a web of interests that cut across class, religion, ethnicity, or other divisions; forms a bulwark through activism and organization against the expansion of state power that might threaten democracy; and inculcates a sense of democratic politics based on interaction, negotiation, consensus, and compromise. Within most less-developed and newly industrializing countries, civil society is weak. Individuals tend to be divided by ethnic, religious, economic, or social boundaries; what sporadic or spontaneous public activity exists does not help generate lasting community institutions. The state is also hampered by this lack of civil society, without which it can become enmeshed in clientelist relationships that prevent the formation of policies that serve society as a whole.

As in the case of administrative reform, building civil society has become a focal point for scholars and political actors involved in development. No longer is the state seen as the sole instrument for democracy and development; public activity is now viewed as an equally important component. A first step in the development of civil society is civic education, in which communities learn their democratic rights and how to use those rights to shape government policy. Beyond education, organizational skills must also be strengthened so that the public is able to mobilize effectively and make its voice heard.

Critical in this effort are **nongovernmental organizations** (NGOs), which are national and international groups, independent of any state, that pursue policy objectives and foster public participation. Although many of the most prominent NGOs, such as Doctors without Borders or Amnesty International, originated in the advanced democracies, a vast array of local organizations has been created and staffed by citizens of the poorer countries themselves. For example, in Quezon City, the Philippines, local organizers formed the Women's Health Care Foundation, creating a number of clinics to provide affordable medical care and outreach.[15] That women played a primary role in starting and running this group is not unusual: in less-developed and newly industrializing countries, women are particularly active in the NGO movement. NGOs not only create the opportunity for the development of civil society, but also enable underrepresented segments of society to organize and expand their rights.

In recent years, NGOs have played a powerful role in many less-developed and newly industrializing countries, tackling a range of issue areas, including human rights, the environment, gender, health, minority rights, and poverty. Their work has been supported in part by foreign aid that was traditionally directed primarily at states. The efforts of NGOs to link up (often via the Internet) with other NGOs in other less-developed, postcommunist, or advanced-democratic countries have given birth to a network of citizen initiatives. Some go so far as to view the spread of NGOs as a sign of an emergent global civil society that functions beyond the limits of any one state, though others again see a kind of neocolonial domination of the less-developed countries by Western NGOs that bring with them particular agendas of social, political, and economic change. The implications of this blurring of domestic and international relations is something we will turn to in the final chapter of this book as we consider the impact of growing globalization.

Promoting Economic Prosperity

Economic prosperity is the third crucial need within the less-developed world. Above all, the diverse countries that fall into this category are defined by their lack of economic development and the pressing problems of poverty among their populations. Over the past half-century, state-driven policies were carried out in most of these countries in order to promote growth. Although such policies were successful in some countries, in many others they resulted only in further debt and economic stagnation. Those success stories that did take place, as in East Asia, occurred under specific conditions that cannot be easily replicated. As a result, liberal economic strategies such as opening up markets and rolling back state power are now promoted for the less-developed and newly industrializing countries. Liberals believe that these policies will help stimulate trade, entrepreneurialism, and growth; others fear that although the industrialized world will benefit from new markets and new sources of cheap labor, these strategies will not generate prosperity for poorer countries but will only perpetuate their dependent status. Are there no other alternatives?

As in the case of civil society, solutions may be found by concentrating on the people themselves, providing policies that can empower individuals economically. In many less-developed countries there exists a strong **informal economy**, meaning a segment of the economy that is not regulated or taxed by the state. Typically the informal economy is dominated by the self-employed or by small enterprises, such as an individual street vendor or a family that makes or repairs goods out of its home. In some cases the informal economy may contribute up to 60 percent of a country's GDP, though by its very nature an informal economy is hard to measure. Women often play a large role in this economy: according to some research studies, in many less-developed countries up to 90 percent of women working outside of the agricultural sector are within the informal economy.

Although the informal economy represents an important source of employment in less-developed countries, it has its limitations. First, by existing outside of the authority of the state, it does not generate tax revenues that could be spent on infrastructure or social welfare. Second, without regulation, informal workers are not subject to labor laws or state employment benefits. Third and perhaps most important, informal economic activity is so small that it often suffers from financial problems, such as a lack of the capital necessary to expand. For example, many self-employed individuals must rely on loans in order to purchase the supplies or tools necessary for their businesses, yet given the small amount of funds needed and the absence of any collateral to secure such loans, banks are usually unwilling to extend credit to such entrepreneurs. Individuals are thus forced to turn to loan sharks, who charge extremely high rates of interest, eating up virtually all the profits that the individual then makes. Businesses operating in the informal economy are thus unable to grow into larger businesses and thereby to enter into the formal economy.

One way to break this cycle is through **microcredit**, a system that involves not an individual lender and borrower, but borrowing groups made up of several individuals. Loans at reasonable interest rates are first provided to some of the group's members; once these borrowers begin to make loan repayments, funds become available to make loans to the next set of participants. Groups thus serve as a means of support and collateral, a combination of business and civil society. Microcredit systems were first developed in Bangladesh by the Grameen Bank, which has since become world-famous for its innovative strategy. These loans are quite small: in Bangladesh, Grameen Bank loans can be as small as $1; the average loan is only around $100. The system of group lending and support produces extremely high rates of repayment (the Grameen Bank reports that 98 percent of its loans are repaid on time), in turn generating new sources of revenue that can be loaned out to new groups. Although microcredit is no panacea, studies indicate that it does help alleviate poverty, decrease economic vulnerability by building personal assets, and assists in increasing women's public participation and independence. Since its creation in the 1980s, microcredit has spread throughout less-developed, newly industrializing, and even advanced democratic countries. One study estimates that there are currently more than a thousand microcredit groups around the world, serving more than 23 million people, though these figures are small given that more than a billion people in the world live on less than $1 a day. Microcredit leaders hope to reach 100 million people by 2005. Their goal may be made easier by the fact that in recent years and in response to criticisms of more traditional lending practices, international aid has been channeled more toward microcredit as part of the greater emphasis on civil society.[16]

In Sum: The Challenges of Development

The material we have studied in this chapter can be applied across politically, economically, and socially diverse parts of the world. Although newly industrializing and less-developed countries differ in their levels of development, almost all share the legacies of imperial rule. The fusion of local institutions with those of the imperial power created challenges as these countries sought to chart their own independent courses. Weak states; conflicts over ethnicity, nation, religion, and gender; and incomplete and distorted forms of industrialization all contributed to instability, authoritarianism, economic stagnation, and overall low levels of freedom and equality. The newly industrializing countries seem to have overcome many of these obstacles, but it is unclear whether their strategies and experiences provide lessons that can be easily applied elsewhere in the world.

In the past most prescriptions for these countries assumed that such solutions must come from the state, for only a centralized institution, it was believed, could amass the power necessary to ensure freedom and equality. Yet in many ways the state in this part of the world became more the problem than the solution, absorbing wealth, functioning in an arbitrary and often ineffective manner, and serving as a source of violent contention between rivals who sought to steal its resources. Thus some now suggest that solutions should come from the bottom up, through decentralized government, civil society, and local financial institutions. Rather than relying on the state to remake society and the economy, more flexible solutions may be possible by empowering society to make its own decisions. Such a plan is much less grandiose—it relies on no huge projects close to the hearts of politicians and donors. It may also be much harder to evaluate—the impact of a $1 loan is much less easily seen than financial support for a large factory or a rural-electrification scheme. Yet its effects may be no less powerful. Even though much of the world remains mired in poverty, instability, and violence, new ways of thinking offer hope for eradicating these problems by helping to forge the policy tools that will enable the citizens of these countries to take control over their own destinies.

NOTES

1 For two excellent studies of imperialism in practice see L. H. Gann and Peter Duignan, eds., *Imperialism in Africa, 1870–1960* (Cambridge: Cambridge University Press, 1969–75); and Nicolas Tarling, ed., *The Cambridge History of Southeast Asia* (Cambridge: Cambridge University Press, 1992).

2 A general discussion of the impact of colonialism can be found in Paul Cammack, David Pool, and William Tordoff, *Third World Politics: An Introduction* (Baltimore: Johns Hopkins University Press, 1993). See also Philip D. Curtin, *The World and the West: The European Challenge and the Overseas Response in the Age of Empire* (Cambridge: Cambridge University Press, 2000).

3 Georgina Waylen, *Gender in Third World Politics* (Boulder: Lynne Rienner, 1996).

4 For a Marxist analysis of dependent development as it applies to Latin America, see Eduardo H. Galeano, *Open Veins of Latin America: Five Centuries of the Pillage of a Continent,* trans. Cedric Belfrage (New York: Monthly Review Press, 1998).

5 See Joel S. Migdal, *Strong Societies and Weak States: State-Society Relations and State Capabilities in the Third World* (Princeton: Princeton University Press, 1988).

6 For a discussion of these issues in Africa see George B. N. Ayittey, *Africa in Chaos* (New York: St. Martin's, 1999).

7 For a discussion of these issues see Dennis L. Thompson and Dov Ronen, eds, *Ethnicity, Politics, and Development* (Boulder: Lynne Rienner, 1986).

8 Charlotte Watts and Cathy Zimmerman, "Violence Against Women: Global Scope and Magnitude," *The Lancet,* April 6, 2002, 1232–37.

9 Ralph Premdas, "Ethnicity and Development: The Case of Fiji," United Nations Research Institute for Social Development discussion paper no. 46 (October 1993), available at www.unrisd.org/engindex/publ/list/dp/dp46/toc.htm.

10 For a discussion of differing paths of industrialization, see Stephan Haggard, *Pathways from the Periphery: The Politics of Growth in Newly Industrializing Countries* (Ithaca: Cornell University Press, 1990).

11 Peter Evans, "Class, State, and Dependence in East Asia: Lessons for Latin Americanists," in Frederic C. Deyo, ed., *The Political Economy of the New Asian Industrialism* (Ithaca: Cornell University Press, 1987), 203–26.

12 United Nations Conference on Trade and Development, *Trade and Development Report, 2000,* available at www.unctad.org/ldc2000/ldc2000.pdf.

13 Pierre du Toit, *State Building and Democracy in Southern Africa: Botswana, Zimbabwe, and South Africa* (Washington: United States Institute of Peace Press, 1995).

14 See the Columbia University Center for Earth Science Network's "Online Sourcebook on Decentralization and Local Government" at www.ciesin.org/decentralization/.

15 See Rina Jimenez-David and Florence M. Tadiar, "Case Study of the Women's Health Care Foundation, Quezon City, Philippines," Family Health International, at www.fhi.org/en/wsp/wspubs/philippine.html.

16 See the Microcredit Summit Campaign at www.microcreditsummit.org, as well as the Web site of the Grameen Bank at www.grameen-info.org.

GLOBALIZATION 10

The central theme of this textbook has been the struggle to balance freedom and equality. Market forces can generate tension in this relationship; when societies clash over how to reconcile these two values, states must confront these problems using their capacity to generate and enforce policy. Democratic institutions presume that freedom and equality are best reconciled through public participation, whereas authoritarian systems withhold such rights. The variety of institutional tools available has led to a diverse political world, where freedom and equality are combined and balanced in many different ways. Here, in essence, is the core of comparative politics: the study of how freedom and equality are reconciled around the world.

But over the past few years this study has taken on a new dimension, one more international in scope. Of course, domestic politics have always been shaped by international forces, such as war and trade, empires and colonies, migration and the spread of ideas. But to some observers this interconnection between countries is changing in its scope, depth, and speed. Linkages among states, societies, and economies are intensifying, and at an increasingly rapid pace, challenging long-standing institutions, assumptions, and norms. This process, still ill-defined and unclear, is commonly known as **globalization**, a term that fills some with a sense of optimism and others with anxiety and dread. Although the extent of globalization and its long-term impact remain unclear, behind it lies the sense that the battle over freedom and equality is becoming internationalized, no longer a concern to be solved by each country in its own way. What does this mean for comparative politics?

In this chapter will we look at the concept of globalization and its potential impact on comparative politics and the ongoing struggle over freedom and equality. We will begin by defining globalization, sorting out what this term means and how we might measure it. Next, we will consider some of the possible effects of globalization, and how it may change political, economic, and societal institutions at the domestic level. We will also ask some questions about the nature of globalization—whether it is in fact something fundamentally new or somehow inevitable. Finally, we will conclude with a discussion of how the old dilemma of freedom and equality may change in a globalized world, leaving us to consider what our future might look like in a world where the boundaries between the domestic and the international have disappeared.

WHAT IS GLOBALIZATION?

One could argue that we have lived in a globalized world for many thousands of years. Even as early humans dispersed around the world tens of thousands of years ago, they also maintained and developed long-distance connections between one another through migration and trade. Such contacts helped spur development through the dissemination of knowledge and new innovations; for example, it is speculated that the technology of written language was created independently only three or four times in human history, in the Americas, in Asia, and in the Middle East. All other written languages were essentially modeled after these innovations as the idea of writing things down spread to other communities.[1] Trade routes, too, forged connections between people who were only dimly aware of each other's existence. For example, in the first century C.E., Romans treasured silk imported from distant China, although they did not fully understand how it was made or where it came from. Where these, then, "globalized" societies?

When we speak about globalization we don't simply mean international contacts and interaction, which have existed for tens of thousands of years. According to political scientists Robert Keohane and Joseph Nye, one important distinction between globalization and these age-old ties is the fact that many of these longtime relationships were relatively "thin," involving a small number of individuals. Although such connections may

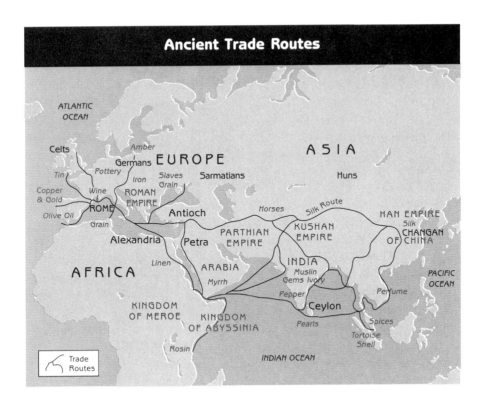

Ancient Trade Routes

ATLANTIC
OCEAN

ASIA

Celts

Amber

Germans EUROPE

Tin

Pottery

Iron

Slaves

Sarmatians

Huns

Copper
& Gold

Wine

Grain

Olive Oil

ROMAN
EMPIRE

ROME

Antioch

Horses

Silk Route

HAN EMPIRE

Grain

KUSHAN
EMPIRE

Silk

Alexandria

Petra

PARTHIAN
EMPIRE

CHANGAN
OF CHINA

AFRICA

Linen

ARABIA

INDIA

Muslin
Gems Ivory

PACIFIC
OCEAN

Myrrh

Pepper

Perfume

KINGDOM
OF MEROE

KINGDOM
OF ABYSSINIA

Ceylon

Pearls

Spices

Tortoise
Shell

Trade
Routes

Rosin

INDIAN OCEAN

have been *extensive* across a vast region, the connections were not *intensive* in their volume or personal impact. In contrast, globalization can be viewed as a process by which this web of global connections becomes increasingly "thick," creating an extensive *and* intensive web of relationships between many people across vast distances. In the twenty-first century, people are not distantly connected by overland routes plied by traders and missionaries; they are directly participating in a vast and complex international network through travel, communication, business, and education. Globalization is a system in which human beings are no longer part of isolated communities that are themselves linked through narrow channels of diplomatic relations or trade. Entire societies are now directly "plugged in" to global affairs.[2]

Globalization presents a number of potential implications for comparative politics. First, because of the thickening of connections between people across countries, globalization breaks down the distinction between international relations and domestic politics, making many aspects of domestic politics subject to global forces. Debates over environmental policy become linked to global warming; struggles over employment are framed by concerns about trade and migration; health care is influenced by pandemics like AIDS. As a result, political isolation becomes difficult or even impossible, and domestic and foreign policy become blurred.

Second, globalization can also amplify politics in the other direction, essentially "internationalizing" domestic issues and events. Given that globalization deepens and widens international connections, local events, even small ones, can have ripple effects throughout the world. Computer viruses released in the Philippines can bring down systems in New York City; a panicky stock market in Russia can trigger an economic downturn in Brazil. These interconnections across space are further amplified by the speed of today's world. Whereas technological change once took years or centuries to spread from region to region, today a new software upgrade can be downloaded worldwide simultaneously. The Internet allows the rapid dissemination of news and ideas from every corner of the globe, no matter how remote. The world lives increasingly in the same moment—what happens in one place affects others around the world soon thereafter.

As a result of this blurring and shrinking of time, old institutions may be threatened. All those institutions we have studied at the state, the economic, and the societal levels are subject to dramatic change as participation, power, and policy rapidly shift. Indeed, the very strength of these institutions—their stability and predictability—may become a liability as they struggle to change. Globalization may make politics more unpredictable. In order to better understand how globalization might affect these institutions, we will return once again to the categories of states, societies, and economies.

POLITICAL GLOBALIZATION

In prior chapters we noted that in historical terms the state is relatively new, a form of political organization that emerged only in the past few centuries. Because of their unique organization, states were able to quickly spread across the globe, supplanting all other forms of political organization. And yet we also noted that if states have not always been with us, it then stands to reason that there may come a time when states are no longer the dominant political actor on the face of the earth. States may at some time cease to exist. Some see globalization as the very force that will bring about this dramatic political change, but whether such a change is to be welcomed or feared is uncertain.

How might globalization weaken the state? Scholars point to a number of different factors that may constrain state autonomy and capacity. First, globalization is associated with the growing power of a host of nonstate entities that boast many of the powers of states themselves. **Multinational corporations**, or firms that produce, distribute, and market in more than one country, such as Microsoft, wield assets and profits far larger than the gross domestic products (GDPs) of most countries in the world and are able to influence politics and economic developments through the goods and services they produce and the wealth at their disposal. **Nongovernmental organizations** (NGOs), which are national and international groups, independent of any state, that pursue policy objectives and foster public participation, such as Greenpeace or Amnesty International, are also able to shape domestic and international politics by mobilizing public support across the globe. To be certain, these organizations do not look like typical states: they have no sovereign power over territory, nor do they command armies of their own. Yet some would argue that this is in fact their greatest advantage: nonstate actors need not be concerned with issues of national security or sovereignty, and as a result they are more flexible and able to wield other forms of influence and power. State autonomy is limited when nonstate actors are able to shape domestic politics.

As globalization gives rise to a host of new actors that rival the state, at the same time states are finding their capacity increasingly circumscribed. In part this problem is due to new nonstate actors such as those described above. But states are also being affected by the deepening of international connections that do not conform to traditional boundaries or rules. Particularly notable in this regard is the Internet. Originally created by the United States government as a way to decentralize communications in the event of a nuclear war, the Internet has grown far past this initial limited objective to become a means through which people exchange goods and information, much of it beyond the control of any one state. States have a difficult time regulating the Internet, because it lacks any one physical location or central authority. Its very nature complicates the ability of states to maintain sovereign control over many areas, such as intellectual-property rights, free speech, or national security. Future developments such as electronic currency may further erode the powers of states by undercutting their ability to print money and levy taxes—both critical elements of sovereignty.

What do these changes mean for state autonomy and capacity? One possible scenario is that the state will be eclipsed by new international actors and institutions that will take on many of the tasks that states normally conduct. In this scenario, a web of organizations, public and private, domestic and international, would shape politics and policy, set standards, and enforce rules on a wide range of issues. The rule of law would become less a preserve of individual states than a set of global institutions created for and enforced by a variety of actors.

Under these conditions sovereignty would decline, as states would no longer be able to act independently within their own territory and would be constrained within the international system by their reliance on the globalized world. Even the final preserve of states—the monopoly of violence—may lose its efficacy in a globalized world. Some argue that many of the vital issues that modern-day people face—environmental degradation, drugs, trade, technological innovation—cannot be dealt with through force. One cannot arrest computer viruses, or enact sanctions against the hole in the ozone layer, and despite the U.S. call for a "war on drugs," there's really no one to declare war against. For globalized states, then, war will become less viable, largely ineffective, and likely to undermine vital international connections. War will thus become the province of isolated states that have little to lose through the use of violence against other countries, the exception rather than the norm. This narrowing of state sovereignty as a result of globalization is what *New York Times* columnist Thomas Friedman has referred to as a "golden straitjacket."[3] In short, political globalization may bring about a more peaceful world order, constraining the tendencies toward violent conflict by constraining the capacity and autonomy of states.

Others, however, see political globalization not as a pathway to peace, but as a source of dangerous fragmentation and conflict. In this view, violence will not disappear from the international system as optimists hope; it will simply change form, much as it did when states themselves first appeared. According to this argument, globalization is fostering the creation of new kinds of violent international actors that in many ways are the exact opposite of the modern state. These groups are decentralized and flexible, hold no territory and exercise no sovereignty, and are able to draw financial and other support from across the globe. In many ways, then, they are not unlike other nonstate actors. Yet unlike an NGO or a multinational corporation, these groups seek to achieve their objectives through the acquisition and use of force, applying it in ways that may be difficult for states or other international actors to counter. Globalized criminal organizations or terrorist groups are perfect examples of this new threat.[4]

For example, in the case of the Islamic fundamentalist terrorist network Al Qaeda, we see a group that is highly decentralized, in which individuals such as Osama bin Laden provide resources and guidance but allow a great deal of individual initiative and responsibility among individual operators. Such decentralization makes it very difficult for state intelligence agencies to gather information on or destroy such networks. The death of a leader, although a potential setback, may not destroy the group itself, since it does not depend on a hierarchical structure of command and control. This decentralization is further aided by globalized technology, such as cell phones, encrypted e-mail, Web sites, and satellite television, which allows terrorists to communicate, disseminate propaganda, access money, and recruit new followers. Although states may at times be able to use conventional force against such groups where they have a physical presence, as in the case of the U.S. attacks on Al Qaeda bases in Afghanistan, more often there is no central location to attack nor any easy way to keep such individuals from simply dispersing and regrouping elsewhere. States, the military capacity of which is geared toward fighting other states, may be ill equipped to battle small groups that can take advantage of globalization to attack and undermine existing institutions.

There are two starkly different visions of the state in a globalized world. In one scenario, the state will become more irrelevant as power shifts to the global level, international cooperation increases, and these developments undermine the logic of war. In the other scenario, the very nature of deepening international connections will help foster new violent organizations that wield the capacity to use force yet lack the liabilities of a state—a territory to defend, a people to protect. Perhaps most disturbingly, September 11 may indicate that both of these predictions could occur at the same time. States may be weakened by their dependence on globalization, losing their capacity and autonomy, while simultaneously threatened by new actors who can turn the very benefits of globalization against them.

ECONOMIC GLOBALIZATION

Politics and the state are not the only realm in which globalization may be taking place; in fact, when many people think about globalization, economics is what typically comes to mind, and it is this area that generates the most controversy and debate. Over the past few decades the world has seen a rapidly developing system of international trade and economic relations, fostered by technological change and dramatic shifts in world politics, such as the collapse of communism and the spread of liberalism. To give one example, between 1992 and 2001 world trade nearly doubled in size, from \$4.7 trillion to more than \$8 trillion.[5]

Increased trade is just part of the picture. Technological change and the liberalization of markets in recent decades have also helped foster a growing internationalization of finance, as investments expand into markets overseas in pursuit of greater profits. Worldwide **foreign direct investment**, or the purchase of assets in one country by a foreign firm, increased from just \$58 billion in 1982 to more than \$1.2 trillion in 2000.[6] As men-

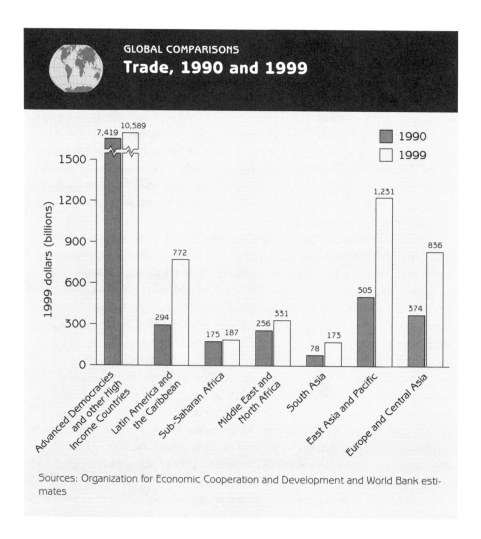

GLOBAL COMPARISONS
Trade, 1990 and 1999

Sources: Organization for Economic Cooperation and Development and World Bank estimates

tioned earlier, globalization is also associated with the emergence of a number of large corporations that dominate global markets. Assisted by more open markets and reduced costs for transportation, large firms such as IBM, Honda, McDonald's, and Johnson and Johnson control assets and make profits in the billions of dollars, often rivaling the GDPs of many countries in which they do business. For example, General Electric's annual profits in 2001 were approximately $13 billion, whereas Mozambique's entire 2001 GDP at purchasing power parity was only $19 billion.

Finally, as in the case of the state, these economic developments are compounded by expanding global communications. The dot-com meltdown notwithstanding, the development of electronic commerce and the ability to link far-flung businesses globally is transforming the way in which markets, firms, and individuals interact. Technological innovations have reduced many of the traditional barriers to trade. Firms and people are able to buy goods and services from around the world, using fewer or no intermediaries. As a result, markets are more open and firms face greater competition. A business in Chile or Thailand, for example, can advertise its goods on-line directly to other firms or individuals anywhere in the world. In the area of investment, too, on-line banking and investment allow people to move their money by computer around the world with a few mouse clicks. Many people liken the significance of the development of the Internet to that of the creation of railroads in the nineteenth century, which helped transform the way in which goods could be produced, marketed, and delivered.

For liberals in particular, these dramatic changes are seen as the mechanism for future global prosperity. In their view, globalization is the true internationalization of liberal values, with their emphasis on open markets and competition for goods and labor. Through the expansion of international economic connections, goods and services, labor, and other resources can be allocated more effectively through a broader market, unfettered by tariff barriers and other obstacles that states might erect. Countries are able to export what they produce best, encouraging innovation, specialization, and lower costs. Jobs are also created as capital flows and transnational corporations take advantage of new markets and new opportunities. In the end, wealth is diffused more effectively through open markets for goods, labor, and capital, increasing standards of living worldwide. Globalization is thus viewed as positive trend, the means to lift billions out of poverty by allowing them to be a part of the global marketplace for goods and labor.[7]

Others view economic globalization with more suspicion. Some equate increased trade with increased dependence, arguing that trade creates con-

THE GLOBALIZATION OF CUSTOMER SERVICE

One of the most fascinating examples of how globalization is changing everyday business is the development of international customer-service centers. Seeking to cut costs, many firms in the United States, such as Amazon.com, are moving their customer-service centers overseas to countries where English is spoken but where wages are much lower. The development of international communications makes routing a call to an employee overseas much cheaper than answering it at home, and improvements in connectivity mean that a phone call to a distant country can sound as good as a local one. Thus, an American calling a company's customer-service phone number or sending an e-mail to customer service may be routed to India. Some call centers even train their employees to adopt American accents to prevent any difficulties in communication and to hide the fact that the call is being answered overseas. Some have derided this mimicry as an example of cultural imperialism, with Indian workers having to hide their true national identities for the sake of their jobs, whereas others view the globalization of customer service as yet another opportunity for countries to find a comparative advantage in the global economy and thereby accrue wealth.

ditions whereby some countries will gain monopoly control over particular goods vital in the international economy, such as software, energy, biotechnology, or pharmaceutical products. The resulting unequal relationships in the international system will allow countries in control of crucial resources to dominate countries whose goods are less critical to the world economy. The globalization of investment and labor markets is also criticized as a system in which firms invest in countries with cheap labor and weak labor regulations in order to increase profits; these moves eliminate manufacturing jobs in the advanced democracies. Workers in both parts of the world thus suffer, as countries engage in a "race to the bottom," lowering standards in order to keep or attract jobs. More generally, the emergence of large, far-flung corporations raises the fear that globalized businesses are increasingly able to avoid government oversight and public accountability. As economic globalization weakens state capacity and autonomy, it is replaced not with a global rule of law, but rather with a small cartel of powerful corporations that lack any national or democratic control.[8] Freedom and equality are thus compromised.

It remains unclear whether economic globalization is a solution or an obstacle to international development, as there is a great deal of data that both sides can muster as evidence to support their arguments. For example, critics of economic globalization point to examples of foreign investment in low-wage countries with weak regulations and low state capacity. Frequently cited in this regard is the North American Free Trade Agreement (NAFTA), which led numerous U.S. firms to move their manufacturing plants and jobs across the border into Mexico. Although Americans certainly have lost jobs as a result of such relocations, these arguments do not take into account the new American jobs created by increased market access to Mexico and Canada. Another argument claims that foreign direct investment by advanced democracies is being targeted at countries with weak regulatory systems, allowing the investing companies to avoid having to comply with strict regulations at home. But whether this argument is true is unclear.[9] More than 75 percent of foreign direct investment takes place between advanced democracies, undermining the assumption that large corporations are investing primarily in less-developed countries to escape high wages and government regulations.[10] The picture of global poverty and inequality is also mixed. Although the percentage of the world's population that lives in poverty has declined and people's life expectancy has risen over the past twenty-five years, others point to a growing gap between rich and poor.[11]

If the economic benefits or the dangers of globalization remain unclear and open to debate, is there any consensus on how globalization is changing economic institutions around the world? One assertion about which many supporters and opponents of globalization do agree is that, as a result of the deepening interconnections between economies around the world, there is a greater chance that local crises and problems may become global ones. The growing linkages of finance, trade, and markets now increase the likelihood that local events will ripple throughout the system. Frequently cited in this regard is the Asian financial crisis of 1997, in which growing concerns about future economic growth led to a sudden withdrawal of capital from the region, wiping out stock markets, throwing economies into recession, and increasing unemployment. This fear soon turned to panic as international investors began to withdraw their funds from less-developed and newly industrializing countries such as Brazil that were otherwise not connected to the Asian crisis. Greater economic linkages may create new opportunities for growth, but with these opportunities may come greater uncertainty and instability. Thus states may still have a role to play in the economic sphere: prosperity may be built not on global connections alone, but also on basic public goods and regulations that manage and minimize risk.

SOCIETAL GLOBALIZATION

Whether globalization and the political and economic transformations it brings become an instrument of greater cooperation and prosperity or one of conflict and hardship may depend on our last category—how societies themselves are transformed by globalization. As with politics and economics, how globalization might affect societal institutions remains uncertain and a matter of debate.

We have explored how political globalization may challenge state sovereignty and power, and how economic globalization binds markets for goods, labor, and capital. Societal globalization is a similar process, in which traditional societal institutions are weakened, creating new identities that do not belong to any one community or nation. As we know from previous chapters, in the premodern past people's identities were rather limited and narrow, focused on such things as family, tribe, village, or religion. Only with the rise of the state did national identities begin to emerge, such that individuals began to see themselves tied to a much larger community of millions, strangers bound together by complex myths and symbols—flags, legends, symbols, anthems, culture. This transformation coincided with the development of sovereignty, whereby borders and citizenship reinforced the notion of national identity—one people, one state.

As globalization proceeds, some argue that these central aspects of individual and collective identity are giving way. Just as the state and domestic economic institutions are being challenged, so too are the traditional identities of the past. New technologies, trade, and communication link people across vast distances, forging relationships between people on the basis of common interests and ideas rather than shared national symbols. Many find the Internet particularly powerful in this regard, in its ability to spread information, ideas, and cultural products to hundreds of millions of individuals around the globe. As a result, people may develop virtual interconnections stronger than the physical ones on which they have historically relied (see the table on page 293).

How might this process shape societal institutions and identities? One possible outcome of societal globalization is the emergence of a global society built on shared values and ideals. As globalization broadens their exposure to new information, choices, and options, people will expand their understanding of what is possible and seek to advance and promote their preferences from this widened palette of choices. For example, a greater understanding of the environment may help build a global consensus for its protection. This increased awareness can in turn foster democracy

GLOBAL COMPARISONS
PERCENTAGE OF POPULATION THAT USES THE INTERNET, 1997 AND 2002

	1997	2002
United States	16.16	59.1
Brazil	.29	7.77
Peru	.26	10.73
Czech Republic	1.9	26.21
Russia	.15	12.42
Sweden	21.34	67.81
Iran	n/a	.63
Kuwait	1.51	9.47
Nigeria	n/a	.08
South Africa	1.6	7.03
China	.001	3.58
Malaysia	.15	25.15
South Korea	1.53	53.8
Worldwide	*1.81*	*9.57*

Source: Nua.com (www.nua.com/surveys/how_many_online/index.html)

through greater participation and activism. As intellectual horizons expand, new ideas and values may take shape that respond to the unique concerns of a globalized world.

The rapid proliferation and impact of international NGOs over the past decade is pointed to as evidence of this emerging global society. For example, the 1990s saw the formation of the International Campaign to Ban Landmines (ICBL), a coalition of more than a thousand NGOs whose activities were coordinated primarily through the Internet. By 1999, the ICBL had succeeded in creating an international treaty to ban the production of and use of land mines, and as of 2002 more than 120 countries had ratified it into law. For its efforts, the ICBL won the 1997 Nobel Peace Price.[12] In the long run, the development of shared information, choices, preferences, ideas, and values may create not just a global society, but a truly global culture, with people no longer primarily bound by local identities but instead connected by a more universal set of norms and institutions.

As you might expect, there are critics of such views, skeptical that increased globalization will be beneficial to social progress. These criticisms are twofold. First, some critics contend that the onslaught of globalization will not generate a shared worldview but instead will overwhelm people with innumerable choices, values, ideas, and information that they are unable to understand, evaluate, or escape. They predict not a more globally enlightened public but rather confusion, alienation, and a public backlash as people seek to hold on to their traditional identities in the face of these changes. Nationalism and fundamentalism in many parts of the world, for example, may be a reaction to a globalized society that people find alien and hostile to their own way of life. This countervailing trend against globalization has been described by the political theorist Benjamin Barber as "jihad," the impulse across many societies (Islamic or otherwise) to violently resist these alien ideas and values.[13] The September 11 attacks can be viewed in this light—as a strike against the values (and perceived source) of globalization rather than on the United States itself. As societal globalization increases in speed and impact, conflicts over ideas and values are likely to intensify, not decline.

A second criticism of societal globalization accepts the view that a world society is not only possible but in fact likely. Although a jihad against globalization is possible, it is unlikely to win in the long run. But is a global society desirable? It may represent little more than a cultural and intellectual race to the bottom, with societies trading their own cultures for a bland culture shaped primarily by consumption. Those things that make each society unique—languages, food, music, history, customs, values, and conflicts—could be absorbed and homogenized by globalization. This outcome is described by Barber as "McWorld," a process in which what is most attractive in each society is sterilized, repackaged, and sold to the rest of the planet, and those things that lack mass appeal are thrown away or driven out, replaced by what satisfies the widest public and the lowest common denominator. Jihad may attempt to stem this tide, but it is too little, too late, in the minds of many.

Furthermore, although the emergence of McWorld may promise greater prosperity and cooperation, it may also weaken the foundations of democratic society. When there are no longer any meaningful differences in ideas, and when choices are limited to the realm of consumption rather than that of values, participation and debate lose their meaning. Both freedom and equality become, in essence, meaningless concepts, since they are not material items that can be marketed, bought, or sold.

GLOBALIZATION: REALITY OR HYPE?

Clearly these heated debates over globalization show that it remains a fuzzy and highly controversial issue. Some believe it will destroy old institutions, creating a world more unequal and less democratic, at worst chaotic and violent, at best bland and uninspiring. Others see within it new sources of prosperity and progress and predict that humans will look and act beyond the local context to see themselves as part of a single community with a shared commitment to freedom and equality. Yet what both of these views share is the belief that globalization is a major turning point in history. But is globalization really all that? Some doubt that globalization represents the kind of fundamental human transformation that many assume, arguing that it is not quantitatively or qualitatively different from past waves of global interconnection, that it is not an unstoppable force. Other waves of globalization have come and gone, it is argued, and there is no reason to think that this time should be any different.

At the start of the twentieth century many countries experienced a surge of economic and other international connections not unlike those we have seen in the past few decades. Consider the development of modern imperialism. The spread of European power into Latin America, Africa, the Middle East, and Asia profoundly reshaped domestic and international relations as Western political, economic, and social systems were transplanted into these parts of the world. Within Europe too, imperialism and the declining costs of transportation helped facilitate the migration of millions of people to North and South America and parts of Africa and Asia. By comparison, the current world of passports, visas, and immigration controls in some ways constrains human mobility far more than it was just a century ago. And those who marvel at the advent of Internet communication forget that the first transatlantic cable connected Europe and North America by telegraph in 1866, spurring a global system of rapid communications and trade. In his famous work *The Economic Consequences of the Peace*, the economist John Maynard Keynes wrote of the dramatic impact of such changes:

> The inhabitant of London could order by telephone, sipping his morning tea in bed, the various products of the whole earth, in such quantity as he

might see fit, and reasonably expect their early delivery upon his doorstep; he could at the same moment and by the same means adventure his wealth in the natural resources and new enterprises of any quarter of the world, and share, without exertion or even trouble, in their prospective fruits and advantages; or he could decide to couple the security of his fortunes with the good faith of the townspeople of any substantial municipality in any continent that fancy or information might recommend.[14]

Sound like the new global economy? The time period Keynes wrote about was that prior to World War I.

Globalization in the early twentieth century also led to worldwide dangers not unlike those discussed today. The worldwide economic boom of the early twentieth century, for example, ended in a global depression much more severe than the Asian financial crisis of the 1990s, and finally culminated in global war. Imperialism and migration also disrupted the old and created new economic, political, and societal institutions across the globe to an extent only imagined today. Although these connections may have been more indirect than those found between people now, they were no less profound in their impact. If anything, their effects were much more dramatic than what we experience today.

Such periods of intense international connection are not isolated to the nineteenth or early twentieth centuries; the conquest of the Americas, the Roman and Ottoman Empires—all were examples of powerful international networks that dramatically reshaped large portions of humanity within a relatively short period of time. These examples suggest that it may be short-sighted of us to think that today's global interconnections are more dramatic than any before. History may help us better understand the present; we should not assume that what is occurring now is so unique that the past has nothing to teach us.

But even acceptance that globalization is not unique in human history does not undermine its potential impact. Perhaps the lessons of past waves of globalization only underscore what a powerful effect current changes are likely to have. But we should also be careful not to assume that what is underway now is somehow an inexorable process that cannot be stopped. To illustrate this point, let us again return to history, and to Keynes. After noting the profound changes that occurred before World War I, he remarked that above all the average individual

regarded this state of affairs as normal, certain, and permanent, except in the direction of further improvement, and any deviation from it as aberrant, scandalous, and avoidable.[15]

Yet this was not to be the case. The onset of World War I disrupted inter-national trade; its effects were further compounded by the world depres-sion of the 1920s and 1930s, World War II, and the Cold War. History suggests, then, that globalization is not unstoppable.

Globalization could be limited or reversed in a number of ways. One is economic or political crisis. The heady period of economic development a hundred years ago was finally undermined by financial collapse in the 1930s. In its immediate aftermath, trade, investment, and migration declined, often as a result of new national barriers that reflected increased isolationism, protectionism, and nationalism. Many of these barriers per-sist to this day, in spite of recent liberalization. For example, between 1901 and 1910 the U.S. accepted nearly 9 million immigrants, but it would not again reach even half that level until the 1970s. U.S. immigration is still below the volume of one hundred years ago. A major global recession could create pressure to roll back many of the elements of globalization that have developed over the past decade. The political crisis brought on by Sep-tember 11 has already called into question the wisdom of a borderless world. The long-term result of September 11 may be the construction of new obstacles to globalization and an increased emphasis on centralized state power. Even supposedly anarchic systems such as the Internet can be controlled by governments through the filtering of information, the tax-ing of transactions, and the prosecution of certain activities.

Finally, further globalization may be stymied by public opposition. Many people's concerns about how globalization might affect such things as the environment, labor standards, and democratic practices around the world are being translated into antiglobalization activism—aided, ironi-cally, by new technology such as the Internet. The protests against the World Trade Organization (WTO) in Seattle in 1999 are perhaps the most notable example of such activism: there, for the first time in the WTO's history, members were unable to begin negotiations on a new round of trade-liberalization measures. Although this failure was not simply, or even primarily, due to public protests, widespread opposition in the street by activists from around the world certainly helped to complicate matters.[16] Such protests may only increase in intensity as globalization proceeds.

Throughout human history societies have gone through periods of inter-national connection and isolation. Some of these contacts have been rel-atively thin, involving relatively few people, but in other cases many millions became directly connected to and a part of a larger world. Although today's globalization may look qualitatively different from waves of globalization in the past, what we are experiencing now may not be an unprecedented or irreversible force. Globalization may fail through its own flaws, or through concerted action against it. Nothing is set in stone.

IN SUM: FREEDOM AND EQUALITY IN A GLOBALIZED WORLD

With these ideas at hand, we can close with some thoughts on the dilemma of freedom and equality. The goal of this textbook has been to study the way in which politics unfolds around the world, shaped by the various institutions that help define economies, societies, and states. The struggle for individual freedom and collective equality is fought at several levels. Within states, this battle takes shape as power is centralized and policies made; within economies, as resources are allocated and wealth distributed; and within societies, as ideas are created and identities given form. The interaction of these institutions and conflicts is the fuel of comparative politics.

The modern world is defined by this struggle between freedom and equality, between the individual and the collective good. No one has yet been able to find a solution that can satisfy everyone; democracy and capitalism, with their emphasis on individual freedom, currently prevail, but problems of collective inequality remain. If our world does in fact become truly globalized, the struggle over freedom and equality is likely to shift from the domestic to international arena. Both values will be measured not just within states, but between them: Does one country's freedom or equality come at the expense of another's? In such a debate, the very meanings of freedom and equality may evolve, as new ways of thinking about individual choice and collective aspirations emerge.

These changes before us are at once uncertain and potentially profound. We stand at the end of one era in comparative politics and at the rise of a new one, whose possible changes may be profound—for good or ill—and whose outcome we cannot foresee. By understanding these forces we arm ourselves with the ability to shape the future and define the course of human progress.

NOTES

1 Jared Diamond, *Guns, Germs and Steel: The Fate of Human Societies* (New York: W. W. Norton, 1997).

2 See Robert O. Keohane and Joseph S. Nye, Jr., "Introduction," in Joseph S. Nye, Jr., and John D. Donahue, eds., *Governance in a Globalizing World* (Washington: Brookings Institution Press, 2000), 1–41.

3 Thomas Friedman, *The Lexus and the Olive Tree* (New York: Farrar, Straus, and Giroux, 2000).

4 John Arquilla and David Ronfeldt, eds., "Networks and Netwars: The Future of Terror, Crime, and Militancy" (Washington: Rand, 2001), available at www.rand.org /publications/MR/MR1382/.

5 World Bank, World Development Indicators 2001 database (www.worldbank.org); International Monetary Fund, *World Economic Outlook 2001* (Washington, International Monetary Fund, 2001), 194.

6 *World Investment Report 2001* (New York: United Nations Conference on Trade and Development, 2001), 2.

7 John Micklethwait and Adrian Wooldridge, *A Future Perfect: The Challenge and Hidden Promise of Globalization* (New York: Random House, 2000).

8 William Grieder, *One World, Ready or Not: The Manic Logic of Global Capitalism* (New York: Simon and Schuster, 1997).

9 See Beata K. Smarzynska and Shang-Jin Wei, "Pollution Havens and Foreign Direct Investment: Dirty Secret or Popular Myth?" (Washington: Brookings Institution, June 14, 2001).

10 *World Investment Report 2001*, 1.

11 See Robert Wade, "Winners and Losers," *The Economist*, April 26, 2001.

12 See the ICBL's Web site at www.icbl.org/.

13 Benjamin Barber, *Jihad versus McWorld: How Globalism and Tribalism Are Reshaping the World* (New York: Random House, 1995).

14 John Maynard Keynes, *The Economic Consequences of the Peace* (New York: Harcourt, Brace and Howe, 1920), 11–12.

15 Ibid., 12.

16 Jeffrey J. Schott, "The WTO after Seattle," in Jeffrey J. Schott, ed., *The WTO after Seattle* (Washington: Institute for International Economics, 2000), 5.

Glossary

ABSTRACT REVIEW *Judicial review* that allows the constitutional court to rule on questions that do not arise from actual legal disputes.

ADVANCED DEMOCRACY A country with institutionalized democracy and a high level of economic development.

ANARCHISM A *political ideology* that stresses the elimination of the *state* and private property as a way to achieve both freedom and equality for all.

AUTHORITARIANISM A political system in which a small group of individuals exercises power over the *state* without being constitutionally responsible to the public.

AUTONOMY The ability of the state to wield its power independently of the public.

BEHAVIORALISM A movement within political science during the 1950s and 1960s to develop general theories about political behavior that could be applied across all countries.

BICAMERAL SYSTEM A political system in which the *legislature* comprises two houses.

BUREAUCRATIC AUTHORITARIANISM A system in which the state bureaucracy and the military share a belief that a technocratic leadership, focused on rational, objective, and technical expertise, can solve the problems of the country without public participation.

CAPACITY The ability of the state to carry out basic tasks such as defending territory, making and enforcing rules, collecting taxes, and managing the economy.

CAPITALISM A system of production based on private property and free markets.

CARTEL A small number of producers that, although each individually is unable to dominate a market, collaborate to do so together.

CENTRAL BANK The state *institution* that controls how much money is flowing through the economy, as well as how much it costs to borrow money in that economy.

CENTRAL COMMITTEE The legislature-like body of a communist party.

CENTRAL PLANNING A communist economic system in which the state explicitly allocates resources by planning what should be produced and in what amounts, the final prices of goods, and where they should be sold.

CHARISMATIC LEGITIMACY *Legitimacy* built on the force of ideas embodied by an individual leader.

CITIZENSHIP An individual's relationship to the *state*, wherein citizens swear allegiance to that state and the state in return is obligated to provide rights to those citizens.

CIVIL RIGHTS   Individual rights that are created by the constitution and the political regime.

CIVIL SOCIETY   Organizations outside of the state that help people define and advance their own interests.

CLIENTELISM   A process whereby the *state* co-opts members of the public by providing specific benefits or favors to a single person or a small group in return for public support.

COLONIALISM   An *imperialist* system of physically occupying a foreign territory using military force, businesses, or settlers.

COMMUNISM   (1) A *political-economic system* in which all wealth and property are shared so as to eliminate exploitation, oppression, and, ultimately, the need for political *institutions* such as the state; (2) A *political ideology* that advocates such a system.

COMPARATIVE ADVANTAGE   The ability of one country to produce a particular good or service more efficiently relative to other countries' efficiency in producing the same good or service.

COMPARATIVE METHOD   The means by which social scientists make comparisons across cases.

COMPARATIVE POLITICS   The study and comparison of domestic *politics* across countries.

CONCRETE REVIEW   *Judicial review* that allows the constitutional court to rule on the basis of actual legal disputes brought before it.

CONSERVATISM   A *political attitude* that is skeptical of change and supports the current order.

CONSTITUTIONAL COURT   The highest judicial body in a political system that decides whether laws and policies violate the constitution.

COOPTATION   The process by which individuals are brought into a beneficial relationship with the *state*, making them dependent on the state for certain rewards.

CORPORATISM   A method of *cooptation* whereby *authoritarian* systems create or sanction a limited number of organizations to represent the interests of the public and restrict those not set up or approved by the *state*.

COUNTRY   Term used to refer to *state, government, regime,* and the people who live within that political system.

COUP D'ÉTAT   A move in which military forces take control of the government by force.

CRONY CAPITALISM   An economic system that shifts valuable state assets and resources into the hands of a small number of elites closely connected to the *government*.

DEMOCRACY   A political system in which political power is exercised either directly or indirectly by the people.

DEMOCRATIC DEFICIT   Loss of direct democratic control resulting from the shifting of state *capacity* to highly autonomous *supranational institutions*.

DEVOLUTION   A process in which political power is "sent down" to lower levels of state and *government*.

DIRECT DEMOCRACY   Democracy that allows the public to participate directly in government decision-making.

ECONOMIC LIBERALIZATION   Changes consistent with *liberalism* that aim to limit the power of the *state* and increase the power of the market and private property in an economy.

ELECTORAL SYSTEM   A set of rules that decide how votes are cast, counted, and translated into seats in a *legislature*.

EMPIRE   A single political authority that has under its *sovereignty* a large number of external regions or territories and different peoples.

ETHNIC CONFLICT   A conflict in which different ethnic groups struggle to achieve certain political or economic goals at each other's expense.

ETHNICITY (ETHNIC IDENTITY)   Specific attributes and societal *institutions* that make one group of people culturally different from others.

EXECUTIVE   The branch of *government* that carries out the laws and policies of a *state*.

EXPORT-ORIENTED INDUSTRIALIZATION   A *mercantilist* strategy for economic growth in which a country seeks out technologies and develops industries focused specifically on the export market.

FAILED STATE   A state so weak that its political structures collapse, leading to anarchy and violence.

FASCISM   A *political ideology* that asserts the superiority and inferiority of different groups of people and stresses a low degree of both freedom and equality in order to achieve a powerful state.

FEDERALISM   A system in which significant state powers, such as taxation, lawmaking, and security, are *devolved* to regional or local bodies.

FIRST PAST THE POST   An *electoral system* in which individual candidates compete in *single-member districts*; voters choose between candidates and the candidate with the largest share of the vote wins the seat.

FOREIGN DIRECT INVESTMENT   The purchase of assets in a country by a foreign firm.

GINI INDEX   A statistical formula that measures the amount of inequality in a society; its scale ranges from 0 to 100, where 0 corresponds to perfect equality and 100 to perfect inequality.

GLASNOST   Literally, openness. The policy of political liberalization implemented in the Soviet Union in the late 1980s.

GLOBALIZATION   The process of expanding and intensifying linkages among *states*, *societies*, and economies.

GOVERNMENT   The leadership or elite in charge of running the *state*.

GROSS DOMESTIC PRODUCT (GDP)   The total market value of all goods and services produced by a country over a period of one year.

GROSS NATIONAL PRODUCT (GNP)   The total market value of all goods and services produced by the residents of a country, including income from abroad.

HEAD OF GOVERNMENT   The *executive* role that deals with the everyday tasks of running the *state*, such as formulating and executing policy.

HEAD OF STATE   The *executive* role that symbolizes and represents the people both nationally and internationally.

HUMAN DEVELOPMENT INDEX (HDI)   A statistical tool that attempts to evaluate the overall wealth, health, and knowledge of a country's people.

HYPERINFLATION   *Inflation* of more than 50 percent a month for more than two months in a row.

IMPERIALISM   A system in which a *state* extends its power in order to directly control territory, resources, and people beyond its borders.

IMPORT SUBSTITUTION   A strategy for economic growth in which a country restricts imports in order to spur demand for locally produced goods.

INDIRECT DEMOCRACY   Democracy in which representatives of the public are responsible for government decision-making.

INFLATION   An outstripping of supply by demand, resulting in an increase in the general price level of goods and services and the resulting loss of value in a country's currency.

INFORMAL ECONOMY   A segment of the economy that is not regulated or taxed by the *state*.

INITIATIVE   A national vote called by members of the public to address a specific proposal.

INSTITUTION   An organization or activity that is self-perpetuating and valued for its own sake.

INTEGRATION   A process by which states pool their *sovereignty*, surrendering some individual powers in order to gain shared political, economic, or societal benefits.

INTERGOVERNMENTAL SYSTEM   A system in which two or more countries cooperate on issues.

JUDICIAL REVIEW   The mechanism by which courts can review the actions of government and overturn those that violate the constitution.

LAISSEZ-FAIRE   The principle that the economy should be "allowed to do" what it wishes; a liberal system of minimal state interference in the economy.

LEGISLATURE   The branch of government charged with making laws.

LEGITIMACY   A value whereby an *institution* is accepted by the public as right and proper, thus giving it authority and power.

LESS-DEVELOPED COUNTRY   A country that lacks significant economic development or political institutionalization, or both.

LIBERAL DEMOCRACY   A political system that promotes participation, competition, and liberty and emphasizes individual freedom and civil rights.

LIBERALISM   (1) A *political attitude* that favors evolutionary transformation; (2) a *political ideology* that favors a limited state role in society and the economy and places a high priority on individual political and economic freedom; (3) a *political-economic system* that favors a limited state role in the economy.

MARKET   The interaction between the forces of supply and demand that allocates resources.

MARKETIZATION   The creation of the market forces of supply and demand in a country.

MERCANTILISM   A *political-economic system* in which national economic power is paramount and the domestic economy is viewed as an instrument that exists primarily to serve the needs of the *state*.

MERITOCRACY   Political authority based on intelligence, talent, and achievement.

MICROCREDIT   A system in which small loans are channeled to the poor through borrowing groups whose members jointly take responsibility for repayment.

MILITARY RULE   Rule by one or more military officials, often brought to power through a *coup d'état.*

MIXED (ELECTORAL) SYSTEM   An *electoral system* that uses a combination of *first-past-the-post* and *proportional representation.*

MODERN   Characterized as secular, rational, materialistic, technological, and bureaucratic, and placing a greater emphasis on individual freedom than in the past.

MODERNIZATION THEORY   A theory asserting that, as societies developed, they would take on a set of common characteristics including democracy and capitalism.

MONOPOLY   A single producer that is able to dominate the market for a good or service without effective competition.

MULTI-MEMBER DISTRICT   An electoral district with more than one seat.

MULTINATIONAL CORPORATION   Firms that produce, distribute, and market their goods or services in more than one country.

NATION   A group of people bound together by a common set of political aspirations, the most important of which is self-government.

NATIONAL CONFLICT   A conflict in which one or more groups within a country develop clear aspirations for political independence, clashing with others as a result.

NATIONAL IDENTITY   A sense of belonging to a *nation* and a belief in its political aspirations.

NATIONALISM   Pride in one's people and the belief that they have a unique political destiny.

NATION-STATE   A *state* encompassing one dominant *nation* that it claims to embody and represent.

NEOCOLONIALISM   An indirect form of *imperialism* in which powerful countries overly influence the economies of *less-developed countries.*

NEOCORPORATISM   A system of social democratic policy-making in which a limited number of organizations representing business and labor work with the *state* to set economic policy.

NEWLY INDUSTRIALIZING COUNTRY   A historically *less-developed country* that has experienced significant economic growth and democratization.

NOMENKLATURA   Politically sensitive or influential jobs in the *state, society,* or the economy that are staffed by people chosen or approved by the communist party.

NONGOVERNMENTAL ORGANIZATION   A national or international group, independent of any state, that pursues policy objectives and fosters public participation.

NONTARIFF BARRIERS   Policies and regulations used to limit imports through methods other than taxation.

ONE-PARTY RULE   Rule by one political party, with other parties banned or excluded from power.

PARTY-STATE   A political system in which power flows directly from the ruling political party (usually a communist party) to the *state,* bypassing governmental structures.

PATRIMONIALISM   An arrangement whereby a ruler depends on a collection of supporters within the *state* who gain direct benefits in return for enforcing the ruler's will.

PATRIOTISM   Pride in one's *state*.

PERESTROIKA   Literally, restructuring. The policy of political and *economic liberalization* implemented in the Soviet Union in the late 1980s.

PERSONAL RULE   Rule by a single leader, with no clear regime or rules constraining that leadership.

PERSONALITY CULT   Promotion of the image of an *authoritarian* leader not merely as a political figure but as someone who embodies the spirit of the *nation* and possesses endowments of wisdom and strength far beyond those of the average individual, and is thus portrayed in a quasi-religious manner.

PLEBISCITE   A nonbinding vote called by a government in which the voters express an opinion for or against a proposal.

POLITBURO   The top policymaking and *executive* body of a communist party.

POLITICAL ATTITUDE   Descriptions of views regarding the speed and methods with which political changes should take place in a given society.

POLITICAL CULTURE   The basic norms for political activity in a society.

POLITICAL ECONOMY   The study of the interaction between states and markets.

POLITICAL IDEOLOGY   The basic values held by an individual about the fundamental goals of *politics*, or the ideal balance of freedom and equality.

POLITICAL-ECONOMIC SYSTEM   The relationship between political and economic *institutions* in a particular country and the policies and outcomes they create.

POLITICS   The struggle in any group for power that will give a person or people the ability to make decisions for the larger group.

POSTINDUSTRIALISM   The shift during the last half-century from an economy based primarily on industry and manufacturing to one in which the majority of people are employed and the bulk of profits are made in the *service sector*.

POSTMODERN   Characterized by a set of values that center on "quality of life" considerations and give less attention to material gain.

PRESIDENTIAL SYSTEM   A political system in which the roles of *head of state* and *head of government* are combined in one executive individual.

PRIME MINISTERIAL SYSTEM   A political system in which the roles of *head of state* and *head of government* are assigned to separate executive individuals.

PRIVATIZATION   The transfer of state-owned property to private ownership.

PROPERTY   Goods or services that are owned by an individual or group, privately or publicly.

PROPORTIONAL REPRESENTATION   An *electoral system* in which political parties compete in *multi-member districts*; voters choose between parties, and the seats in the district are awarded proportionally according to the results of the vote.

PUBLIC GOODS   Goods that are used by most or all in society and which no private person or organization can own.

PURCHASING-POWER PARITY   A statistical tool that attempts to estimate the buying power of income across different countries by using prices in the United States as a benchmark.

QUALITATIVE METHOD   Study through an in-depth investigation of a limited number of cases.

QUANTITATIVE METHOD   Study through statistical data from many cases.

QUASI DEMOCRACY   Rule by an elected leadership through procedures of questionable democratic *legitimacy*.

QUOTA   *Nontariff barriers* that limit the quantity of a good that may be imported into a country.

RADICALISM   A *political attitude* that favors dramatic, often revolutionary change.

RATIONAL-LEGAL LEGITIMACY   *Legitimacy* based on a system of laws and procedures that are highly institutionalized.

REACTION   A *political attitude* that seeks to restore the *institutions* of a real or imagined earlier order.

REFERENDUM   A national vote called by a government to address a specific proposal, often a change to the constitution.

REGIME   The fundamental rules and norms of *politics*, embodying long-term goals regarding individual freedom and collective equality, where power should reside, and the use of that power.

REGULATION   A rule or order that sets the boundaries of a given procedure.

RENT-SEEKING   A process in which political leaders essentially rent out parts of the *state* to their patrons, who as a result control *public goods* that would otherwise be distributed in a nonpolitical matter.

REPUBLICANISM   *Indirect democracy* that emphasizes the *separation of powers* within a *state* and the representation of the public through elected officials.

RULE OF LAW   A system in which all individuals and groups, including those in government, are subject to the law, irrespective of their power or authority.

SEMI-PRESIDENTIAL SYSTEM   An executive system that divides power between two strong executives, a *president* and a *prime minister*.

SEPARATION OF POWERS   The clear division of power between different branches of *government* and the provision that specific branches may check the power of other branches.

SERVICE SECTOR   Work that does not involve creating tangible goods.

SHOCK THERAPY   A process of rapid *marketization*.

SINGLE-MEMBER DISTRICT   An electoral district with one seat.

SOCIAL DEMOCRACY   (1) A *political economic system* in which freedom and equality are balanced through the state's management of the economy and the provision of social expenditures; (2) A *political ideology* that advocates such a system.

SOCIAL EXPENDITURES   State provision of public benefits such as education, health care, transportation, etc.

SOCIETY   Complex human organization, a collection of people bound by shared *institutions* that define how human relations should be conducted.

SOVEREIGNTY   The ability of a *state* to carry out actions or policies within a territory independently from external actors or internal rivals.

STATE   (1) The organization that maintains a monopoly of force over a given territory; (2) A set of political *institutions* to generate and execute policy regarding freedom and equality.

STRONG STATE   A state that is able to fulfill basic tasks such as defending territory, making and enforcing rules, collecting taxes, and managing the economy.

STRUCTURAL ADJUSTMENT PROGRAM   A policy of *economic liberalization* adopted in exchange for financial support from liberal international organizations; typically includes privatizing state-run firms, ending subsidies, reducing tariff barriers, shrinking the size of the state, and welcoming foreign investment.

SUFFRAGE   The right to vote.

SUPRANATIONAL SYSTEM   An *intergovernmental system* with its own sovereign powers over member states.

TARIFF   A tax on imported goods.

TOTALITARIANISM   An *authoritarian* system with a strong ideology that seeks to transform fundamental aspects of the *state, society,* and the economy using a wide array of organizations and the application of force.

TRADITIONAL LEGITIMACY   *Legitimacy* that accepts aspects of *politics* because they have been institutionalized over a long period of time.

UNICAMERAL SYSTEM   A political system in which the *legislature* comprises one house.

UNITARY STATE   A *state* in which most political power exists at the national level, with limited local authority.

WEAK STATE   A state that has difficulty fulfilling basic tasks such as defending territory, making and enforcing rules, collecting taxes, and managing the economy.

INDEX

Note: Page numbers in italics refer to maps, boxes, and charts.

309